Broken Wings

Tragedy and Disaster in Alaska Civil Aviation

G. P. Liefer

hancock
house

ISBN 0-88839-524-8
Copyright © 2003 G.P. Liefer

Cataloging in Publication Data

Liefer, G. P. (Gregory P.)
Broken wings : tragedy and disaster in Alaska civil aviation / G.P. Liefer.

Includes bibliographical references and index.
ISBN 0-88839-524-8

1. Aircraft accidents—Alaska—History. 2. Aeronautics—Alaska—History. I. Title.
TL553.525.A4L53 2003   363.12'4'09798   C2003-911178-4

We acknowledge the financial support of the Government of Canada through the Book Publishing Industry Development Program (BPIDP) for our publishing activities.

Published simultaneously in Canada and the United States by

HANCOCK HOUSE PUBLISHERS LTD.
19313 Zero Avenue, Surrey, B.C. V3S 9R9
(604) 538-1114 Fax (604) 538-2262

HANCOCK HOUSE PUBLISHERS
1431 Harrison Avenue, Blaine, WA 98230-5005
(604) 538-1114 Fax (604) 538-2262
Web Site: www.hancockhouse.com *email:* sales@hancockhouse.com

Contents

Part IV: Southwest Peninsula and the Aleutians

Part V: Southcentral Region

Part VI: Interior And Western Region

Bibliography

Index

Acknowledgments

Many individuals contributed their time and resources toward the production of this book, which originally began as a personal interest in a few old aviation wrecks in the Interior of Alaska. That initial curiosity eventually expanded into years of research on all aircraft accidents throughout Alaska's colorful aviation history. As the facts and details of many of these tragedies were uncovered, it became apparent that their stories needed to be told.

Special thanks to my wife Liz, whose love and encouragement kept me motivated and whose invaluable editing skills made the final outcome even better. For my daughter, Lauren, whose smile and constant enthusiasm keep me in focus. Thank you for teaching me that a hug can make any frustration disappear.

I'm also very grateful to Carl Addington for his computer expertise and the valuable assistance he provided in scanning, downloading documents, photo editing and producing maps used in the book.

Randy Acord, an Alaskan aviation pioneer, who helped immensely by explaining the old airway systems and navaids, also deserves special mention. His memories of many of these accidents, as well as his collection of maps and old aeronautical charts, were invaluable.

The following people and groups also deserve particular mention for their contributions:

Caroline at the University of Alaska Fairbanks photo archives; the librarians at the Noel Wien Public Library in Fairbanks; Kathleen Hertel at the Anchorage Museum of History and Art; Leanne Walther at the Colorado University in Boulder; David Pfeiffer and research assistants at the National Archives and Records Administration in College Park, Maryland; Dianne at the Embry Riddle Aeronautical University Library; Ken Furuta at the Arizona State University Libraries; Cynthia Cook at the Library of Congress; Jason Fodor, U.S.A.F. instructor pilot; Barry Cottam and

Tim Cook at the National Archives of Canada; Nick Williams at the Transportation Safety Board of Canada; Caj Frostell at the International Civil Aeronautics Organization; research staffs at the National Transportation Safety Board, the Department of Transportation Library, General Microfilm and the NTIS; Ron Dupas and Ralph Kunadt for the use of their excellent aircraft photos, as well as the many other individuals who were gracious enough to contribute photographs and anyone else whom I may have failed to mention.

In memory of my uncle, Milton Ronald Schmitz.

Introduction

Aviation first arrived in Alaska in 1911, when a schoolteacher in Nome built a multi-winged aircraft from plans he purchased while traveling in the United States. He spent a considerable amount of time on the project, working out of a garage, before an actual attempt at flight was made on May 9. The strange looking craft with its 32-foot wingspan failed to get airborne, however, probably in part due to the fact the schoolteacher had no previous flight experience. It was later sold without ever getting off the ground.

The first successful flight in the territory occurred in Fairbanks in 1913. A tractor biplane was shipped north from Seattle and flown by pilot James Martin for an aerial exhibition during the Fourth of July holiday. Unfortunately, the endeavor was not as productive a venture as first envisioned by the local businessman who sponsored the project, making far less profit than anticipated. Apparently, most of Fairbanks's inhabitants were content to observe the demonstration from their rooftops instead of paying money to watch from a makeshift airfield on the edge of the city. Only five flights were accomplished over a three-day period before the airplane was dismantled and returned to the states with its pilot.

For the next nine years aviation was absent from Alaska, except for a flight of four military aircraft demonstrating the feasibility of an air route to Asia in 1920. The next attempt to establish a permanent aviation presence was not until June 1922, when Otis Hammontree began operating a Boeing C-11S seaplane out of Anchorage. Less than a month later, the first commercial flying business was started in Ketchikan by aviator Roy Jones with a surplus Curtiss MF Flying Boat purchased from the Navy. The Northbird Aviation Company quickly gained a foothold, leading the way for other commercial aviation enterprises.

Once the practical aspects of air transportation in the region were realized, daring pilots began venturing into every part of the territory with their small, open-cockpit biplanes. Accidents were frequent, but not unexpected, considering the conditions the aircraft were subjected to. Landings and takeoffs were made on all conceivable types of terrain, from gravel bars, grass fields, beaches and tundra, to rivers, lakes and open ocean. Airfields as we know them today did not exist. Hazardous weather conditions were a constant and often devastating threat. Most accidents were not fatal, however, normally resulting in only minor damage to the aircraft. When a severe crash did occur and repairs were not feasible, every usable part was salvaged to keep other aircraft in the air. On the rare occasions where a death was involved, it was a significant event impacting everyone in the aviation community.

Flying in the early days required skill, confidence and a thrill of adventure. There were no communication or navigation facilities, no accurate maps and only limited weather information and simple cockpit instruments. Still, aviation continued to expand in the territory. Flying progressed from small, fabric covered, wooden airplanes, to large, all metal multi-engine aircraft.

Alaska saw even greater advances in aviation with the advent of World War II. Modern airfields were constructed in almost every community and along all major air routes. Low-frequency airways and radio communication networks were established, providing instrument flight capability in the worst of weather conditions. After the war, civil aviation expanded dramatically with the availability of surplus military aircraft and ever-improving technology. In only a few years, air travel became a common occurrence.

Alaska encompasses an enormous expanse of towering mountain ranges, glacial ice fields, open tundra, thick rain forests and rugged coastline, most of it in remote and difficult locations. The climate is equally diverse, with temperatures ranging from 90° F in the summer to -70° F in the winter. High winds and heavy seasonal accumulations of snow and rain are common in many areas. Pilots often encounter dangerous weather conditions of turbulence, icing, low clouds and zero visibility, all of which are especially dangerous when taken for granted.

As technology improved and the numbers of aircraft increased, accidents became more frequent and even more extensive. Fatalities escalated as faster and larger aircraft began carrying more and more people. In the early years, aviation accidents involved only a handful of occupants at the most. By the 1960s, however, aircraft capacity had expanded to over 100 passengers, increasing to three times that amount today. From 1928 through the mid-1930s, Alaska averaged less than three fatalities a year involving civil aircraft. That number progressively increased through the 1940s, 1950s, 1960s and 1970s, peaking at 156 aircraft fatalities in 1978. By the 1980s the number had begun to decrease, averaging approximately forty-three deaths and twenty-one fatal aircraft accidents between 1983 and 2000. In the year 2000 there were thirty fatalities in fifteen fatal accidents.

Some of the aircraft which have crashed over the years have never been found, others were left where they were, either totally destroyed or in a location which was unsuitable for salvage. Today there are over 6,600 documented military and civilian aircraft wrecks that once existed across the vast areas of the state. Many are still there.

This book details the most significant accidents in Alaskan civil aviation history, including all major crashes involving ten or more fatalities through the year 2000. It spans almost seventy years of flight, from the early bush pilots to modern day commercial airliners. All the accidents resulted in fatalities and in some cases extraordinary feats of survival. Many resulted in a complete loss of life. A few remain a mystery even today.

Dauntless Spirit

SEPTEMBER 16, 1929

Aviation in Alaska provided the means to open vast expanses of remote territory. Pioneer aviators led the way with fragile, open-cockpit biplanes, flying into uncharted areas with only the thrill of adventure to guide them. They blazed overland routes through rugged mountain ranges and across wide stretches of open tundra. Each flight was a risk. There were no radios for communication, no navigation aids to guide the pilots through inclement weather or at night, and no weather facilities to forecast changing conditions. Navigation was by dead reckoning alone, in every extreme of weather, through even the coldest months of winter. It was the exploits of these pilots that opened the frontier to the outside world, bringing people, mail, and much needed supplies in a matter of hours and days instead of weeks and months. Alaska was changed forever.

Russel Merrill was one of the first pioneer bush pilots in Alaska and the first to open the South-central region to aviation. After his discharge from the Navy as a Lieutenant Junior Grade in 1918, he nurtured aspirations of a civilian flying career. Over the next few years he continued flying and honing his pilot skills with the Naval Reserve Flying Corps while employed as an engineer in San Diego. As the Alaskan territory was being introduced to aviation in the early and mid-1920s, the eventual expansion allowed him an irresistible new opportunity for adventure.

Along with his business partner, Roy Davis, Merrill started a flying business in Seward in August 1925 with a Curtiss Model F Seagull flying boat. They flew into Anchorage for the first time on August 20, when they touched down on Cook Inlet and taxied to the city dock. The following week they also made the first civilian flight across the Gulf of Alaska and into the town of Kodiak. Unfortunately, the airplane was destroyed by a storm a few days later while anchored off a small island north of Kodiak, all but ending their first flying business.

After a return to the United States for another aircraft, Merrill and Davis flew back to Alaska in 1926 with an Aeromarine 40 flying boat, still determined to establish a flying service in the region. On the flight north that airplane was severely damaged in Ketchikan, ending another business opportunity. Salvage and repair costs were not financially feasible, and both men ended the brief partnership on good terms.

It seemed to Merrill as if his goal of remaining in Alaska as an aviator would be delayed indefinitely. He was in the process of leaving the territory again when another opportunity suddenly materialized. A new flying service being established in Anchorage desperately needed another pilot and inquired if he was available. Merrill gladly joined Anchorage Air Transport, and in June 1927 he joined fellow pilot Ed Young in flying the company's two Travel Air biplanes. One was a model 7000 with an open-cockpit for the pilot and an enclosed cabin for four passengers. The other smaller airplane, a model 4000, had an open-cockpit for both the pilot and two passengers. Both had detachable pontoons, wheels and skis.

While working for the company, Merrill quickly established a reputation as a skilled and reliable aviator. He was the first to fly in many areas of Alaska and helped open the Kuskokwim region of the Interior to routine flying service. It was Merrill who also discovered an important air route through the Alaska Range on the western side of Cook Inlet that still bears his name today.

Most of the struggling aviation companies in Alaska were incorporated under one name in August 1929. Alaska Airways became the predominate flying service in the territory after purchasing Wien Alaska Airways in Nome, Rodebaugh Company in Fairbanks and Anchorage Air Transport. Famous Alaskan aviator Carl Ben Eielson headed the company, and the list of pilots soon included other famous pioneer aviators such as Joe Crosson, Ed Young, Frank Dorbandt, S.E. Robbins, Matt Nieminen and, of course, Russel Merrill. Other lesser-known pilots of that time, like

Harold Gillam, would later earn praise and fame from their own daring exploits.

Merrill remained in Anchorage as the only pilot, still flying the same airplanes on the same routes, but under the different management of Alaska Airways. His days were just as hectic as before, flying as often as the daylight and weather permitted. He flew because he loved it. Everyday risks and occasional survival situations were all part of the bold adventure. Often he would overnight at some remote trapper's cabin or native village while en route to a distant destination, or while waiting for weather conditions to improve. Occasionally he even spent the night alone on some remote lake or river with only the stars for company, but that was all part of the routine. Like every pilot in Alaska he had become accustomed to surviving on his own when required, and always carried extra provisions for exactly that possibility. If by chance he was stranded because of engine or mechanical problems, Merrill knew other bush pilots would not hesitate in searching for him or in providing assistance.

It was still dark when he awoke at 0300 on September 16, 1929. Merrill ate a hearty breakfast with his wife before leaving for the airplane, assuring her he would be back in a couple of days as long as the weather cooperated. He had two scheduled flights in the morning, then a long cross-country flight to a mining camp near Bethel in western Alaska in the afternoon. It would require spending the night somewhere en route, probably along the Kuskokwim River, but he did not mind. There were plenty of hospitable trappers and natives along the route who would welcome him into their homes, eagerly inquiring of any news he brought from the Outside.

After pre-flighting the float-equipped Travel Air 7000, Merrill loaded his mechanic and a local hunting guide for the short flight south. They departed at 0530 as the sun began breaking over the horizon. A light breeze was blowing inland off the water as they climbed over Turnagain Arm toward the Kenai Peninsula. Broken clouds dotted the sky above them and the distant shoreline was already visible in a flat line across the inlet. The higher snowcapped Kenai Mountains stretched the length of the peninsula southeast of their flight path, in a solid line that intercepted Tustumena Lake, their destination.

Numerous small lakes were scattered across the flat terrain

around the many rivers that flowed away from the mountains. Tustumena Lake was easily the largest lake in the area, encompassing over sixty square miles in the southern half of the peninsula. It lay in a prime hunting area that was becoming well known for brown and black bears, abundant fishing and record-size moose. The hunting guide whom Merrill was flying had a camp already established there and was going back to prepare for the arrival of some well-paying clients. His camp was in the perfect location, isolated in pristine territory, yet still only seventy miles south of Anchorage, allowing for a short trip when the need arose.

It did not take long for them to reach the lake, land and unload before departing again. There was not enough time for much small talk at the lake with more missions still to fly, and Merrill took off as quickly as he could, still carrying his mechanic. They touched down in Anchorage at 0900, stopping the engine only long enough to load more supplies and another hunting guide for the next destination near Rainy Pass, located northwest of Anchorage in the Alaska Range. The mechanic went along again on the flight, and Merrill was grateful for the company and help with the cargo. After another quick turnaround at the second hunting camp, they arrived back in Anchorage around mid afternoon, ready for a well-deserved break and a hot meal.

The last flight of the day would be the longest and Merrill wanted a brief rest before he left. He intended to land about three hours into the flight somewhere along the route, then continue to the Nyac mining camp on Bear Creek, near Bethel the next morning. Remaining in Anchorage and delaying the flight until the 17th was a possibility, but it would still mean spending a night away from home because of the distance involved. The mine had already ceased operations until a new compressor could be delivered, and delaying the flight another day would only aggravate their situation. There was also a cargo of live foxes waiting in Bethel for transport to a fur farm on the Kuskokwim River on Merrill's return trip. In addition, he carried fifty pounds of mail that needed to be delivered along the way to Bethel. Keeping everyone waiting while he was perfectly capable of flying just did not seem right to him.

With the aircraft freshly serviced and loaded with the heavy compressor, Merrill lifted off the water alone at 1610, flying west over Cook Inlet toward the high peaks of the Alaska Range. As he crossed over the open stretch of water, the tide was almost near its highest level, but he only glanced briefly at the surface. His eyes were already focused on the cloud formations that surrounded the distant peaks, studying them for any indication of dangerous winds. He intended to fly up the Chakachatna River, then through the mountain pass he had discovered years before which led into the Kuskokwim region on the other side of the mountains. The weather in the area was always a concern, but he knew that if necessary, he could always land beside one of the trapper cabins on the large lake below the pass and wait until conditions improved.

Russel Merrill and the Travel Air 7000 he flew disappeared that evening, never to be found. No one suspected he was missing until the 18th, and even then most of his friends assumed he had only experienced a mechanical problem that forced him down somewhere in the Interior. His family was worried, of course, but they understood that those particular situations were not uncommon. Everyone was confident he would be located as soon as a search was initiated.

Since Russel Merrill was the only pilot flying out of Anchorage at the time of his disappearance, Alaska Airways had to send some of their other pilots from the northern cities to look for him. As the head of the company, Eielson himself decided to fly down from Fairbanks, arriving in Anchorage on the 19th to begin the search. On the 20th he flew along Merrill's assumed western route to the village of Sleetmute on the Kuskokwim River, a little over half the distance to Bethel. Eielson took along a mechanic as an extra set of eyes, but they saw no sign of Merrill or the airplane, and the village had no news of him.

Other pilots arrived in Anchorage on the 21st. Joe Crosson decided to participate in the search for Merrill instead of continuing on to his Alaska Airways job in Fairbanks. The only airplane available in Anchorage was the smaller Travel Air 4000, primarily used for landing on short fields and sandbars, and so he had the wheels quickly replaced with pontoons. Harvey Barnhill also arrived the same day, flying a New Standard biplane that had just recently been assembled at the Alaska Airways hangar in Fairbanks. They branched off on different routes, enabling them to cover more of the territory that Merrill might have flown over. By that time he had only been missing for five days, and they were all still confident he was safe and waiting to be found. It was common knowledge that Russel carried enough food aboard his airplane for two weeks, and as long as he was not injured there was little to worry about.

Over the next few days the search pilots and their observers covered every conceivable route Merrill might have taken on his flight, including any diversions he might have made because of bad weather. Every attempt came up empty, with not a single clue to indicate his whereabouts. The primary route between Anchorage and the Kuskokwim River, through Merrill Pass, was covered four times, and the area around Cook Inlet several times as well. When those flights proved unsuccessful, they expanded the search north into the Susitna Valley, over Skwentna and Rainy Pass. They even began dropping notes to hunting parties and remote cabins to ask if anyone had seen or heard Merrill's airplane on the 16th. No one had.

By the 26th the search crews were becoming concerned and began extending their flights farther away from Anchorage. They hoped Merrill had somehow made it farther toward Bethel without being seen or heard in the villages and scattered cabins of the region. Crosson flew all the way to the mining camp at Nyac, only sixty-five miles from Bethel, but with no luck. He then tried an area farther east of the Kuskokwim area where Merrill kept several caches of gasoline. There was no sign of him.

The search along the western shore of Cook Inlet became more intensive as the Interior flights came up empty. Spirits were temporarily lifted when villagers at Tyonek, only forty miles west of Anchorage on the opposite shore of the inlet, signaled a positive reply to a search aircraft that had dropped a note asking about Merrill. They spread a brief message on the ground that was interpreted by the pilot to mean they had seen an aircraft drifting in the inlet with the tide. However, a boat sent to investigate returned with the news that the villagers had probably not seen an aircraft at all, but only natural debris that was floating with the current.

That news might not have been so easily dismissed if a report had not arrived from Seward at about the same time, claiming a ship captain had seen signal rockets off Cape Resurrection, on the other side of the Kenai Peninsula. Speculation arose from some that Merrill had diverted his flight south along the inlet, where he was probably forced down onto the water. The wind and tides could then have carried the airplane around the peninsula, from where he would have attempted a signal.

Several search ships soon combed the area around Cape Resurrection and a general alert was issued to all vessels to be on the lookout for any signs of the missing pilot or airplane. At the insistence of a local newspaper in Anchorage, the Territorial Governor dispatched a Coast Guard cutter on October 7 to assist in the search around Seward. No evidence was ever found of Merrill, his airplane or anyone else in distress in the vicinity of Cape Resurrection.

While attention shifted toward Seward for a few days, the Alaska Airways pilots in Anchorage continued the search for their lost comrade. Other people began coming forward, claiming wreckage resembling a small airplane had been seen drifting in Cook Inlet on the day of Merrill's disappearance. The pilots intensified their flights over the inlet, expanding the area even further south along the Alaska Peninsula and again along the previously searched routes leading into the Interior. Most of the aerial coverage concentrated on the western side of Cook Inlet, since the outgoing tides usually moved in that direction and the shoreline followed part of Merrill's proposed flight route.

There was also a possibility that Merrill might have attempted to walk out if he was forced down east of Chakachamna Lake, on the inlet side of Merrill Pass. A well-used trail existed between the lake and Trading Bay, and he could possibly have covered the distance on foot if he was not injured. However, subsequent searches along the trail and coastline found no sign of him.

Finally, on October 20, there was some confirmation of Merrill's fate. A local trapper near the village of Tyonek had found a piece of fabric from the missing airplane on October 3, after it washed up on the beach. He was unaware of the significance at the time and continued with his hunting. He returned to the village on the 20th and mentioned the discovery to others. A mechanic who had stitched and painted the fabric only a week before the airplane vanished positively identified it as belonging to the aircraft. It appeared to have been cut from the tail section of the aircraft and speculation arose that Merrill might have used it as a makeshift sail to try and reach shore.

The next day, Harvey Barnhill landed in front of the village to inquire further about the sightings on the 17th. Upon seeing Barnhill's airplane on the beach as a comparison, the natives became convinced that the object they had previously seen in the inlet was indeed an airplane. It was concluded by the search pilots that Russel Merrill must have landed on Cook Inlet after experiencing some sort of difficulty, but was unable to reach shore. A storm that swept through the area that night probably destroyed the airplane, taking whatever wreckage remained to the bottom or out to sea.

The search for some sign of Merrill's body continued for another week, but there was no longer any hope that he had survived. At the end of October the search was finally halted. Over 10,000 air miles of Alaska had been covered during the six week search, with many of the routes being overflown numerous times. The search area had stretched from Bethel to Anchorage, from the Susitna Valley to the Alaska Peninsula, and from Cook Inlet to Seward. His friends and family reluctantly admitted it was finally over.

Russel Merrill left a legacy of dedication and personal service to the people of Alaska. The Anchorage Municipal Airport was renamed Merrill Field in his honor in 1930. A plaque bearing his name is still mounted at the base of the control tower today.

Legend of the Arctic

NOVEMBER 9, 1929

During the early years of aviation in Alaska, no aviator was as well known or as well respected as Carl Ben Eielson. His exploits helped open up the vast northern regions of Alaska and made him a hero among Arctic pilots. He first earned his wings in the Army Air Corps in 1919 and was released from duty shortly after when there was no longer a need for pilots. After attending college and receiving a teaching degree, he headed north for Alaska, becoming a teacher in Fairbanks in September 1922. Almost immediately the lure of aviation enticed him away from teaching and filled him with dreams of founding a flying service in the Interior.

With assistance from local businessmen to finance the Farthest-North Airplane Company and the purchase of a Curtiss biplane, he became the chief pilot for a new flying service in 1923, subsequently making the first commercial flight in the region that summer. Early the next year he accomplished the first mail delivery flight between Fairbanks and McGrath, and later started the first official airmail service in Alaska. Eielson's demonstration of the feasibility of practical aviation service all but ended the era of much slower dog team delivery systems as the primary means of winter transportation.

In 1926 Eielson became the first pilot to land at Point Barrow on the North Slope and fly over the Arctic ice pack in an attempt at crossing the Arctic Ocean. In 1928 Eielson and the famous explorer Hubert Wilkins became the first pilots to successfully fly across the Arctic Ocean to Europe, and the first to fly over the opposite end of the earth into the Antarctic region. In a time when little was known about cold-weather flying, Ben Eielson forged the way for a new era in aviation, leading the pack of great Alaskan pilots who followed.

By 1929, Eielson had become the general manager and vice president of Alaska Airways, a new airline formed from several smaller air services in the territory. One of the airline's first major contracts was acquired when the U.S. fur ship *Nanuk* became trapped in the sea ice off the coast of Siberia that winter. He signed a contract for $50,000, requiring his airline to deliver supplies to the fifteen stranded passengers aboard the ship and transport the valuable cargo of furs back to Alaska. Although the lucrative terms could provide the success his company needed, Eielson knew flying would be an extremely hazardous undertaking for that time of year in the Arctic.

The *Nanuk* was located almost 400 miles northwest of the Seward Peninsula, near the North Cape of Siberia, over 1,100 miles from Fairbanks. Flights would have to proceed across the narrow stretch of the Bering Strait separating Alaska from Asia, where weather patterns were notoriously unpredictable. Fog, icing conditions and severe storms were not uncommon. Temperatures could easily reach -50° F or less, with winds gusting over sixty miles per hour. Furthermore, only limited flying hours were available during that time of year. Darkness was prevalent and the sun would soon disappear over the horizon until late January, providing only a few hours of ambient light each day.

Initially, Eielson decided to send two airplanes in relief of the *Nanuk*. He flew a Hamilton H-45 Metalplane, accompanied by a young, but extremely experienced mechanic named Earl Borland. Pilot Frank Dorbandt flew the second airplane, a Stinson, with mechanic Bud Bassett. Their operation was to be based out of the coastal settlement of Teller on the Bering Strait while providing the relief flights, but several difficulties prevented them from reaching the *Nanuk* until October 26.

Dorbandt arrived first and waited for Eielson, who had been delayed for repairs on his flight from Fairbanks. Two days later the Hamilton landed with the experienced Arctic pilot and his mechanic, loaded with extra gasoline for the return trip and groceries for the stranded crew. A warm welcome ensued and a festive atmosphere circulated throughout the ship in anticipation of a return to civilization.

The next morning both pilots prepared their airplanes for the return flight by preheating the engines and removing the seats for loading of the cargo. Large bales of white fox fur had been packed in advance for air transport by the ship's crew, and being the most valuable, were to go out on the first flight. Six of the ship's passengers were added after the furs, with just enough room left atop the stuffed bales for them and a small amount of personal baggage.

Both pilots departed within fifteen minutes of each other, with only their flying skill guiding them across the Bering Strait. No weather forecasts were available, and anticipating the weather patterns from one point to another or one hour to the next was almost impossible. More than anyone, Eielson knew that successful flying in the Arctic, especially in the winter, was often by experience and occasionally by instinct. Having the proper judgment in any particular situation was often the difference between arriving safely at a destination or not. It was not uncommon for a pilot to set his airplane down in a remote area during bad weather and wait for better conditions. Emergency equipment, rations, and the knowledge of how to survive in the Arctic environment were essential.

An hour into the flight both pilots and their passengers encountered just such a situation. Blizzard conditions forced both airplanes down near Cape Serdze, where they were stranded for the next five days. Luckily, they were able to land near an Eskimo village that welcomed them into their sparse homes. Eielson and Dorbandt supplied the eager hosts with news and stories, sharing each other's food and company until the weather finally cleared.

On November 5 conditions improved. After digging the airplanes out from the snow and heating the engines, Eielson continued on in the Hamilton with Dorbandt following. The return flight to Teller was uneventful, allowing a safe arrival on the Alaska coast that afternoon. By the next day the weather had again deteriorated, leaving any subsequent relief flights to the *Nanuk* on hold. Thick fog prevailed around the village of Teller for several days, and without any weather forecast available the enroute conditions remained unknown. The *Nanuk* was able to send wireless reports of the current weather observed around the ship, but the crew had no equipment for measuring or forecasting the actual atmospheric conditions, or what those conditions might be elsewhere along the Bering Strait.

Each morning the airplanes were prepared for flight in anticipation of improving weather, and each day the pilots returned from the airplanes as the fog surrounded them in a thick blanket. By November 9, Dorbandt became frustrated enough to let his emotions overcome his common sense. The others thought he was only letting off steam when he boasted that he would not be kept on the ground any longer. Eielson, who was much more experienced and patient, knew the weather was still unsuitable for any attempt to reach the *Nanuk* and voiced strong objections against trying. In any case, Eielson did not take Dorbandt's statement seriously or he would have probably grounded him on the spot. He was as surprised as the others later that morning when the sound of Dorbandt's departing Stinson echoed through the fog. Foolish or not, Dorbandt and Bassett were now airborne over the Arctic sea ice.

When Eielson realized that the company's less experienced pilot had taken off against his objections, he reluctantly followed. A second aircraft was essential for safety in case the other encountered any difficulty. Without even a current weather report from the *Nanuk*, Eielson and Borland departed a half-hour behind Dorbandt in the Hamilton.

Only a few minutes after the sound of Eielson's airplane faded in the distance, Dorbandt returned to Teller after being unable to continue across the Bering Strait. He confirmed that the weather was terrible, just as Eielson had predicted. There were assurances all round that the experienced pilot and his mechanic would also return once they encountered the very same conditions, but they did not. Carl Ben Eielson and Earl Borland were completely unaware of Dorbandt's return. Perhaps they encountered a momentary break in the weather and decided to press on for the *Nanuk*, or maybe they were determined to catch the other airplane before it got into trouble. No one will ever know for sure. They were never heard from again.

That night the temperature reached -40° F with the winds gusting upwards of seventy miles an hour. When Eielson and Borland did not return and the *Nanuk* reported no news of them, the other pilots assumed they had landed somewhere on the ice to wait out the storm. The Hamilton Metalplane carried plenty of provisions and survival gear for just such a situation. A search would be launched as soon as the weather cleared. There was little doubt that both would be found safe in a few days, none the worse for the ordeal and eager to continue in the relief of the *Nanuk*.

When the few days had turned into weeks, and news of the famous Arctic aviator's disappearance spread worldwide, an international search was organized to find the missing hero and his mechanic. Unfortunately no matter how many airplanes and pilots were committed to the effort, the weather would not cooperate. While one of the worst storms in memory continued to batter the Bering Strait, the search was limited to a few dog teams sent out from the *Nanuk* and Native villages along the Siberian coast.

Aircrews began congregating from around Russia, Canada and Alaska, only to be denied the opportunity of a search by the unrelenting weather. Skilled and daring pilots who willingly risked their lives for the sake of another, sat in frustration while their airplanes remained grounded.

Three new modern Fairchild 71s were shipped from Seattle for the search, with experienced Canadian airmen sent along to fly them during the operation. A few Russian airplanes and pilots along the Siberian coast were also sent to assist in the search at the urging of the United States government. Additional aircraft would later depart from the Russian interior to participate. The few Alaskan pilots experienced in Arctic flying were either already waiting at Teller for a break in the weather with the rest of the pilots, or en route.

As the weeks passed with the airplanes still grounded, more and more dog teams were organized and sent out from the Native villages. The world literally held its collective breath for word of Eielson and Borland, still hoping they were alive somewhere in the frozen wasteland.

Reports began filtering back from the dog teams that Natives along the Siberian coast had heard Eielson's airplane on November 9, within fifty miles of the fur ship *Nanuk*. It was good news in that it at least confirmed they had reached the Russian side of the Strait, narrowing the search area. Other unsubstantiated and totally inaccurate reports had smoke signals being spotted from the sea ice and rumors of the missing men being safe and waiting comfortably in a trapper's cabin until the weather cleared. No matter how brief or false the reports, it at least kept the waiting aircrews focused and determined in finding the truth.

It was not until December 16, thirty-seven days after Eielson's disappearance, that the first aerial search departed from Teller on the Alaskan side of the Bering Strait. Only Joe Crosson and Harold Gillam, flying open-cockpit biplanes with observers along as extra pairs of eyes, managed to depart with extra fuel and rations in the hope of locating Eielson. However, they were turned back after only a two-hour flight and could not depart again until December 19. Crosson was already a well-known and experienced Arctic pilot in his own right, and a good friend of Eielson. Gillam, however, was a new pilot with only one cross-country flight under his belt when he joined the search, but he later earned a reputation as one of Alaska's most skilled aviators. He too would perish in inclement weather on a flight in Southeast Alaska in 1943.

The air route to the *Nanuk* was long and dangerous, extending from the western tip of the Seward Peninsula for fifty miles across the Bering Strait, past the Diomede Islands to East Cape, Siberia. From there the aircraft would have to follow the barren coast north for another 300 miles, before finally reaching the stranded fur ship off North Cape. Only a few scattered settlements were located in the remote region in case of an emergency and they were typically inhabited by more polar bears than humans.

On December 19, Gillam in a Stearman biplane and Crosson in a Waco, attempted again to follow each other across the sea ice to the Siberian coast. Strong winds and limited visibility soon forced them down near a remote Eskimo village for the night. They encountered even worse weather the next day en route to the North Cape, where they planned to concentrate the search. They were separated in blizzard conditions but joined up again the following day at the *Nanuk*.

While they waited on the ship in frustration, another fierce winter storm delayed the search even further. By then more reports had come in of local natives hearing Eielson's airplane on November 9 near the Amguema River, not far from the *Nanuk*. The airplane was heard circling near the coast, possibly looking for a place to land as nightfall approached. Search attempts continued to be hampered by the extreme weather conditions, however. Over the next five weeks, Crosson and Gillam were limited to only eight hours of flight.

There was a brief break in the weather on December 23, which allowed Crosson and Gillam a few hours of flight time. Another airplane flown by Dorbandt even managed to make the flight across from Teller, but no sign of Eielson's airplane was spotted by any of the three aircraft. Search efforts were further complicated with news that the Russian pilots would not assist in the search until the middle of January, when the sun returned above the horizon. Of the three new Fairchilds that were shipped from Seattle, one crashed on takeoff from Fairbanks and another was reported missing en route to Teller. The search for Eielson on the U.S. side of the strait was now stalled while aircrews focused their attention on the other lost aircraft.

On January 15, the missing Fairchild unexpectedly flew into Nome after its crew made repairs on the airplane, which had been damaged when it crashed in bad weather. It was not until January 21 that the two remaining Fairchilds finally reached Teller to join in the search. By then two Russian airplanes had also arrived at North Cape, and another nine were reported en route.

Since mid-December Crosson and Gillam had remained at the *Nanuk*, flying whenever possible in the open-cockpit biplanes during the brief breaks between winter storms. The first real day of decent weather occurred on January 25, when a clear sky revealed a brilliant sun hanging over the horizon. Flying on a parallel course about four miles apart, they followed the coast for a considerable distance before moving further inland. An hour into the flight Crosson and Gillam sighted an unusual shadow out of place on the ice and landed nearby. It was a snow-covered wing from Eielson's Hamilton, torn loose during impact and now protruding at a strange angle from the ground. The fuselage was nearby, broken in half by the force of the crash and now lay almost completely buried under a hard drift of snow.

The aircraft had struck a small island in a marshy lagoon approximately 10 miles inland from the coast. It had been heading in a southeasterly direction when it impacted the ground. The right wing was torn loose and the landing gear demolished, leaving the fuselage resting at a 045° angle and the left wing pointing in the air. Ben Eielson and Earl Borland were not found inside the cockpit, but it was obvious their bodies had been thrown clear during the crash. It was also apparent that they could not have survived the force of impact. The damage from the crash was too severe, and supplies they had been carrying on board were strewn about the area unopened. Their bodies were hidden somewhere under the packed snow and it would take some time until they too were eventually found.

After seventy-seven days the missing airplane had finally been located, ninety miles from the *Nanuk*, its intended destination. Borland's body was not located until February 13. Eielson's was found farther away on the 18th, over 100 feet from the wreckage. Both men had died on impact. The largest international search in history at that time had drawn to a tragic close.

What caused the crash of the world's most experienced Arctic pilot? Today's aviation accident investigators would undoubtedly conclude it was pilot error, and certainly they would have a strong case, but no one will ever know for sure. Even the best pilots can have a brief moment of inattention or a second of lapsed judgment. Mistakes are rare but they can still happen. Good pilots learn from their mistakes and go on to become great pilots. Eventually even a great pilot will do something to remind himself that he is not infallible. Whether it is fate, luck or simple error, that particular something usually serves as a reminder that knowledge, experience and skill are not limitless. Sometimes the reminder can prove to be unforgiving and completely disastrous.

There was no sign of mechanical or structural failure on the airplane that would suggest any problems prior to impact. It had hit right wing first while in a slight bank, with the throttle in the full forward position. The broken altimeter showed a false reading of 1,000 feet, 950 feet higher than the actual elevation at the crash site. Hands on the clock in the cockpit had stopped moving during impact and were fixed at 3:40, when twilight would have prevailed over the landscape.

At the time, Joe Crosson thought the accident was probably caused by an inaccurate altimeter. As Eielson flew into the colder air mass approaching from Siberia, the continued decrease in temperature would have given the altimeter a higher reading than the actual altitude above the ground. Eielson would have mistakenly assumed he was significantly higher than he really was. Since the throttle of the airplane would normally be set slightly back from the forward position for cruise flight, it is feasible that Eielson saw the mound of earth in front of him just prior to impact, realized how low he was and applied full power in an attempt to climb.

The weather was certainly a contributing factor to the terrible accident. Visibility was extremely poor and with the onset of night-fall Eielson would have been forced to set down somewhere on the tundra until the following day. Finding references over ice and snow, with fog masking the horizon and clouds shielding much of the ambient light, was difficult enough during the day, but impossible at night. Several reports from villages in the area had in fact stated that the airplane had flown over them as if circling for a place to land. Eielson had no accurate or current weather reports and was forced by circumstance to fly blindly into an unknown situation. The only reliable weather reports in the area were from Russian stations, but they were not even made available to the search crews until almost two months after Eielson's disappearance.

Fatigue might also have been a problem. Eielson had been up since early that morning preparing for departure. At the time of the crash he had spent four-and-a-half hours in the air, most of it probably straining his eyes to maintain a reference with the ground. His airplane only had basic instruments that necessitated visual flight. Navigational aids were unheard of, communication radios were not yet available and accurate maps were nonexistent. Flying was strictly by the seat of your pants.

The body of Ben Eielson was given a hero's welcome as it made the long journey back through Teller, Nome and Fairbanks. Memorial services were conducted throughout the territory in honor of his achievements. Thousands of mourners paid their respects as his casket continued the trip by air and rail to his hometown of Hatton in North Dakota. Alaska's greatest Arctic pilot was gone, but his memory and exploits lived on in the thoughts of those that followed. Eielson Air Force Base near Fairbanks, named in his honor, is a fitting tribute to the pioneer aviator who opened the Arctic to aviation.

The Search for Paddy Burke and Pat Renahan

OCTOBER 1930

Whenever an airplane went missing during the early years of aviation, a search quickly became the focal point of the flying community. Finding and rescuing lost or injured survivors was more than a temporary diversion for pilots of that era. It was a priority born from a brotherhood of fellow aviators who routinely risked their lives for each other. No one understood the dangers of flying in the harsh and unforgiving climate of the north more than they did. When a pilot was missing or an airplane damaged, assistance was always available, for each of them knew the next incident might be their own.

In 1929, a veteran World War I aviator named Paddy Burke, one of Canada's most famous bush pilots, began flying into the panhandle of southeastern Alaska. Aviation companies already had a strong foothold in the area, servicing the coastal towns and islands between Juneau and Seattle, and several more were expanding into the remote interior of British Columbia with mining and exploration contracts. Experienced pilots were in great demand throughout the region and Burke was considered one of the most skilled airmen available.

He was first hired in 1928 by the newly formed Airland Manufacturing Company of British Columbia to support their flight operations in Canada. By the summer of 1930 he was based out of Atlin, north of Juneau, flying an open-cockpit Junkers F-13. His flights often took him deep into the Canadian interior and along the adjoining coastal region of Alaska. The German-built Junkers, like most airplanes in the territory, had floats installed for easy access to the abundant coastal bays and interior lakes and rivers.

It was a dangerous business, requiring a daring and knowledgeable pilot. Burke already knew that navigation was dependent on dead reckoning alone, often using terrain features and landmarks in the region that were not even shown on official maps. In contrast to the stretch of islands along the Alaskan coast, much of the interior of British Columbia had not been surveyed at that time and the charts for the area were very inaccurate. Numerous landmarks were not depicted and many major mountains and rivers were often shown in error. More than anyone, Burke knew that any pilot foolish enough to trust a map of the region would eventually become lost.

Paddy Burke experienced the dangers of being stranded in the remote territory on more than occasion, but one particular incident in August 1930 is worth mentioning because of its similarity to his fatal flight a month later. On August 17, he disappeared with a prospector named Sam Clerf after encountering high head winds and running low on fuel northeast of Teslin, British Columbia. Forced to land on a small lake, the pair spent ten days awaiting rescue before finally being spotted by another airplane on the 27th. Fuel was brought out to the lake the next day and both airplanes returned safely to Atlin. The Junkers F-13 that rescued Burke was flown by W.A. Joerss, a former German World War I fighter pilot and friend who would play a role in Burke's next disappearance. The incident clearly demonstrated the vulnerability of the airplanes and their pilots flying in the remote region. Circumstances could quickly turn a simple flight into a survival situation at any time.

Less than a month later, on October 10, Burke departed Atlin, British Columbia, ninety miles north of Juneau, with a prospector named Bob Martin and a mechanic, Emil Kading. The airplane was chartered by Martin to consult with a partner at Liard Post, and would continue the next day to look at some mining property in the area before returning to Atlin. Several sluice boxes the prospector had brought along were stored in the cargo area, and to make room for them, Burke was forced to leave behind the emergency rations and snowshoes he usually carried. Only a few provisions were kept aboard, along with a rifle, a few rounds of ammunition and three sleeping bags. It was a terrible mistake they would all regret.

Burke was not feeling well when they departed, but he did not want to delay the flight and figured they would be back the next day, when he would be able to get the rest he needed. They reached Liard Post safely, encountering a few snow flurries along the way, but by the next morning the weather had deteriorated even further. Burke was optimistic they could still navigate around the worst conditions and make it back safely to Atlin by way of Teslin. After all, he had flown the same route under identical circumstances many times before.

After takeoff the in-flight conditions worsened considerably, and at one point they were forced down on the Liard River by a blinding snowstorm. Continued flight was impossible for a couple of hours until the visibility finally improved enough for another attempt. After departing once again in marginal weather, they followed the river for several more miles until being forced down a second time. During the landing one of the pontoon floats hit a submerged rock in the river, puncturing a hole in the thin metal that began filling with water. It was not a large hole, but the river's fast current and lack of a shallow bank to pull the airplane up on, would not allow an expedient repair. Stranded for good, they had no option except to wait and hope for rescue.

For the next two months an extensive search for the missing men was front-page news. Each day became a testament not only to their own physical endurance but also to the dedication of fellow airmen who never relented in a quest to find them. Isolated in the wilderness with no provisions or shelter and only limited survival equipment, the three men struggled with increasingly harsh conditions that ultimately ended in tragedy for one of them.

When the news that Burke was overdue on a flight first filtered through the local communities, most people were not overly concerned. It was not uncommon for inclement weather to strand an airplane for a few days on some remote lake or river. Few people doubted he was in any serious trouble and assumed he would be back in Atlin once the weather cleared.

After a week had passed and there was still no news of Burke or his missing airplane, it became obvious that something serious might have happened after all. The other pilots in the region quickly began a search, but with no immediate success. As the news spread down the coast and through the interior of Canada, more and more aviators joined in the hunt for the well-known pilot. Frank Dorbandt, who was also involved in the search for Carl Ben Eielson in 1929, joined the Burke search almost immediately. Additional airplanes from competing airlines were sent from as far as Seattle and Whitehorse.

The search intensified with the onslaught of winter, bringing tragedy to some of the aviators involved. Pat Renahan, a close friend of Burke, disappeared on a flight up the coast with a mechanic and a wealthy miner named Sam Clerf, the same man who had been with Burke during the previous month's flight. Clerf insisted on joining the search since he was familiar with the Liard River area and Burke's habits as a pilot. They were en route from Seattle to Ketchikan on October 28, and were last seen after a stop in Butedale, British Columbia, south of Prince Rupert. The airplane vanished sometime that evening. The crew of a fishing boat later reported spotting them flying low over the water at dusk, about twenty miles south of Ketchikan. They were never seen again.

Two other airplanes sent north along the Stikine River in support of the Burke search had mishaps near the village of Telegraph Creek. A Fairchild 71 was damaged beyond repair after the airplane impacted the trees during takeoff, resulting in the pilot fracturing both legs. The second aircraft that accompanied it, a Consolidated Fleetster, tried taxiing across the lake to assist, but broke through a patch of soft ice, where it remained submerged for the remainder of the search. Only the wings extending over the surface of the ice stopped it from sinking completely.

W.A. Joerss again joined the search for Burke in another Junkers airplane, accompanied by fellow pilot R.I. Van der Byl and a mechanic. In a strange situation, the airplane landed at a remote lake on November 12, but was unable to lift back off because of icing. Every time they taxied for departure the water spray contacted the metal surface of the airplane and froze, adding several hundred pounds to their takeoff weight. Each time they would break the ice free, unload some of the cargo and try again, without success. Finally Van der Byl decided the only hope was for Joerss to attempt a takeoff by himself and to leave them to snowshoe out on their own. They would stay in a trapper's cabin at the lake until dogsled teams could be arranged to bring them out.

Joerss was successful in taking off and in arranging assistance for his friends at an Indian village, but after arriving in Vancouver alone, the local population thought he had deliberately abandoned his friends and called him a coward. His license was revoked on the spot, probably more out of resentment of him being on the wrong side during World War I, than of anything he did wrong to his friends. Not until his two companions walked into Fort St. James after twenty days in the wilderness and explained the circumstances was his reputation restored.

With the disappearance of Renahan, the air crews had to divide their search areas. The few airplanes from the coastal areas concentrated on Renahan's route between Ketchikan and Prince Rupert, while the Interior pilots remained focused on Burke's flight in the Liard River area. By November 5 a Coast Guard cutter was dispatched from Ketchikan to search the inland waters, and two Canadian Royal Air Force airplanes were sent north from Vancouver Island on November 11. On the 14th, two U.S. naval amphibians were also dispatched from San Diego to assist in the Renahan search. Unfortunately weather and maintenance delayed their arrival until November 23. By November 28 the Canadian airplanes had already given up and departed for Vancouver. After a few days the U.S. Navy airplanes also admitted defeat and headed south on December 3.

During the days following Renahan's disappearance, several sightings were reported from areas along the coast. A lighthouse keeper on Lucy Island reported hearing an airplane pass over about 1900 on the night Renahan disappeared, flying very low in the dark and falling rain. A local Native also reported seeing the airplane flying very low that evening in the same area. Another witness claimed he heard a loud crash that night on the north side of Gravina Island, only a few miles across the narrows from Ketchikan. A villager in Metlakatla said he also heard a low-flying airplane over Duke Island, approximately thirty miles further southeast. Extensive air and sea searches of those areas could not find any evidence of the missing airplane.

A few weeks later a pastor on Annette Island, fifteen miles south of Ketchikan, brought in two airplane wheel assemblies he had found on the beach. The tires were still inflated with air and had been floating with the tide before being deposited on the shore. They were later identified as coming from the cargo compartment of Renahan's airplane, where he had stored them for later use in the Burke search, as replacements for the floats during ground operations.

By the middle of December the search effort had been drastically reduced. Aside from an occasional flight by local pilots over Renahan's route, a small Coast Guard cutter and a few private fishing boats were the only hope of finding any sign of his missing airplane. It was accepted that he had either crashed in the water or into one of the coastal islands. Since the area had been covered numerous times with no signs of survivors, it was concluded that all three men had probably perished.

Paddy Burke was a different matter. Many of his fellow pilots were still convinced he could be found alive. The Burke search area was much larger and more remote than Renahan's had been, leaving open the possibility that Paddy and his two companions were still waiting to be rescued somewhere in the wilderness.

In late November an experienced Canadian pilot named Everett Wasson finally spotted Burke's airplane on an isolated stretch of the Liard River, frozen in the ice. It appeared to have landed safely, but there were no signs of survivors or tracks leading away from the river. After landing on a nearby lake, Wasson hiked to Burke's airplane where he found a message carved into a tree, dated October 17. It stated the crew had no food remaining and were walking west toward Wolf Lake. Ironically there was an Indian village in the opposite direction, only thirty miles down river from the airplane.

For the next few days Wasson concentrated his search in the direction the three men had headed. On December 7 he spotted a signal fire and two men frantically waving their arms. With the help of two companions aboard his airplane he dropped a couple of boxes of food near the men, then landed at the closest lake, some ten miles away. They were unable to reach the survivors until the following day. When they finally found the two starving men, the extreme ordeal both had suffered became apparent.

Burke was not with them. He had died on November 20, too weak from illness and starvation to continue. In the twenty-three-day period after leaving the airplane, the three men had survived on one duck and four squirrels. Because of the heavy snow and their declining strength, they walked only three or four miles a day. Burke had grown sicker each passing day and Martin's toes became frostbitten. As the youngest of the three, Kading was left to break trail, cut firewood and care for the other two.

On November 15 they managed to shoot a caribou that had wandered into camp, but by then Burke was so weak he could not even eat. When he died, the others hid his body from scavenging animals and struggled on as best they could for the next few weeks. By the time they were found they were very close to death themselves. They had been lost for two months under extreme conditions. Their strength and desire to survive were all but gone. The last remaining rifle bullet was fired from their gun to signal the rescue party as it approached through the woods.

Both survivors from the Burke flight were flown back to Whitehorse and eventually recovered. Paddy Burke's body was located and retrieved by Wasson several days later, and is now buried in Atlin, British Columbia.

Pat Renahan and his two passengers were never found. Months after their disappearance a small piece of the fuselage was recovered on an uninhabited island near Ketchikan. A two-foot piece of blue fabric and a tie rod were identified as belonging to the missing float-plane. Natives supposedly found a decomposed body in the same area along the shoreline, but it sank while they were attempting to tow it into town. It was felt that Renahan and his passengers had perished when the airplane crashed in Dixon Entrance the night they disappeared. Ironically, the airplane Renahan flew was a Lockheed Vega, sister ship to Wiley Post's *Winnie Mae*, which set around-the-world speed records in 1931 and 1933. Wiley Post would encounter his own tragic fate in August 1935.

Even though the Burke tragedy did not actually occur in Alaska, it is included here because many of the ensuing search efforts were organized and flown out of the coastal communities of Ketchikan, Wrangell and Juneau. The incident is also significant because of its similarity to many later aircraft accidents in Alaskan history, and because it directly influenced the loss of Pat Renahan.

Wiley Post and Will Rogers

August 15, 1935

By 1935, Wiley Post had already made a name for himself with two around-the-world speed records. The first was made in 1931 in a Lockheed Vega he had named the *Winnie Mae*. He shared the record with his partner, Harold Gatty, when they flew around the globe in just over eight and a half days. Post's second around-the-world speed record was a solo flight in 1933. Using the same Lockheed Vega, he completed the trip in only seven and a half days, once again using an easterly flight route that took him through Siberia and Alaska.

Strangely, both record flights were delayed in Alaska when the airplane sustained minor damage. The accident from the first flight occurred on the Seward Peninsula when the propeller was bent during landing, requiring a temporary repair before they continued onto Fairbanks for a replacement. The second flight's mishap happened while landing at a mining camp in the territory, when the airplane's right landing gear was broken off during a rough landing. Luckily, the local miners made hasty repairs, allowing Post to complete the historic flight in record time.

Wiley Post's third accident in Alaska would be fatal. In August 1935 he was accompanied by his friend Will Rogers, a well-known American humorist, on what was supposed to be a leisure flight from Seattle to Point Barrow. The flight took them through stops in Juneau, Dawson City and Fairbanks, where they rested a few days before continuing on toward the northern Eskimo village on the Arctic coast. Many of the local residents in Fairbanks watched with enthusiasm as the two celebrities departed from the Chena River in front of town. None of the spectators could have predicted that the flight would end in tragedy.

The airplane was an Orion-Explorer, a low-wing hybrid built from an older Lockheed Orion 9E, aptly referred to as "Wiley Post's Bastard" by a few of his acquaintances familiar with its history. Purchased by Post in February 1935, it was completely rebuilt with new wings, engine, propeller and fuel tanks. The new modifications were inspected and approved by the Department of Commerce, which limited the airplane to long-distance and special test flights.

Post wanted to add pontoon floats to the aircraft, but Lockheed engineers disapproved of the change since it would dangerously alter the airplane's aerodynamic profile, making it extremely nose heavy and impossible to control during potential in-flight engine malfunctions. The facts plainly did not deter Post from continuing with the modifications for long, since he added a set of EDO 5300 floats he had acquired in Seattle a short time later. Post clearly understood the risk the floats imposed on the airplane. In fact, his statements to other pilots after they were installed confirmed what the Lockheed engineers had told him. He also justifiably assumed the Department of Commerce would not approve of the new modification and failed to have them inspected.

On August 15, Post and Rogers departed Fairbanks from the Chena River with partially filled fuel tanks, intending to fill them completely at a large, nearby lake, which provided a much longer takeoff distance. Several witnesses stated that Wiley Post made a very steep and unnecessary climb after taking-off from the winding waterway, before heading east for Harding Lake some forty miles away. They landed without incident a short time later and began the refueling operation. Even though this took a significant time, Post did not bother to obtain a current weather report from Point Barrow, even though his good friend and skilled Alaskan pilot Joe Crosson, advised against flying without one.

Had he checked with Point Barrow, Post would have learned that the 1330 local observation reported dense fog and zero visibility at the village, extending along much of the northern coast. Instead, the experienced aviator and his passenger departed around 1445 with no current weather forecasts for the route, relying on a false sense of over-confidence from the clear skies and unlimited visibility around Fairbanks.

Approximately three hours later, the airplane landed in a shallow lagoon beside a coastal river south of Point Barrow to ask for directions. Apparently they had become lost flying above a thick cloud layer, but continued northwest until a break in the clouds allowed them to descend and follow an unknown river. Unsure of exactly where they were, they landed near a group of Eskimo hunters spotted near the coast. Post and Rogers both exited the airplane after shutting down the engine to talk with the men and stretch their legs. Upon learning that they were only fifteen miles south of their intended destination, they conversed for a time with the hunters before heading back to the aircraft. Post even made a point of checking the engine before climbing back aboard.

When the Lockheed Orion lifted from the water a few minutes later, it made a sharp right turn, climbing approximately fifty feet above the water before the engine suddenly quit. The airplane fell out of the sky in a nose low attitude, striking the water at a slight angle before cartwheeling and hitting the surface again in an inverted position. Both occupants died instantly from the impact. One of the hunters reportedly ran all the way to Point Barrow with the news, shocking the world with the tragic announcement of Wiley Post's and Will Rogers' death.

From first-hand accounts and a subsequent government investigation of the accident, it became apparent that the engine did in fact fail shortly after takeoff, causing the airplane to plummet into the lagoon. Why the engine failed, is unfortunately a matter of speculation. Crash investigations in 1935 under the Bureau of Air Commerce were still in their infancy and could not provide any detailed analysis of airframes or powerplants.

The Lockheed Orion flown by Post was never fully investigated for either structural failure or internal component failure of the engine. Field investigators did not have the proper training or equipment needed for proper accident analysis. The airplane was never removed from the crash site for examination, and it is doubtful whether an accident investigator even visited the actual crash location. The findings of the accident board were based on statements from people involved with the aircraft's initial purchase, modification and subsequent flight to Alaska, as well as weather reports and eyewitness accounts at the time. This was standard procedure for that period and in no way implies a less than professional investigation by the accident board. Their findings directly substantiated all the evidence at hand.

In his book about early aviators in Alaska, *Cowboys of the Sky*, Steven C. Levi suggests that the engine failed because the airplane had simply run out of gas. He based his theory on the fact that Wiley Post had departed from Fairbanks with only partially filled fuel tanks, which were found completely dry several days after the crash. That assumption is not entirely correct since the airplane was completely fueled at Harding Lake before continuing the flight toward Point Barrow. The approximately three hours that passed before the airplane crashed would have left plenty of usable fuel remaining for continued flight. As for the tanks being dry when checked several days later, it would seem likely the remaining fuel had simply leaked out while the airplane remained upside down in the lagoon.

Other, more plausible, theories suggest the engine failed because of excessive cooling or condensation and icing of the carburetor after the aircraft landed in the lagoon. Many of the experienced Alaskan pilots of that time thought engine cooling was probably the cause, since the Wasp motor installed in the Orion had a tendency to cool very quickly. If Post had overlooked that fact, ignoring the effects of the chilly 40° F outside temperature at the time, the engine could have misfired on takeoff and resulted in the subsequent fatal loss of power.

One interesting theory explained in a letter from an Arctic ship captain to the accident board, suggested "wind holes" had caused the fatal crash. These "wind holes" were reportedly strong Arctic winds swirling in unpredictable patterns along the coast near cliffs and high terrain. He was probably referring to what are now called "Williwas," but the facts do not support his statement. The land area was relatively flat around the lagoon, not at all conducive to the type of winds he suggested, and first-hand accounts do not mention any unusual air currents or turbulence that day. In fact, the witness statements confirmed that the airplane's flight path after takeoff until impact was exactly what would be expected if the engine had actually failed.

Wiley Post was an experienced aviator. Some might suggest he took unnecessary risks when flying, but he certainly did not become successful in setting around-the-world speed records by being overcautious. He flew because he loved it and taking risks was part of the adventure of flying. It is easy in hindsight for us to fault his decisions on that fateful flight, but no one can fault the enthusiasm he brought to aviation. At least he died doing what he loved best.

His Luck Ran Out

JANUARY 5, 1943

One of the most legendary pilots of his era, Harold Gillam established a reputation for effortlessly flying in the worst weather imaginable early in his career. Many who knew him regarded his abilities as a pilot unmatched. Others considered him a danger to aviation and one who made a habit of taking unnecessary risks. No one questioned his fearlessness in the air or his seemingly uncanny ability to survive any situation. Some thought he was the luckiest pilot alive, but his exploits were certainly more than luck. His success at flying in conditions that grounded other pilots was a testimony of unequaled performance that could only come from exceptional skill and dedication. Whatever his peers thought of him, in many ways he was a predecessor to instrument flight before the introduction of modern instrument systems.

Even though Gillam would become an extraordinary aviator in Alaska aviation history, his early adulthood began under much different circumstances. After running away from home in Nebraska and a youthful stint in the Navy aboard a destroyer, he began working as a painter in Seattle, Washington after his discharge in 1923. There he first became fascinated with stories of Alaskan adventure and opportunity from the travelers passing through the Seattle area. Before long he ventured north himself and began working for the Alaska Road Commission. Eventually he started his own freight company with some used Caterpillar tractors and began hauling supplies into the numerous gold mines around Fairbanks. Some of his work involved operations around the local airfield where he became interested in the assortment of strange-looking airplanes.

He became infected with the flying bug like so many other young men of his day, but access to an airplane and flight instruction was neither easy nor cheap. As aviation continued to expand in Alaska, Gillam decided he wanted in on the experience. His tractor business was doing well enough to allow him a few flying lessons in 1927. By May 1928 he had accumulated enough money to purchase a used Curtiss JN-4D biplane from California while on a trip south. He accumulated several hours of flight instruction in the airplane before heading back to Fairbanks, bringing along a former naval aviator as the instructor for a flying school that he intended to start in the Interior. His own flight training would be contingent upon the schedule of the school and his tractor business.

Danny Danforth, the young pilot who had accompanied Gillam north, was giving Harold some flight instruction in a borrowed Super Swallow biplane on July 25 when they experienced engine trouble and crashed. The airplane was damaged, but luckily neither of them sustained more than a few bruises. They continued with their plans for the flying school using the Curtiss biplane Gillam had purchased for that reason, and started the first class in August. Even with the school in operation Gillam still managed to work in a few hours of his own flight training around the four other students. That group included Arthur Hines and Percy Hubbard, who would later start their own flying business in the Interior.

On September 10, 1928, Gillam was at the controls on a flight with Danforth when the biplane stalled during a low-speed turn. Before Danforth could grab the controls and recover, the aircraft spun into the ground, injuring both of them. Danny Danforth died the following day, while Gillam recovered in a few weeks from a painful back injury and broken bones in his hand. The newly established flying school was now out of operation with its only airplane demolished, but Gillam was not deterred from pursuing his aviation dreams.

Before he was even able to fly again he purchased a second aircraft, a used Swallow biplane, and was soon in the air whenever the opportunity allowed. He soloed for the first time that fall, made his first cross-country flight in February, and also became a respected airplane mechanic at the airfield. The new job allowed him to remain around aviation full-time, and even to accompany other pilots on many of their flights around the Interior while gaining valuable experience himself.

By the winter of 1929, Gillam was still working as a mechanic, not yet officially certified as a pilot. He also acquired additional stick time whenever he could by riding with other pilots on their flights. When Carl Ben Eielson was reported missing in November while flying supplies to a fur ship off the northern coast of Siberia, Gillam persuaded Joe Crosson, an experienced bush pilot and chief pilot for Alaska Airways, to let him fly another airplane north to assist with the search. He had only a total of forty flight hours under his belt at the time and was not even licensed to fly. At first Crosson was reluctant, but he finally agreed to let Gillam tag along in another airplane. Crosson was amazed when Gillam flew through a blinding snowstorm to reach the fur ship *Nanuk* on the Arctic ice flow. As the Eielson search continued into January, Gillam continually

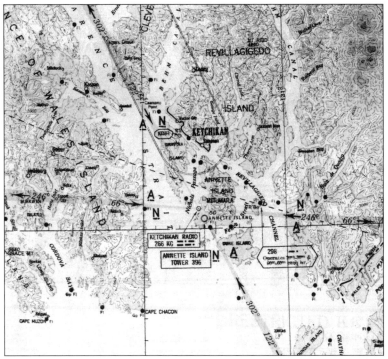

Ketchikan World Aeronautical Chart, showing Raido Range legs at Annette Island.
Photo: Courtesy of Randy Acord - Not To Be Used For Navigation Purposes

impressed the more experienced pilots and established a reputation as an exceptional aviator.

When Gillam and Crosson found Eielson's airplane in late January, and the bodies were finally recovered, Gillam returned to Fairbanks. With his name now becoming well known in Alaska he decided to start his own flying business in the mining areas along the Copper River Valley. Gillam Airways began flight operations a short time later after he finally obtained his official pilot certification. The company started with two Swallow biplanes in the spring of 1930, and over the next few years it expanded the size and service into the coastal region of Cordova and Valdez. His reputation for flying boldly in inclement weather and at night continued to grow.

Accidents were frequent during his first few years, however. He damaged numerous airplanes on the many rough runways and almost inaccessible landing strips in the region. By the time he left for more productive pastures after several years of flying in the area, he had little profit to show for his efforts.

Harold Gillam returned to Fairbanks in 1935 and established Gillam Air Service. Whether it was flying daily high altitude flights for the U.S. Weather Bureau measuring atmospheric conditions over the Interior, hauling supplies to Point Barrow for a Russian expedition, searching the Polar icecap for the missing explorer Levanevsky, or delivering mail on the first regularly scheduled flights to the Kuskokwim region, he always accomplished the missions in the worst conceivable weather. His success at flying in conditions others shied away from was more than luck and good eyesight, as some pilots claimed. He worked hard at being a bad-weather pilot by studying charts and weather patterns, plotting accurate routes, calculating times and headings between points, and experimenting with radio signals for navigation. His airplanes were also some of the first in Alaska to be equipped with cockpit instruments for flying in inclement weather.

During the rapid build-up of the Alaska territory during World War II, Gillam was unable to obtain one of the lucrative government contracts for his airline and was forced out of business. Instead, he went to work flying as the chief pilot for the Morrison-Knudsen Construction Company, which was in the process of building a number of emergency military airfields along the southeast coast and Interior of Alaska. New advances in instrument flying had already taken place, providing a much more accurate means of navigation in inclement weather than Gillam had first experimented with. If he was to remain flying, he realized he had to keep pace with the technology.

Even though several modern instrument airways and airfields had been under construction by the Civil Aeronautics Administration in Alaska since 1940, Gillam did not become a certified instrument pilot until 1942. He was always reluctant to abide by what he perceived as government intrusion into aviation, often ignoring basic requirements until being reprimanded. Even after receiving his instrument certification, his tendency to do things his own way continued getting him in trouble with the agency in charge of civil aviation. On more than one occasion in the months preceding the accident, he had charges filed against him for violating prescribed flight procedures on airways and during instrument approaches.

It was most probably his tendency to disregard what he perceived as intrusive flight regulations, and overconfidence in his own infallibility that contributed more to the tragic accident in 1943 than anything else. He was a man used to flying by his own intuition and skill. Government agents and inspectors telling him how to conduct his flights, file his flight plans and perform his landing procedures did not sit very well with him. Although it can be said he was the predecessor in some respects to the instrument flying techniques being used during World War II, he never fully accepted or anticipated the increased regulations that would accompany them.

On January 5, 1943, Gillam departed Seattle in a twin-engine Lockheed Electra for Anchorage, with a fuel stop planned at Annette Island, twenty miles south of Ketchikan, Alaska. Aboard were five passengers, some survival equipment, and a small amount of luggage. Gillam received a forecast of a strong storm system moving into the coastal region around Ketchikan. He disregarded the warning, even though several other flights going north along the coast had already been canceled. The flight controller at the Seattle airport was reluctant in issuing an instrument clearance to Gillam, but eventually agreed and allowed the takeoff after a lengthy argument.

Overcast conditions were expected over most of the coastal route with occasional light rain and moderate icing in clouds. Light turbulence was also expected at higher altitudes. In-flight winds were forecast out of the west at thirty to thirty-five knots above

Radio Range Stations were the early navigation facilities used for instrument flight. Similar to the modern systems of today, the stations transmitted a low frequency signal, or airway beam, that was received by a direction finder system inside the aircraft. Pilots of that era referred to navigating on the low frequency airway as flying "the beam."

Ground stations that transmitted the airway signals used an arrangement of four towers, approximately fifty yards apart, all set on the same frequency, but each emitting a separate course leg or direction in relation to the facility. When an aircraft's receiver was tuned to the proper frequency, it would be displayed as a fixed-card needle indication on the pilot's corresponding cockpit instrument, allowing the aircraft to track the airway signal.

An audio or aural signal from the station was also transmitted on the frequency from each tower. The airway,

6,000 feet, and at reduced velocities below that level.

After receiving a cross-country flight clearance, Gillam departed Seattle along the Victoria leg of the Seattle Range. The aircraft ascended through the broken clouds at 3,000 feet and proceeded north visually along the coastal islands. About thirty minutes after departure they passed Victoria and climbed to 9,000 feet. Three hours later the flight entered a solid overcast and Gillam proceeded on instruments, tracking the "A" side of the southeast leg of the Annette Radio Range.

As Gillam proceeded inbound to the Annette Radio Range, he crossed what he thought was the southeast leg of the station, when in reality he had crossed the east leg. The Fraser River aeronautical chart he was using was outdated and did not reflect the new changes in the course leg directions. The southeast leg of the radio range had been changed from 117° to 122°, and the northeast leg from 027° to 066°. Gillam had also labeled the bi-sectors on his chart with true headings instead of magnetic, which was a difference of 029°.

At no time during the four-hour flight did Gillam establish contact with any ground facilities to either obtain current weather information or transmit position reports. Nor was any attempt made to verify the correct radio range headings at Annette. There were no problems with the aircraft radio and it was determined after the accident to be transmitting and receiving normally.

44

After crossing what he thought was the "cone of silence," Gillam continued flying the same heading for approximately three minutes, then executed a 180° turn back to the previous position. The airplane was at 7,000 feet, over a thick cloud cover, in icing and strong wind conditions. Gillam became confused by the signal he was receiving and turned to a course of 011°. In an attempt to verify their position, he was preparing to use the airplane's direction finder equipment when the left engine quit.

An emergency radio call was transmitted at that time, informing the controller at Ketchikan they were in trouble, but would continue tracking outbound from the station to look for a break in the overcast.

The left engine was feathered and the right engine advanced to full throttle to compensate for the loss of power. By that time they were losing altitude rapidly, passing through 5,000 feet. One of the surviving passengers reported it was extremely foggy, but there was an occasional small hole in the clouds they could see through.

Shortly afterwards the aircraft encountered a violent downdraft that knocked them several thousand feet lower in a matter of seconds. No further radio contact was made as Gillam fought to maintain control of the aircraft. They broke out of the overcast at approximately 2,500 feet, still on a northerly heading, with a forested mountain lying directly ahead. Gillam had time to shut down the right engine and pull the air-

which fanned out from the station at an angle of a few degrees, had a separate audio code for each side of the arc. One side was called the "A," and the other the "N." As an aircraft approached the tower the audio signals increase in intensity and overlapped. Once the aircraft crossed over the tower, it passed through a "cone of silence" within the perimeter of the four towers of the radio range station. When the aircraft flew outbound from the station, it would track a different leg or tower signal. The "A" and "N" audio signals would then be reversed, and would fade in intensity as the distance from the tower increased.

craft into a stall before they hit. The right wing separated as it clipped the tops of two taller trees, swinging the aircraft at a right angle before they impacted the snow-covered slope.

The airplane came to rest in a small depression in about twelve feet of snow. A tree, which had been sheared during the crash, fell and broke over the partially crushed fuselage. The cockpit was also badly damaged. Gillam impacted the forward console with his head, sustaining a deep cut in his forehead that left him stunned and bleeding. All the passengers were injured, some seriously. Two of the men escaped with only cuts and bruises, but another had a broken leg, and the fourth had a broken collarbone. The lone woman was in the worst condition, having been jammed between the seat and fuselage. After a couple of hours they managed to free her, but she had lost a lot of blood as her wrist had been almost severed during the crash.

Everyone was badly shaken from the accident. They administered first aid as best they could to each other, giving the most care to the woman. Her injuries were life-threatening and she was in obvious shock, but there was little the others could do except make her as comfortable as possible until help arrived. A shelter was prepared under the wing and food distributed as nightfall approached. They were all hopeful for rescue the following day.

Gillam had sustained a concussion in the crash, but he wasted little time in recovering from the shock. The passengers were his responsibility and he organized the others into clearing snow, preparing a fire and improving the shelter. He was convinced that they had impacted one of the mountains on Annette Island not far from the military airfield and that they would soon be rescued. His biggest concern was the woman who was extremely weak from loss of blood and shock. Her need for immediate medical attention was obvious, but he could only reassure her and wait for help. They all made sure she was kept warm and comfortable, trying to keep up each other's spirits at the same time.

Food at least was not an immediate problem. There was almost twenty pounds of canned and dried food recovered from the airplane, as well as plenty of matches, some canvas tarps and a rifle. A few flares were also found, and during the next few days they used most of them trying to signal aircraft heard in the area, but the low cloud cover rendered them useless. The men's frustrations turned for the worse when the injured woman died on the night of the 7th. She had remained hopeful and uncomplaining throughout her suffering until she silently passed away.

By January 9 Gillam had given up on being sighted by a rescue airplane. Their location remained hidden under a blanket of clouds, and the persistent rain dampened their spirits more and more each day. That evening the weather cleared for a while and the next day was even better. Since he was in the best physical condition, Gillam decided to hike up to the top of the ridge to see if he could identify any landmarks and possibly build a signal fire. From there he would continue down the mountain to the nearest shore, where a passing boat could eventually be signaled. He took only a few provisions, some matches and a couple flares with him, along with a parachute for shelter. Most of the remaining supplies were left for the others. They watched him disappear into the thick timber, never to be seen alive again.

The four men settled into their shelter, confident Gillam would return with help in a few days. When he had not returned by the 16th, their concern for their own survival became predominant. They were convinced something must have happened to Gillam, and if they were to be rescued it would have to be from their own efforts. Reluctantly, the least injured man, Percy Cutting, left the others and began the journey down through the forested slope in the opposite direction from which Gillam had traveled. He had hardly any food but managed to reach the edge of Smeaton Bay after a couple of days. There were no signs of anyone being in the area, and after waiting for two days he left a signal cloth attached to a bush on the beach before returning for the others. He managed to bring back four grouse he had shot with the small-caliber survival rifle he had taken along.

After hiking back up the mountain to the crash site, Cutting was exhausted. He recuperated after the ordeal for a few days before deciding to leave again, since it seemed their only hope of rescue. Of the other three survivors, only Joseph Tippets was strong enough to accompany him. Before leaving they moved the other two men several miles into a new camp beside a cleared area farther down the hill, where they could hopefully be seen by a passing aircraft.

Six days passed after Cutting returned from the beach, and by then they all knew a chance of rescue was quickly running out. The trip could not be delayed any longer. The remaining food supplies, only a couple of bullion cubes and a spoonful of tea, were left with the two injured men. Survival now depended on Cutting and Tippets finding help. Eventually a vessel or airplane searching for them would surely move into the area where it could be signalled. None of them knew that the search had been called off several days before.

The search for the missing airplane had begun almost immediately after it disappeared, but because Gillam sent no position reports, the aircraft's exact location could not be determined. Over forty military and civilian airplanes searched the surrounding islands and coastal mountains near Annette, while a Coast Guard cutter and numerous private fishing vessels combed every bay and inlet along the coastal route from Seattle. Compounding the search was some of the worst winter weather the area had experienced in many years. After two weeks of intense efforts failed to locate any evidence of the airplane, it was determined that Gillam and his passengers must have crashed into the ocean, taking all evidence of the accident to the bottom. The search was reluctantly terminated.

Cutting and Tippetts reached the edge of Badger Bay in Boca de Quadra Inlet and managed to stumble upon a trapper's cabin where they found a little food. For the next several days they survived near the shore eating mussels and a raven they managed to shoot. They even tried patching an abandoned boat they found to seek help, but it sank underneath them and they barely made it back to the beach. On February 3 a local fisherman from Ketchikan finally spotted the pair of survivors frantically waving their arms from the shoreline. Exhausted, with frostbitten feet and hands, they were taken to Ketchikan despite their insistence on wanting to return to the crash sight for the other survivors.

News of their rescue was quickly broadcast and a new search for the missing men was immediately launched. The camp was sighted later that evening on an inland mountain between Smeaton Bay and Boca de Quadra, thirty miles northeast of the airfield on Annette Island. Both survivors were seen waving from the ground as the rescue airplane flew over and dropped supplies nearby. A Coast Guard rescue party was able to reach the crash sight on foot on February 4 after hiking up from Smeaton Bay. They were accompanied by Cutting and Tippetts, who had spent only a few hours in the hospital before demanding to return with the others for their friends.

Another rescue party reached the camp the next day from Boca de Quadra to assist with transporting the injured survivors. Both Dewey Metzdorf and Robert Gebo were near death when they were finally located. Three more days were spent at the camp restoring their weakened health and preparing a trail to get them off the mountain. Each man had lost over fifty pounds.

Susan Batzer, the only passenger to perish in the tragedy, was forced to be left in the airplane after she died without a proper burial. The other survivors were too weak and injured to dig a suitable grave. Her body was not recovered from the wreckage until March, when the airplane was again uncovered after lying under several feet of winter snow. Susan's remains were taken to Ketchikan and later shipped to her hometown for burial.

Harold Gillam's body was later found inside the tree line near the shore of Boca de Quadra Inlet, only a mile from where Cuttings and Tippet were rescued. He had made a camp near a small creek while waiting for a passing ship. His body was still wrapped in the silk parachute he had covered himself with for warmth. He appeared to have passed away while sleeping, probably from exposure and injuries sustained in the crash. A pair of boots remained propped on a stick beside the long extinguished campfire, and his underwear hung nearby in the branches of a tree. Two pieces of cloth that Gillam had placed on the beach as a signal eventually led to the finding of his body.

Alaskans mourned the loss of Harold Gillam as they did with all the pioneer bush pilots. His luck had finally run out. Many of his peers agreed it was pilot error, but if his engine had not quit he might have made it after all, and defied the wrath of nature one more time.

Missing near Yakutat

NOVEMBER 4, 1948

Alaska's aviation history is filled with tales of the many aircraft that have disappeared along the vast expanse of the Interior and endless miles of uninhabited coastline. One of the more remote regions, and one repeatedly affected by powerful weather patterns blowing in from the Gulf of Alaska, is the southeastern coastal area between Cordova and Sitka. Along the 400-mile stretch of land and sea lay one of North America's largest accumulations of glaciers and high mountains, covering hundreds of square miles. The ice fields are seemingly endless, extending in every direction within the rugged coastal range, while many of the peaks reach well over 10,000 feet, completely encased with snow. In the few places where the mountains and glaciers do not meet the sea directly, the usable land is narrow and exposed to open ocean, continually battered by every extreme of weather. Much of the flying distance along the route is over open water, in an area well known for harsh storms and unforgiving seas. Looking at the enormous stretch of territory on a map, it is easy to imagine how an aircraft could vanish without a trace.

A Pacific Alaska Air Express DC-3 left Yakutat early in the morning on November 4, 1948, bound for Seattle with an intermediate stop at Annette Island. Approximately one hour after departure the airplane made a position report to Gustavus Radio, stating they were 128 nautical miles southeast of Yakutat, passing Spencer Intersection at a cruising altitude of 10,000 feet and estimating their next reporting point at Sitka Station in thirty-four minutes. Nothing further was ever heard from the flight. It disappeared without a trace, remaining a mystery even today.

The aircraft originally departed Anchorage at 2226 the previous night, making a scheduled stop in Homer before arriving at Yakutat. A pilot and co-pilot were the only crew members on board, along with ten passengers who initially boarded the airplane in Anchorage. Four more passengers were added at the first stop in Homer, and one more while in Yakutat. The flight from Anchorage and Homer proceeded without incident, touching down in Yakutat at approximately 0300 in the morning. After being fully serviced with fuel for the next leg of the journey, it lifted off again at 0407 for the next stop at Annette Island.

A weather forecast obtained on the ground in Anchorage for the entire route showed a minimum ceiling of 2,000 feet in light rain showers between Yakutat and Sitka, with scattered cloud layers from 9,000 to 12,000 feet. Light to moderate turbulence was predicted below 12,000 feet, but no turbulence expected above that level. The next portion of the flight had basically the same conditions from Sitka to Annette, with several broken and overcast layers from 3,000 to 12,000 feet in light rain showers and turbulence. Winds at their cruising altitude of 10,000 feet were estimated as 190° at twenty-six knots near Yakutat, and 220° at thirty-nine knots near Annette. In-flight icing was not anticipated, since temperatures were unsuitable for the build-up of either aircraft or carburetor icing. Even though the weather briefing was over four hours old by the time of the flight's departure from Yakutat, the crew elected not to obtain a current forecast.

When the Pacific Alaska Air Express flight failed to report passing Sitka an hour after their estimated time of arrival, the Civil Aeronautics Administration office issued an emergency warning to all stations along the flight route. At that time search and rescue services from the Air Force and Coast Guard were also notified. Almost immediately an airplane from the nearest Coast Guard station was launched to overfly the last reported position of the missing airliner. Another Coast Guard aircraft joined the effort later that day, assisted by a third airplane from the 10th Rescue Squadron at Elmendorf Air Force Base in Anchorage.

They found no evidence of the DC-3 the first day, and by the next morning the Coast Guard dispatched two additional airplanes from Washington and California. Only a single aircraft from the 10th Rescue Squadron was available at that time. The unit's other

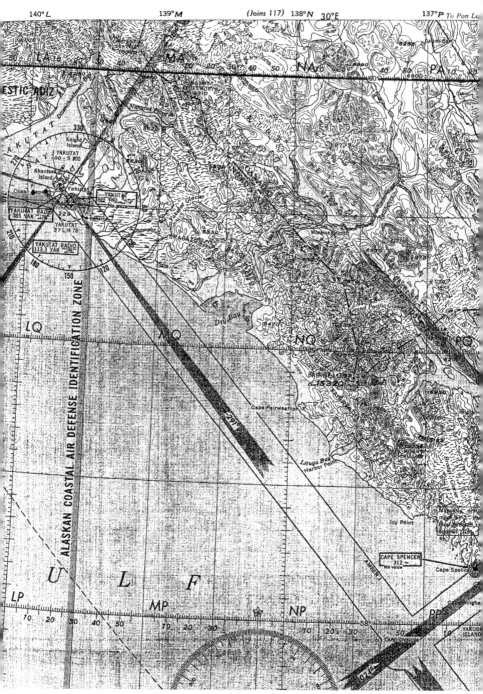

Mount Fairweather World Aeronautical Chart. Airway system from Yakutat to Cape Spencer. (*For illustration only—not to be used for navigation purposes.*)

assets were already committed to a search for a missing Navy PBY in the Aleutians and another missing Navy airplane near Vancouver Island. Even so, by November 6 over forty aircraft were associated with the three separate search efforts, including several from the Canadian Air Force. Numerous ships also joined the hunt in the waters near Yakutat, combing the open ocean and shoreline where the airplane might have gone down.

There was a good possibility that the DC-3 might have made a precautionary landing along one of the more southern coastal islands if it had developed a problem, especially if it had passed Sitka and continued onto Annette without making a position report. A two-week supply of food and survival equipment was carried on the airplane for just such an emergency. Fishing gear, a rifle and ammunition, twenty blankets, axes and two portable radios were always on board for any unforeseen difficulty.

The major search effort eventually moved southeast around the larger accumulation of islands when no evidence was found elsewhere along the route. Hope of finding the airplane increased when a rumor of residents hearing a possible airplane crash on Prince of Wales Island was reported. However, the report was later determined to be false.

Winter storms carrying snow and heavy rain impeded the search attempts of many of the aircraft, but by November 24 the entire route along the airway to Annette had been checked several times, including an extensive air and sea search of both the Yakutat and Sitka areas. All other potential leads were equally unsuccessful. After failing to uncover any signs of the missing DC-3 over a several week period, the effort was reluctantly canceled.

Military and civil aircraft continued flying the route during the following months. Their crews always kept a sharp watch for evidence of the missing airplane, but with no success.

Small pieces of material from a DC-3 type aircraft were found some time later near Chichagof Island, 160 nautical miles southeast of Yakutat, but they could not be identified as coming from the Pacific Alaska flight. Speculation increased among many of the local pilots that the airplane had crashed into the ocean shortly after its last position report, but no positive findings were ever uncovered to support that conclusion.

The official Accident Investigation Report, released over a

year later, found there was insufficient evidence to determine a probable cause of the accident. The crew had reported nothing unusual during the flight from Anchorage. Neither had the previous crew experienced any mechanical problems with the aircraft. Maintenance and service personnel verified that the airplane was in good flying condition. Its last major overhaul had been completed earlier in the year, and it had accumulated 4320 total hours, a significant number of hours but not excessive, since leaving the assembly line in June 1943.

There was a possibility that the aircraft encountered unforecast, extreme weather conditions in flight, but the weather patterns in the area at the time did not support that conclusion. A navigation error could have contributed to the accident, but, again, there was no evidence of any prior difficulty with the on board navigation systems or cockpit instruments. Subsequent flight checks of the navigation facilities at Yakutat, Gustavus and Sitka, also found them to be operating normally and within tolerance.

The only discrepancy that was found by the accident investigation board involved the co-pilot. Richard Wilson had been hired only two months previously and was listed by the company as a pilot-mechanic, holding an airman certificate with a multi-engine and instrument rating. The Civil Aeronautics Administration, however, only had him listed as a student pilot with a separate aircraft and engine mechanic's license. His mechanic's license number on file at the Civil Aeronautics Administration was the same number shown on a separate airman certificate kept at the Pacific Alaska Air Express office. Whether he was actually certified as a multi-engine instrument pilot was never confirmed. Perhaps it was only a clerical error, but if he really was only a student pilot, the lack of proper qualification and experience would certainly have contributed to the accident.

Captain Andrew Kinnear's qualifications were not in doubt. He had 3,600 total flight hours, most of which were in multi-engine aircraft. On ten previous occasions he had flown the same Anchorage to Seattle route, several times under similar weather conditions. Of the ten previous flights the captain had made over the same area, four were with the same co-pilot, Richard Wilson.

What really happened to the missing Pacific Alaska Air Express flight will probably never be explained. It was the one of the first civil aircraft to disappear in that area, and only one of many that followed. Over the years the accident was forgotten, pushed into the back pages of history by the passing of time and more dramatic aviation events that unfolded in the decades to come.

Lost off Cape Spencer

JULY 20, 1951

Somewhere between Cape Spencer and Anchorage a Canadian Pacific Air Lines DC-4 vanished without a trace. In the sphere of world aviation it was just another statistic, but in Alaska it added to the growing mystery of aircraft disappearing along the southeastern coast. Whether it was a victim of weather or navigation will never be known. The vast expanse of open ocean and coastal mountains between Juneau and Anchorage is an area of many mysteries.

In 1951 the Korean War was an intense struggle that had not yet resolved itself into a stalemate along the demilitarized zone separating the two Korean countries. The shipment of troops to the area was, of course, a priority for the armed forces. An overseas airlift was established for moving soldiers in and out of the war zone from the United States, via a transition point in Japan. Referred to as the "Great Circle" airlift, the flights between North America and Japan became a major operation for the United States and Canada. Commercial airline companies from both countries were contracted for the scheduled service, easing the heavy burden already placed on military assets.

Vancouver was the operations base for Canadian Pacific Air Lines Limited, and the hub for all Korean airlift flights departing from North America. U.S. troops scheduled on the airlift were first routed through military bases in Washington State before continuing onto Vancouver for one of the four weekly flights. From there it was a relatively comfortable trip by air to Anchorage for a rest and refueling stop, then on to Tokyo, Japan.

The four-engine commercial airliner departed Vancouver at

1643 Alaska Standard Time, on July 20, carrying thirty-one passengers and six crew members. Among the passengers were twenty-six from the U.S. military, two from the Royal Canadian Navy, and three civilians attached to the U.S. Army. All six crew members, including the airplane captain, first officer, flight navigator, flight engineer, radio operator and a flight attendant, were Canadian. They were experienced and familiar with the route.

A weather briefing received by the captain before departure did not show any significant hazards between Vancouver and Anchorage. The only thing of importance was an occluded front in the Gulf of Alaska, 150 to 200 miles west of Yakutat. A freezing level of 9,000 feet was forecast between Cape Spencer and Yakataga, along with various layers of overcast cloud conditions. No severe icing was expected, but there was a possibility of increased turbulence in the vicinity of the occluded front as it moved northeast toward the coastline.

After departing from Vancouver, the Canadian DC-4 proceeded by instrument flight rules along the coast, first transitioning into Alaskan territory south of Annette Island. It followed the Amber One airway past the Sitka Radio Range and continued toward Anchorage. A position report over the Sitka station was delayed by twenty-three minutes due to radio interference, and the captain instead transmitted the information to the Yakutat station once they were within range. A few minutes later, approximately four and a half hours after the flight's initial departure from Vancouver, the captain reported over the Cape Spencer Intersection, at 9,000 feet, and estimating their arrival over Yakutat at 2200 hours. He did not mention any in-flight problems. Nothing further was heard from the aircraft.

Numerous attempts at radio contact were initiated by air traffic control when the aircraft failed to report passing Yakutat, but no answer was received. Another pilot flying in the area would later report that the radio conditions were extremely weak, and the low-frequency airway signal from Yakutat was fluctuating considerably during that period of time.

At 2244, search and rescue facilities were alerted. During the next few days of the search, heavy cloud cover blanketing the coast up to an altitude of 12,000 feet hampered flights between Juneau and Anchorage. Persistent rain and thick ground fog in many areas

57

further limited the search. Even so, two Coast Guard cutters arrived in the Gulf of Alaska to begin a sweep of the offshore waters, and several aircraft managed to overfly the 500-mile route between Cape Spencer and Anchorage.

During the first day of the search on the 21st, the aircraft not deterred by the weather concentrated along the barren southeastern coast and high peaks north of the airway course. In addition to the Coast Guard airplanes and ships dispatched from Juneau and Kodiak, the 10th Rescue Squadron at Elmendorf Air Force Base in Anchorage had two aircraft involved and another three waiting to join once the conditions improved. The Army base in Fairbanks had another two aircraft standing by, as did McChord Air Force Base with two B-17s specially configured for search and rescue missions. Unfortunately, the inclement weather did not improve for several more days, limiting any extensive operations in the area.

On the second and third days of the search the aircraft were as busy dodging clouds and each other as they were looking for any signs of the missing airplane. Flights were forced to fly below the lower cloud base, skimming a few hundred feet over the water or cruising above the cloud tops at 8,000 feet, able to search only the highest peaks of the coastal mountains.

There was still hope of locating survivors, but continuing foul weather conditions only added to the searchers' frustration. Survival gear had been carried on board the missing DC-4, including three life rafts and an emergency radio in case the aircraft was forced to ditch, leaving the possibility that the occupants were still alive and awaiting rescue. The search crews knew that if the airplane had gone down somewhere in the Gulf or along the coast, there was still hope. Those positive thoughts kept them motivated and focused on the mission. Talk of more fatal consequences would only frustrate the search efforts further.

By July 24 the clouds finally dispersed over the search area between Cape Spencer and Yakutat, allowing eighteen airplanes to systematically cover the offshore waters and inland mountains. Clear skies and unlimited visibility were a welcome change that provided an excellent opportunity for locating the missing airliner. A total of twenty-seven aircraft were involved by that evening, many flying past midnight through the summer twilight to take advantage of the good conditions.

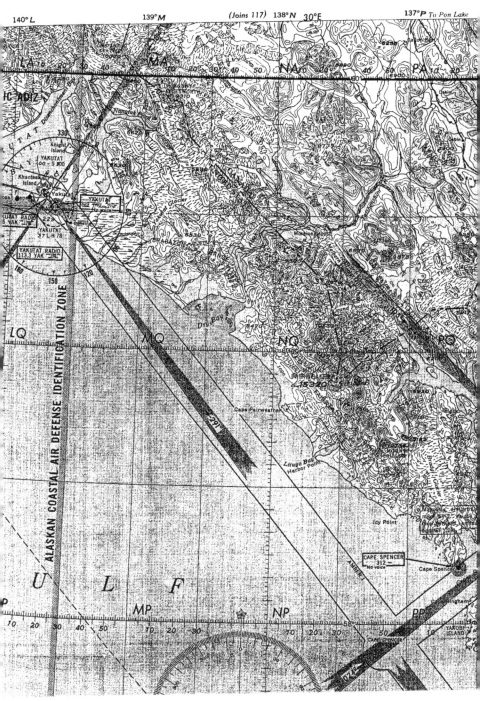

Mount Fairweather World Aeronautical Chart. Airway system from Yakutat to Cape Spencer. (*For illustration only—not to be used for navigation purposes.*)

Three different Coast Guard cutters were involved in the search effort by the 24th as well. Private and commercial fishing vessels joined them in combing the Gulf of Alaska. Planes of different makes and sizes from the U.S. military, Coast Guard, Canadian Armed Forces, Canadian Pacific Airlines and civilian agencies flew over their search areas again and again, but without any luck. Occasionally an aircraft would bank sharply and descend over a promising sighting, only to discover another clump of kelp floating at sea, or a large rock on a barren hillside casting a strangely shaped shadow.

Another aircraft, which was not involved in the search, disappeared near Yakutat on the 27th. The pilot was supporting a group of scientists conducting glacial studies in the St. Elias Mountains. The aircraft was a single-engine Norseman flown by Maurice King, a well-known and experienced Alaskan bush pilot. Two other occupants were also onboard. The airplane vanished without a trace in marginal weather on a short flight to Malaspina Glacier near Mount Hubbard. Determined aircrews, already looking for the missing airliner, included the second missing airplane as an equal priority in their widening search patterns.

On the 30th, the search for the DC-4 concentrated closer around the Yakutat area when word was received from a radio operator in Whitehorse, Yukon, stating that the airliner had sent another possible message the evening it disappeared. He said a strange transmission had been passed from an unidentified aircraft about an hour after the missing DC-4's last position report near Cape Spencer. The message was received about the time the airplane should have arrived over Yakutat Station. The pilot of the aircraft requested that the controller relay to Elmendorf Air Force Base in Anchorage to have hot meals ready for the crew and passengers when they arrived. Even though the controller did not remember the airplane's call sign, he was convinced the radio call was from the missing Canadian Pacific aircraft.

At first the story seemed like an encouraging lead, especially since no other aircraft were reported inbound to Elmendorf Air Force Base during the same time. Extra military aircraft were even dispatched to the Yakutat area when the authenticity of the story seemed certain. It was discounted the very next day, however, when the radio operator admitted he could not be sure of what day he actually received the message. A subsequent check by the accident investigation team with the military personnel at Elmendorf Air Force Base, revealed that no radio messages with that particular request had been received.

As the exact day of the transmission could not be verified, it would seem logical that investigators would inquire whether other inbound aircraft to Elmendorf Air Force Base over the several day period before and after the airplane disappeared might have sent the message. Strangely, there is no evidence that this was ever done.

About the same time as the false lead near Yakutat, another false report had the missing DC-4 over Prince of Wales Island, about 200 miles south of the primary search area. Several residents of Craig, a small community on the west side of the island, stated they heard a large aircraft flying over the town on the night the airliner disappeared. However, it seemed unlikely the aircraft would have turned back after reaching Cape Spencer Intersection, especially without any communication with air traffic control as to its intentions. If there had been an in-flight emergency, other landing areas closer to Yakutat were certainly available. The report was dismissed almost as soon as it materialized.

No legitimate clues to the disappearance of the aircraft were found until the 31st, when an oar, similar to those carried on emergency life rafts, was spotted floating near Yakutat. Unfortunately, the surface ship sent to the area for positive identification could not locate it. The possibility that it came from the missing airliner seemed even more probable on August 4, when a yellow life raft was reported a few miles south of Cape Spencer, near Chichagof Island. Two people aboard a commercial aircraft stated they clearly saw the raft floating several hundred feet from shore. However, it too could not be verified. A Coast Guard cutter dispatched to the area found no trace of the raft when it arrived.

Over the next several days other potential clues were found, only to be dismissed after closer investigation. A fisherman found a case of Army rations near Yakutat, supposedly from the missing aircraft, but there was no evidence that military rations were carried aboard the aircraft. One of the most promising leads was found on August 6, when a ground search party walking the beach near Yakutat, stumbled on the apparent remains of a human leg. It seemed to be a positive clue, especially when a pair of trousers was located a short distance away. Those finds also proved erroneous after a few days. The leg and foot bones were determined to be from a bear, and the trousers were positively identified as belonging to a fisherman who had fallen overboard in the same area many months before.

Weather continued to hamper the search efforts throughout the summer and fall with intermittent storms rolling in from the sea. The area was well known for its extreme conditions, and when thick clouds or rain were not prevalent, high winds and turbulence usually were. Even so, a large number of aircraft persisted with the search. Through the middle of August, over twenty aircraft were still involved each day, limited only by weather and increasing hours of darkness. Thousands of flight hours were flown by military and civilian crews, many under difficult conditions that could easily have taken their own lives.

On August 14, three Royal Canadian airplanes involved with the search operation returned to their bases in British Columbia. A Canadian civil aircraft, which had disappeared near Vancouver Island with seven occupants, was still missing and the R.C.A.F. airplanes were needed there. Some U.S. military and Coast Guard airplanes also diverted from the southeast coast to look for a Navy airplane that disappeared in the Aleutians, but a large number of aircraft still continued their search efforts around Yakutat. A concentrated search for the missing DC-4 lasted through the end of October, until the operation was officially called off on the 31st.

Aircraft from six different military and civilian agencies had been involved from the outset, including numerous private citizens searching with their own airplanes and boats at significant personal expense. At the time it was one of the largest search operations in Alaskan history. Local pilots paid extra attention when over flying the area for years to come, but no one ever sighted any evidence of the missing aircraft.

During the official investigation following the accident, the investigation team could only rely on statements from Canadian Pacific personnel in Vancouver as to the airworthiness of the missing DC-4. Interviews with maintenance and service personnel at the point of departure indicated the aircraft did not have any major problems to limit it from overseas flight. All logbooks pertaining to the aircraft were on board when it vanished, but this was normal procedure at the time.

Checks of the radio range stations at Sitka and Yakutat after the flight's disappearance found them both to be operating normally. Captain Fox, the pilot-in-command, had over 10,000 total flight hours, of which 320 were flown during the previous three months. First Officer Thomson was also very experienced with over 6,000 hours. He had flown 194 hours over the previous three-month period. All six crew members were properly trained and qualified, with the exception of the navigator, who had not yet been issued a navigator certification from the Canadian Department of Transport. However, he had previously held a British navigator's license which expired a week before the flight. His total flight time while serving as a navigator was approximately 900 hours, 250 of which were during the three months prior to the flight's disappearance.

Lost and Found

August 21, 1958/August 23, 1979

Clarence Rhode was one of the best-known and most respected government officials in Alaska at the time of his disappearance. A staunch conservationist who worked in fish and wildlife management throughout his adult life, Rhode was also the predominate influence in the use of aircraft in wildlife enforcement. Rising through the ranks of the Alaska Game Commission, and later the Fish and Wildlife Service, he earned a reputation as a no-nonsense individual dedicated to conserving Alaska's wildlife through strong but fair management.

Growing up in Washington State, Rhode learned to appreciate and respect the outdoors at an early age. The experiences he gained working with his father in a fish hatchery, and later as a deputy game warden, helped shape his views on wildlife management.

He arrived in Alaska in 1934, only twenty-one years old and with no college education, and began working for a meager salary with the U.S. Forest Service in Seward. Times were tough during the Depression, even in Alaska. His salary was not enough to afford a decent place to sleep and barely kept him fed. A storeroom in the Forest Service building served as a temporary residence for several months until he finally earned a decent raise.

Whatever brief inconveniences were placed before him, Rhode either overcame or ignored by relishing in the splendors of Alaska. The expanses of unspoiled territory, abundance of wildlife and local pioneer spirit captivated him like so many others before. Other officials did not share his enthusiasm, however, and instead allowed the exploitation of the seemingly endless resources without any concern for the future. Rhode knew differently. He could envision a land stripped of its natural fish and game by uncaring bureaucrats and ineffective management, much like Washington State had been, and his aim to avoid a similar fate for Alaska soon became his life's work.

In 1935, Rhode began work with the Alaska Game Commission, the predecessor to today's U.S. Fish and Wildlife Service. He quickly advanced through the organization as a hardworking, talented young man. In only a short time he was a certified game warden and acting assistant to the Regional Executive Officer.

By 1939 the lure of aviation had taken hold of him, becoming an on-going love affair that consumed much of Rhode's free time. After learning how to fly, he continued to improve his pilot skills until he became an experienced bush pilot. Much of his apprenticeship in the air was under the tutelage of Sam White, one of Alaska's most respected aviators and a legendary game warden, who was the first territorial agent to use aircraft in the performance of his duties.

Eventually Clarence Rhode earned commercial and instrument ratings, allowing him to earn extra income and flight experience while working for different air services around the territory during his annual leaves. During World War II, he flew cargo and passengers along the dangerous Aleutian route and assisted many lend-lease pilots transporting aircraft across Alaska to the Soviet Union.

By 1947 Rhode's career as a wildlife agent and supervisor had progressed to the highest position in the Alaska Game Commission when he was appointed as Regional Director and Executive Officer. He wasted little time in improving and expanding the operation. One of his first priorities was to acquire surplus military equipment and aircraft for use in wildlife enforcement and management. He helped build a high-frequency radio network that was second in quality only to the military's, and ensured that available aircraft were put into use in Alaska where they were desperately needed by the Fish and Wildlife Service.

As the Regional Director, Clarence also insisted that every wildlife agent be a qualified pilot with his own assigned aircraft and that qualified biologists be included in his staff. The proper management of fish and wildlife resources became a priority. His modern ideas of game conservation helped preserve much of what Alaskans have available to them today, but his influence went far beyond the policies of just the Fish and Wildlife Service. Rhode also helped establish a wildlife management program and a wildlife research unit at the University of Alaska in Fairbanks in 1949. Later, he even became a faculty member responsible for graduate training in wildlife management.

By 1957, his name was one of only a few individuals considered for the National Director position at the Fish and Wildlife Service in Washington, D.C. Rhode was relieved when his lack of a college degree became the decisive factor against his appointment. Leaving Alaska was a decision he was happy he was not forced to make.

Even though he continued to hold the highest Fish and Wildlife Service position in Alaska, Rhode's duties did not prevent him from flying and assisting other agents with their own field work. In August 1958, he flew a Fish and Wildlife Service Grumman Goose north from Juneau into the eastern Brooks Range to conduct Dall sheep counts and establish fuel cache sites for later use by field agents. The aircraft was one of his personal favorites and he was one of the most experienced pilots in the organization qualified to fly it. Fish and Wildlife agent Stan Fredericksen from Fairbanks and Clarence's twenty-year-old-son Jack, a student at the University of Washington, accompanied him on the flight.

On the flight north from Fairbanks on the 20th, Rhode sent a position report over the Middle Fork of the Chandalar River and another once they reached their destination at Porcupine Lake, deep in the Brooks Range. Situated in a mountain pass at the 3,000-foot elevation between the Canning and Ivishak rivers, the lake was a perfect staging area for reconnaissance flights into the eastern portion of the range. Over a mile long, the lake was more than adequate for twin-engine amphibian operations.

After arriving at Porcupine Lake, no further radio communication was received from Rhode, probably because of severe atmospheric interference that blocked out all communication over much of northern Alaska for the next few days. They did, however, visit other groups in the area. That same afternoon, they flew approximately forty-five miles northeast into Lake Peters and Lake Schrader on the northern edge of the Range, near Mount Chamberlin. They talked for a few hours with a local hunting guide and a group from the International Geophysical Society before departing west, presumably back toward Porcupine Lake. It was the last confirmed contact ever made with Clarence Rhode.

When the aircraft did not return to Fairbanks as scheduled on the 21st, and no communications were received over the next few days, an aerial search was initiated over the Brooks Range. At first there was no immediate concern for their welfare, it being assumed that the twin-engine amphibian had been forced down with mechanical problems on some remote lake that precluded any radio contact. The aircraft carried plenty of emergency gear for the three men, including rations, sleeping bags, a tent and a survival weapon. All three men were also experienced outdoorsmen who would have had little trouble surviving on their own.

Much of the search area in the eastern portion of the Brooks Range was hampered by bad weather through the end of August. Snow had already begun falling in the higher elevations, accompanied by low clouds and fog in the mountain passes and valleys. Limited visibility prevented aircraft from searching many of the more remote areas in the mountains where Rhode might have been forced down.

The Air Force's 71st Air and Sea Rescue Squadron at Elmendorf Air Force Base in Anchorage was commanding over a dozen aircraft involved in the air search each day, sometimes over twice that amount. By August 25, additional aircraft from the military, Fish and Wildlife Service, Civil Aeronautics Administration and several northern communities were involved in a massive, coordinated effort. The area between Bettles and Fairbanks and the north and south slopes of the eastern range were searched extensively during the first few days, but with no evidence of the missing airplane being found.

The days grew shorter during the first weeks of the search, but very few gave up hope Rhode and his two companions would eventually be found alive. But as August turned into September speculation became less optimistic. The lakes and rivers in the Brooks Range were already starting to freeze during the night with the approach of winter, and snow continued moving lower into the valleys and mountain passes, potentially covering any evidence of the missing airplane. The chance of survival for the three men was also diminishing with each progressive day of falling temperatures. Although they were adequately equipped to survive the mild fall conditions, severe winter weather was an entirely different predicament.

On September 1 the clouds finally broke, providing the first day of good flying weather and clear radio reception. Aircraft searched the valleys deep inside the mountains where they could not fly into before, covering all the critical areas in the eastern half of the Range. Every mountain pass and every possible air route between the river drainages was overflown several times. All the lakes and slopes of each valley were covered for any potential clues to the disappearance, but nothing was found.

On September 6, the search shifted to the western half of the Brooks Range after a hunting guide who arrived in Fairbanks from his camp on Chandler Lake stated that he had seen the Fish and Wildlife Service aircraft on August 21. The airplane was observed flying over the lake around noon, heading in a northwesterly direction. Even though Chandler Lake was over 150 miles west of Rhode's base camp at Porcupine Lake, the Grumman Goose carried more than enough fuel for the round trip. It was certainly conceivable that the crew had decided on scouting other areas much farther west than originally intended.

By the middle of September, no evidence of the missing airplane had been found in the western area of the Range either. Worsening weather conditions became a serious problem for most of the search aircraft, and the effort was temporarily halted from several locations because of the dangerous landing conditions. Once the ground had frozen completely, the local search aircraft switched to skis and the search was resumed.

Military and other government and civilian aircraft continued searching through November, until flying became unsafe in the extreme conditions. Temperatures were by then plummeting to -40° F at times, while low clouds and high winds continued plaguing much of the search area. On December 1 the search was officially called off, but aircraft still conducted occasional flights over the area when the weather would allow it.

The following summer, another air search was begun once the snow melted from the mountain passes. Fish and Wildlife Service personnel even combed a few of the remote valleys on foot. Over 400 aircraft had been involved in the three-month search the previous year. Other airplanes resumed flights in July 1959. Again, nothing was found of the aircraft or men. For the next twenty-one years the disappearance of Clarence Rhode remained a mystery.

On August 23, 1979, two hikers near the saddle of a high mountain pass separating the upper Ivishak and Wind River Valleys discovered the burned wreckage of an aircraft. At first they assumed it was a previously known crash, but on closer inspection the evidence revealed a different story. Even though most of the fuselage was destroyed by impact and fire, one wing was left intact with a partially crushed engine lying nearby. A large duffel bag containing survival gear was also found outside the burn area. Other debris littered the crash site in a small area around the wreckage.

Human remains were also found later, but one significant find was a partially burned metal briefcase containing the aircraft's flight logs. The two hikers read the entries written by an unfamiliar pilot named Clarence Rhode, surprised that the details concerned events that took place twenty-one years previously. The final entry showed the aircraft departed from Porcupine Lake at 1010 on August 21, 1958, returned at 1135, then departed again at 1326 for an unspecified destination.

The hikers knew from their map that Porcupine Lake was only around twenty miles northeast of the airplane's wreckage. Apparently the pilot had flown west from the lake into the Ivishak valley, then southwest toward the mountain pass before crashing a couple hundred feet below the summit on the eastern side of the canyon. They were amazed the wreckage had remained undiscovered for so many years.

When the hikers were picked up two days later in the next valley by a local air service, they showed the flight logs with the aircraft's registration number to the pilot, who reported the find to the Fairbanks flight service station. News of the discovery quickly spread, finally bringing to an end the twenty-one-year-old mystery of Rhode's disappearance.

On August 28 officials from the National Transportation Safety Board, Fish and Wildlife Service and Rhode's surviving son flew to the crash site by helicopter. Even though most of the wreckage had been consumed by fire, enough evidence remained to determine the probable cause of the crash. It was apparent that the airplane hit while in a left turn, impacting almost nose first into the 040° slope. Damage inflicted on the propellers indicated both engines were operating at cruise power during the impact. The throttles were also found in a forward position.

Numerous five-gallon fuel cans stored in the nose compartment and cabin area had been crushed by the impact, causing almost instantaneous vaporization and subsequent ignition. Most of the fuselage that was not destroyed by the severe collision was consumed in the post-crash fire. A few items that had been thrown clear on impact were found relatively intact, including the duffel bag, briefcase and Rhode's personal flight bag. After twenty-one years, the bag still contained readable maps and Fish and Wildlife Service paperwork.

There was no indication of any in-flight fire or mechanical problems with the aircraft. The evidence suggested weather conditions in the pass at the time of the accident were probably marginal, forcing Rhode to turn around in the canyon. The aircraft's height above the ground and proximity to the surrounding mountains would have precluded an attempt at climbing above the weather, placing the trapped aircraft in a dangerous predicament. It seemed as if the airplane had simply run out of room to maneuver and crashed. There was also the possibility high winds were prevalent at the time, causing strong downdrafts that forced the aircraft into the slope.

For twenty-one years the airplane crash site eluded discovery from other aircraft flying over the area. The initial search in August 1958 was hampered by poor weather and by September 1 snowfall had probably covered evidence of the wreckage. Any subsequent flights over the years would only have been able to see the debris during the few months when snow was melted from the slope, and even then the aircraft's scattered pieces would have blended in with the rock- and lichen-covered surface.

The mountain pass where Rhode's airplane crashed is also one of the highest in the eastern Brooks Range. Because of its elevation and surrounding terrain it was not used much by low flying aircraft. Other less dangerous routes in the adjoining valleys were usually frequented instead. As Rhode was flying southwest in the valley, he would have made the final turn into the narrower canyon only a mile north of the pass. By the time he realized weather conditions blocked the intended route, it would have been too late.

It is possible that the change in the search area west of the crash location a few weeks after the airplane's disappearance had some effect on the outcome. From the entries found in the flight log it was doubtful if Rhode's airplane was anywhere near Chandler Lake on the 21st, 150 miles west of the actual wreckage. Other hunters on Nelikpuk Lake, near Chandler Lake, would have seen the aircraft if it was in the area, but they reported no such sighting. In fact, the guide of the hunting party near the lake had previously arranged with Stan Fredericksen, the Fish and Wildlife Service agent accompanying Rhode, to meet the guide at Nelikpuk Lake if they were flying in the area.

By the time the search effort was diverted further west, the Ivishak and Wild River areas to the east had already been searched and light snow partially covered the higher passes, but additional flights over the area might eventually have noticed the crash site before the heavier snows fell later in the month. However, after twenty-one years of speculation, at least the mystery had finally been solved.

The discovery leaves hope that the dozens of other aircraft that have vanished somewhere in Alaska over the past seventy years may also be found in the future.

The Disappearance of Boggs and Begich

OCTOBER 16, 1972

A moderate northwest wind blew across the runway as the white twin-engine Cessna departed in a shallow climb away from the Anchorage airport. It turned downwind and flew eastward into Turnagain Arm toward Portage Pass, disappearing into the low clouds, never to be seen again. On board were an experienced Alaskan pilot, two U.S. Congressmen and a congressional aide. The date was October 16, 1972, only three weeks away from the federal election.

Democratic Party faithful attending an extravagant fundraiser at the Anchorage Westward Hotel the previous night had high hopes for the political future of Alaska Congressman Nick Begich. Running for his second term in office, Begich was accompanied in Alaska by Louisiana Representative Hale Boggs, who had taken the freshman legislator under his wing. As the second-ranking Democrat in the U.S. House with twenty-eight years in office, Boggs's presence was influential in raising money for Begich's re-election campaign.

The intention of maintaining his party's dominance in the House of Representatives in the next election would certainly have been a priority for Boggs. If the Democrats could have continued their majority in Congress through 1978, when the then current Speaker of the House was expected to retire, Boggs's aspirations for the prestigious position would have become reality. The $250 per person cocktail party and $25 a plate dinner they hosted had attracted over 400 supporters and raised more than $20,000 for Begich's campaign. Another fundraiser was planned for the next evening in

Juneau before they continued on to Washington. But they never arrived.

Pilot Don Jonz, owner and chief pilot of Pan-Alaska Airways in Fairbanks, was transporting the important passengers himself instead of assigning another pilot. He had asked for current weather conditions along the proposed route of flight from the Anchorage Flight Service Station at 0656 that day. In addition to the current terminal forecasts at Juneau, Sitka, Yakutat and Cordova, Jonz received the current area forecast and winds aloft through 12,000 feet. The area forecast included a significant weather advisory for Cook Inlet listing moderate to locally severe turbulence with strong winds, showers, and strong updrafts and downdrafts. The Flight Service briefer also informed Jonz that Portage Pass on his intended route of flight was forecast to be closed.

With 17,000 flight hours to his credit, Don Jonz was a highly rated and competent aviator. He had over fifteen years of flying experience in Alaska, most of it in the Interior, and had written several aviation articles on flight techniques in icing conditions. In the previous six months he had flown over 600 hours, most of them while operating out of Fairbanks where his company was based. Jonz had a reputation as a superb pilot and as someone who could always get the job done. He was rumored to do things his own way at times, in disregard of an occasional regulation, but no one could dispute his flying skills.

There was no indication from witnesses at the airport that Don Jonz seemed at all concerned about the weather. After talking with the flight service station briefer, he refueled the airplane around 0800 and repositioned in front of the control tower. Congressmen Nick Begich and Hale Boggs arrived with Russel Brown a short time later and boarded the aircraft. A small amount of personal baggage was added prior to departure. The controller cleared N1812H for a visual flight rules downwind departure from runway 24R, and watched as the Cessna 310 took off at 0859, turning southeast along Turnagain Arm.

There were no other sightings of the plane, but pilot Jonz did contact the Anchorage flight service station again at 0909 to file a visual flight rules flight plan and receive updated weather reports. He stated their intended route of flight was along airway V-317 to Yakutat, then direct to Juneau. The estimated time en route was given as three hours and thirty minutes with a six-hour fuel endurance. True airspeed was given as 170 knots. When the flight service station operator asked if emergency gear and a locator beacon were onboard, Jonz replied "Affirmative."

Weather observations from the current sequence reports were given to Jonz for Cordova, Yakutat, Juneau and Sitka, showing little change from the previous reports he had received at 0656. Current terminal and area forecasts were again passed to him, still listing Portage Pass as closed to visual flight rules traffic. The hazardous weather advisory for Cook Inlet had been amended to include a forecast of moderate icing in clouds from 6,000 to 15,000 feet over the area. At the time Jonz received the updated information, the flight would still have been a few miles west of Portage Pass. He did not question any of the reports. After that, no further communication was received from the airplane.

It is significant to note that the official National Transportation Safety Board aircraft accident report released in January 1972 stated that an Air Force helicopter, over Turnagain Arm at 0840, was intending to fly through Portage Pass when the pilot reported encountering moderate to severe turbulence at 500 feet a few miles west of the pass. The pilot of the helicopter also claimed a headwind of fifty-five knots and a solid overcast at 700 to 800 feet, with visibility deteriorating ahead of him. His attempted flight through Portage Pass was then abandoned for an alternate route he selected toward his destination of Seward.

The pilot report sent from the helicopter might have influenced Jonz's decision to continue through the pass, but the flight service station specialist did not relay it to him, nor did Jonz at any time ask for pilot reports pertaining to his route of flight.

At 1315 that afternoon, the Coast Guard Command Center in Juneau advised the Air Force Rescue Coordination Center (RCC) in Anchorage that the flight was overdue. The RCC immediately began conducting communication checks with all airfields and facilities along the intended route, to determine if the aircraft might have diverted from the stated route on the flight plan. By 1345 it was determined that none of the stations had any knowledge of the overdue airplane's whereabouts. The flight was officially declared missing and an Air Force HC-130 was launched within the hour to begin a preliminary search.

As news of the airplane's disappearance spread, early speculation was that it had probably gone down somewhere in the Whittier area, on the eastern side of Portage Pass. A dockworker in the town of Whittier told the city police he had heard a light airplane pass over around 0930 that morning. Jonz's airplane would have been the only one in the area at that time.

Many local pilots felt Portage Pass was the most dangerous leg of the V-317 airway. The lower elevation was at approximately 3,000 feet, with steep mountains rising on either side. Pilots proceeding visually from Anchorage into Prince William Sound usually flew down Turnagain Arm and across the pass. Weather was always an important factor in any decision to transition through that area. Winds are often funneled into the pass at high velocities, causing increased turbulence and strong vertical drafts on either side of the steep terrain. Adequate visibility and cloud clearance are especially important for any pilot to maintain a safe distance above the ground. Any attempt at transitioning through the pass in marginal weather conditions would definitely not be in a pilot's best interest.

There was a possibility that Jonz had switched from visual flight to instruments on the airway after encountering instrument meteorological conditions. Without a pressurized cabin Jonz would still have been restricted from flying above 10,000 feet, forcing the aircraft to remain at lower levels forecast for high turbulence and icing. If he had decided to continue under instruments for the duration of the flight, he would also have been in violation of the applicable federal aviation regulations. Federal aviation regulations part 135, dealing with Air Taxi and Commercial Operators of Small Aircraft, restricted all flights to visual flight rules unless two pilots were aboard, or the aircraft was equipped with an autopilot and the pilot had demonstrated competency in using the autopilot under instrument conditions. The Cessna 310 Jonz flew was equipped with a functional VHF omni-directional range and automatic direction finder receiver for instrument flight, and an oxygen system was on board the aircraft, but it had not been serviced with oxygen. In addition, there was no autopilot installed or anti-icing capability on the aircraft, except for a heated Pitot tube.

Whether Jonz actually had an emergency locator transmitter and emergency equipment on board came into question after the flight was declared missing. Even though he had stated to the flight service station specialist that the airplane carried those items, Jonz's personal emergency locator transmitter was found after the search began in the cabin of another Pan-Alaska Airways airplane in Fairbanks. One witness did state that Jonz had carried an object aboard in his briefcase at the airport in Anchorage that could have been an emergency locator transmitter, but it was a different color from those used by his company. Employees who were inside the cabin shortly before the flight's departure also stated there were no survival equipment packages or containers inside. Pan-Alaska Airways only had three containers packed with survival equipment on hand for all their aircraft. All three of those containers were found in the Fairbanks office after Jonz's airplane was missing. Alaska law specifically prohibited any flights within the state unless equipped with an approved emergency locator transmitter, and required minimum items of survival equipment on board during any cross-country flight.

By the evening of the 16th several aircraft were already involved in the search for the missing airplane, and the Air Force RCC in Anchorage was organizing an in-depth, coordinated effort along the 24,000 square miles of coastline for the following day. Over thirty military and civilian air patrol aircraft were available on the 17th, as well as four Coast Guard cutters being dispatched from their home ports along the coast. Unfortunately, the weather was not very cooperative over much of the search area and impeded any flights around Portage Pass for several days. Most of Prince William Sound was also being raked by high winds that whipped whitecaps across the waves, making visual sightings of wreckage or survivors extremely difficult.

There was some promising news the next day when a helicopter flying in the Juneau area monitored two separate emergency locator transmitter signals from the Mansfield Peninsula, fifteen miles southwest of the city. Two subsequent searches of the area, however, could not locate any signs of survivors or the missing aircraft.

There was little improvement in the weather through Wednesday, the 18th, and aircraft were still unable to search Portage Pass. Over thirty aircraft were involved in the search the first two days along most portions of the search area, and by Thursday eighty-seven total aircraft had joined the operation, logging over

300 hours that day alone. With the weather limiting search efforts around Portage Pass, the operation concentrated most of their assets farther out in Prince William Sound.

There were additional reports in the first few days that possibly placed the flight somewhere in the Juneau area. Several workers at a logging camp about eighty miles southwest of Juneau, on the outer coast of Chichagof Island, told the Coast Guard they had heard a small airplane in the area on the day the missing flight was en route to Juneau, followed by a loud booming noise. A private pilot flying in the area had also heard the booming sound near the Clear Creek logging camp, and at the time transmitted over the radio for anyone in distress to click their microphone. He stated that he did receive a responding click. Three Coast Guard helicopters were dispatched to the area, but none of the crews observed any indications of possible wreckage.

By the 20th an Air Force spokesman confirmed the missing airplane probably did not carry an emergency locator transmitter or any of the emergency gear that was required to be onboard. An emergency locator transmitter would have been automatically activated during a crash if it was operating correctly. Since the missing aircraft was thought to have not carried an emergency locator transmitter, it would seemingly discredit reports of subsequent emergency transmitter signals as coming from the missing airplane. In addition, since no further communication was received from the airplane after 0909 on the morning it disappeared, most of the people involved in the search remained convinced the airplane went down somewhere in the Prince William Sound area.

As the search for the missing Cessna stretched further into the week, requests for additional assistance would certainly have been sought by the congressmen's influential friends in government. The House of Representatives in Washington D.C. kept a sharp vigilance over the fate of Boggs and Begich, even so far as conducting daily briefings on the status of their two missing comrades. Not surprisingly, it did not take long before other military assets outside of Alaska began joining the search.

An SR-71 spy plane was soon dispatched to take infrared photographs of the entire area from an altitude of 80,000 feet. Several thousand photographs were taken of the entire search area in a short amount of time, with no success in identifying the missing aircraft.

Two RF-4C Phantoms, equipped for all-weather, all-night surveillance, were also sent north to participate, with the same results.

By October 22, six days into the search, focus shifted to the southeastern Panhandle. Portage Pass had finally been covered by Army ground search teams on the 19th and 20th, and subsequent helicopter flights found no evidence of the missing airplane. Extensive overflights and surface searches of Prince William Sound had also proven fruitless. Even if the airplane had gone down in the water, it was determined that any survivors would already have perished from exposure.

Confusing reports of mysterious Citizen Band (C.B.) radio broadcasts were also coming forward from several individuals in California, possibly placing Jonz's flight somewhere near Juneau on the day it disappeared. Five different C.B. owners in four cities claimed to have monitored radio broadcasts from a person who stated he was a pilot in Alaska experiencing in-flight difficulties. All five individuals believed they had talked with the pilot of the missing Cessna 310 carrying the two congressmen, even though Jonz's name and the aircraft's identification were never used in any of the transmissions. Stranger still, the radio broadcasts were received nearly eight hours after the airplane's fuel endurance would have been exhausted.

The five C.B. operators only monitored pieces of the pilot's transmissions at different times. Some of the C.B. operators stated that the pilot told them he was experiencing high headwinds and low fuel. Only one of the five operators acknowledged receiving a separate transmission that explained that the airplane had landed on an airstrip in bad weather before proceeding on with the flight later in the day, only to encounter even worse conditions. During the pilot's first broadcast he supposedly identified himself as "Alaska Mobile," stating he was in need of assistance over water, 100 miles from land and with only fifteen minutes of fuel remaining. Seconds later the pilot said he was putting the airplane down, then declared they were going to hit the rocks.

Another C.B. operator only monitored a broadcast about fifteen minutes after the airplane reported going into the rocks, and said the transmission stated there were three injured passengers on board and the airplane was "slipping." All five operators stated they did not consider the broadcast a hoax. They also said the pilot explained he was lost in an area approximately twelve miles southwest of Juneau.

A thorough investigation of the strange broadcasts was conducted by the Air Force, but no conclusive findings were reached, or at least published. The Final Mission Report from the Alaskan Air Command and the National Transportation Safety Board aircraft accident report do not mention the broadcasts.

From the conflicting statements made by the five C.B. operators it seems highly unlikely the broadcasts were authentic. For the pilot of an aircraft in obvious distress not to identify himself or the airplane's registration is unlikely, especially hours after the flight plan had expired and the airplane would have been listed as missing. In all, the investigation followed up over eighty-eight different leads, none of which resulted in any evidence that revealed the location of the missing airplane or its occupants.

By November 11, twenty-seven days into the search, every possible route the airplane might have taken was covered at least three times, and the primary search area along the route filed in the flight plan was covered sixteen times. On November 24, thirty-nine days into the search, the mission was finally suspended. By then the highest probability search areas had been covered at least thirteen times, revealing no clues.

When the mission was finally concluded, the air search had encompassed over 325,000 square miles. Aerial infrared and optical photographs were taken of the entire search area, and an electronic monitoring aircraft was in the air continuously for the first twelve days. Military and CAP aircraft alone flew over 3,607 hours in support of the mission. Private and commercial aircraft not directly involved in the search certainly logged thousands of other hours over the area in the conduct of their normal business, keeping a lookout for the missing airplane and monitoring possible distress calls.

In addition to the extensive air coverage flown during the search effort, ground searches were also conducted in Portage Pass, and sea searches performed in Prince William Sound and along the coastal areas leading into Juneau and Sitka. Commercial and private fishing boats were alerted by the Coast Guard and Alaska Commercial Fishing Organizations to report any sightings concerning the missing aircraft, and would certainly have kept extra vigilant during that time.

There are many theories on what could have happened to the twin-engine Cessna on October 16, 1972. Many of the accusations point to the pilot who had a history of disregarding regulations when it suited him. Jonz's airline transport pilot license had been suspended by the Federal Aviation Administration in 1966 for violating several regulations, but was reissued in 1968, listing him as a completely qualified and certified pilot. He also had a previous mishap several years before when an airplane he was piloting crashed in the Brooks Range.

His previously published articles on flying in icing conditions were very informative, yet demonstrated a somewhat cavalier attitude in his opinions. However, those facts by themselves do not necessarily make Jonz a bad pilot or a safety risk. No one can argue he was very experienced and knew his limitations. Maybe this one time he took them for granted.

Certainly there can be no doubt Jonz was aware of the poor enroute conditions on the day in question, conditions that were not at all conducive for visual flight rules. He was also well aware of the requirements for emergency gear, an emergency locator transmitter and for flying in instrument conditions with only one pilot, if that was his intention. What decisions he actually made in flight and why, will probably never be determined. If he did encounter problems or diverted from the filed flight plan, normal procedure would have been to notify a Flight Service Station or air traffic controller. That was obviously not done, thus raising even more questions.

The possibility of a catastrophic mechanical failure of the airframe or engines can also not be ruled out, either from the extreme forces encountered during the existing weather conditions or an already pre-existing deficiency in the aircraft. However, during the National Transportation Safety Board's accident investigation, the aircraft maintenance records and statements from a company maintenance inspector showed the aircraft to be fully airworthy. The aircraft's last annual inspection had been completed approximately eleven months previously and a 100-hour inspection was completed the day before the flight disappeared. A refueler and tower personnel at the Anchorage Airport also testified the airplane appeared and sounded normal on the morning of the 16th.

A fascination with the airplane's disappearance has never completely died among some individuals. Amateur historians, psychics and conspiracy theorists still occasionally come forward with some new clue that is eventually disproved. One conspiracy theory even has Congressman Boggs linked with the supposed cover-up of President Kennedy's assassination. Some theorists believe Hale Boggs was deliberately silenced before he could reveal information that would not only discredit the findings of the Warren Commission, but would also disclose evidence of the real perpetrators behind the president's assassination.

Today, the fate of Don Jonz, Congressmen Begich and Boggs, and Russel Brown still remains a mystery. Speculation among the aviation community is that the airplane probably came apart in the air due to turbulence and icing, then either crashed into the water and sank or impacted a snow-covered mountain, where it was subsequently hidden from view. Hundreds of miles of ocean, coastal mountain ranges and forested islands can hide many secrets. Perhaps someday a beachcomber, pilot or hunter will finally find some evidence that explains what happened on that fateful day. It is also just as likely that the circumstances will forever remain a mystery.

Crash on Tamgas Mountain

OCTOBER 26, 1947

In the early years of aviation in Alaska and throughout World War II, there were many aircraft accidents involving fatalities. Commercial airliners were no exception. For many years the flying industry in the territory continued expanding its operations with only a few occasional deaths, but never experiencing a major aviation disaster that resulted in a significant loss of life. Most civilian fatalities involved only small single or dual-engine aircraft, usually while landing at a multitude of unimproved dirt airstrips or during flight in inclement weather.

Once the military and Civil Aeronautics Administration began constructing modern radio range stations and airfields across Alaska in the early 1940s, the capabilities of aircraft using those facilities expanded considerably. Commercial aviation took a back seat to military commitments during the war years that followed, but by the war's end those same advances in aviation technology were fueling a rapidly growing airline industry. The territory of Alaska was ripe for expansion.

By the war's end modern airfields had been established in every large city, along numerous coastal islands and even in several remote villages of the Interior. Many of the military-style transport aircraft developed during the war were soon converted and used in great numbers for civilian passenger service. With the network of navigational aids and communication systems established in the territory, instrument flying soon became routine in every type of weather for most commercial aircraft. As technology progressed, the capability of aircraft also expanded, allowing larger numbers of people to be carried over greater distances. Along with the new advances came the increased potential for disaster. Alfred Monsen was a well-known and respected pilot in Alaska. He first arrived in the territory in 1917, and began working for the Alaska Railroad before learning how to fly in 1928. During the early years of aviation he established himself as a skilled bush pilot while operating along the southeastern coast. Monsen remained in the area after joining Pan American Airways in 1932, when the airline purchased the smaller company with whom he was employed at the time. His flight experience in the territory was invaluable and Pan American kept him assigned in Alaska throughout his career. In 1941 he was one of the first Pan American pilots to open a new air route between Seattle and Alaska. By 1947 he was the oldest and most experienced airline captain in the company's Alaska flight division.

On October 26, 1947, Captain Monsen and his crew were flying a Pan American DC-4 from Seattle to Juneau, with an intermediate stop scheduled at Annette Island. Including Monsen, the airplane's crew consisted of a first officer, a flight engineer and two flight attendants. Thirteen passengers occupied the seats in the cabin, including an infant who was returning with his parents to Juneau. The airplane carried slightly over 800 pounds of cargo, mostly baggage, and plenty of fuel for the routine flight. The fuel tanks held over twelve hours of usable fuel, more than twice the amount needed to reach their destination of Juneau.

At 1030, the flight took off from the runway at Seattle under clear skies. All four engines were running smoothly as they reached their cruising altitude of 9,000 feet. The passengers were relaxed and enjoying the spectacular view as the aircraft continued along the airway to Annette. About an hour into the flight the view was lost as a thick cloud cover over the coast surrounded them, obscuring any further outside references. Turbulence soon followed, bouncing the airplane with an occasional jolt that was strong enough to keep anyone from dozing off. Most of the passengers were inexperienced with flying and remained on edge, but the crew considered it fairly routine. Even the light icing they were encountering would not have concerned the crew. They knew the aircraft was easily capable of operating in much worse weather conditions.

As the flight continued toward Annette Island, stronger than predicted winds pushed the aircraft faster than anticipated along the airway. The Pan American weather forecast they received in Seattle had mentioned enroute winds of thirty to forty knots, but the actual velocity was much stronger. The increased winds made for a rougher ride, but they also put the flight ahead of schedule, which certainly made everyone aboard happy.

Captain Monsen knew the weather conditions upon arrival at Annette would be fairly standard for that time of year. An occluded weather front was moving from the west toward the southeastern coast, bringing the usual low ceilings and persistent rain along with it. Winds on arrival at the airport were forecast to be eighteen knots, with visibility two miles and an 800-foot overcast ceiling. In-flight turbulence was not supposed to be a factor once they descended out of their cruising altitude for the approach. Even so, Monsen did not take the weather for granted. He had flown into Annette many times during his career, in all types of weather. More than anyone, he understood the potential hazards involved.

Three hours out of Seattle, when the Pan American DC-4 was approaching Annette Island, the flight received a current weather observation at the airfield from their company radio operator. A 1,400-foot ceiling was reported, with scattered lower cloud levels. Visibility was three miles with rain and southeast winds at sixteen knots, gusting to thirty-five knots. The winds were stronger than originally forecast, but the crew did not expect any significant problems with the approach, except for a possibility of increased turbulence during the descent.

After the crew received the current weather observation, air traffic control cleared the flight to descend and cross over the radio range at 7,000 feet, then proceed with the published instrument approach.

When flying the outbound leg of the approach on the 140° radial, aircraft were required to execute a procedure turn or course reversal back inbound on the 320° radial to the airfield. Because of mountainous terrain to the east and northeast of the airfield, aircraft were required to remain west of the inbound course when executing the procedure turn. The approach had been standardized at Annette for years and had been flown hundreds of times by numerous military and civilian pilots.

Captain Monsen acknowledged the approach clearance from air

traffic control and confirmed crossing the station a short time later at 1338, at an altitude of 7,000 feet. Five minutes later the flight advised Annette radio that it was experiencing extreme turbulence and was canceling the approach, proceeding instead to Juneau. At that time the controller asked the pilot to verify their current altitude. There was no reply. After continued attempts at contact, air traffic control issued a distress alert to all stations at 1401. Nothing further was heard from Captain Monsen or his crew.

By 1430 an initial search of the area had begun and the Civil Aeronautics Board was notified of the situation to begin an official investigation. A weather front hitting the coast at the time of the accident delayed many of the search efforts until the following day, but two military aircraft were dispatched from Ladd Field in Fairbanks that evening to assist. Three Coast Guard cutters also left their home ports to begin a sea search for the missing airplane.

At Annette airfield, many of the local aircraft could not even launch the first day to begin a search around the island. Winds steadily increased throughout the evening, reaching gusts of fifty-five knots as the storm passed though the area. Three hours after the DC-4's disappearance, another commercial airliner arrived and reported encountering light turbulence at 6,000 feet, which steadily increased to severe turbulence as it neared the ground. The crew also said they experienced moderate icing between 9,000 and 7,000 feet during the descent.

Two hours later at 1900, a military airplane confirmed similar weather conditions when it departed from the airfield. The pilot reported extreme turbulence near the ground, which gradually decreased during the climb until reaching smooth air at 6,000 feet. Severe icing was also encountered between an altitude of 4,500 and 6,000 feet, forcing the pilot to return to Annette because of excessive ice accumulation on the aircraft.

By the following morning low clouds still obscured many of the higher mountains, but the weather had cleared enough to allow an extensive search of the coastal region between Annette and Juneau. A Coast Guard amphibian aircraft was the first to launch from Annette that morning and begin a search of the immediate area. Six additional aircraft from Alaska Coastal Airlines soon began assisting as well. The company temporarily suspended all their commercial operations in the area while looking for the missing airplane.

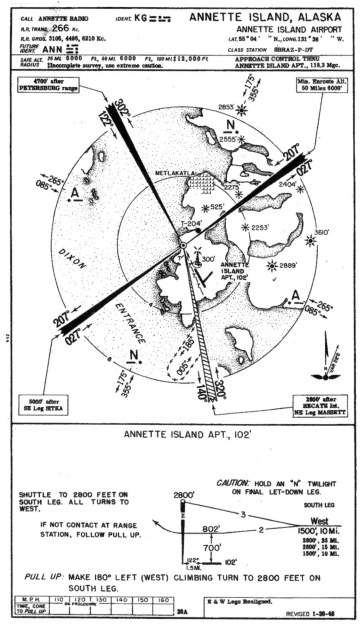

Jeppesen Standard Instrument Approach Procedure at Annette, similar to actual instrument approach at the time of the accident (Note a 1 degree difference in Radio Range legs from what existed at the time of the accident.)

Excerpted from Jeppesen Airway Manual, Copyright 1948 E. B. Jeppesen

(*For illustration only—not to be used for navigation purposes.*)

Before noon, two Pan American airplanes had also joined the operation, with another two en route. The Fish and Wildlife Service even dispatched two of their aircraft to assist with the search and the Canadian Air Force offered the services of an additional airplane. Five military aircraft were dispatched from the 10th Rescue Squadron in Anchorage the same day and began operating from Gustavus, west of Juneau. A total of nineteen civilian and military aircraft were involved by day's end.

Numerous ships also began a systematic search of the waters between Annette and Juneau where the airplane might have gone down. In addition to the three Coast Guard cutters dispatched the day before, vessels from the Forest Service and Fish and Wildlife Service joined the effort. Commercial fishing boats in the area were advised to be on the alert for any signs of the missing aircraft.

Initially, on the day following the commercial airliner's disappearance, a portion of the search focused around the Juneau area. Misleading reports had placed the Pan American flight close to that area the afternoon it disappeared. Several residents supposedly heard a circling aircraft near the northwest tip of Admiralty Island, only a few miles from Juneau. Another report had the aircraft over Funter Bay, twelve miles west of Juneau around 1400. Others stated that they heard explosions in the vicinity of Juneau, near Douglas Island, that sounded like thunder, but could have been an aircraft explosion. By the second day of the search, however, all the reports were investigated and determined to be without merit.

The weather gradually improved through the 28th, then worsened again that evening with increased rain showers and low clouds. When the other areas failed to turn up any evidence of the missing airplane, search efforts began to concentrate around Annette Island. By the 30th, nothing had been found and small search parties began combing the shoreline of Annette Island by boat and on foot. Numerous vessels were by that time involved in the effort as well as thirty-nine airplanes from the military and civilian sectors. But not the slightest hint of what happened to the Pan American flight was revealed.

Finally, on the evening of the 30th, a promising report came in from a Ketchikan man who had returned from a camping trip on the northeast side of Annette Island. He stated that he had seen the missing airplane on the 26th, flying south over the island, inland toward Tamgas Mountain. The search immediately focused in that area, and search teams were sent out at first light the next morning from Annette.

For the first time since the airplane had initially disappeared, the clouds that had been obscuring the island's highest mountain finally cleared, allowing a search airplane to investigate on the 31st. At 0645, five days after the Pan American DC-4 had vanished, the wreckage was spotted on the north side of Tamgas Mountain, six miles east of the airfield and less than 200 feet from the summit. It was immediately apparent that no one could possibly have survived the impact. Pieces of the aircraft were scattered over a wide area on a rugged, snow-covered slope, with larger sections of the fuselage lying broken and torn apart by the violent impact. The complete destruction was obvious to the observers circling overhead.

Ground parties reached the crash site that night and began a preliminary investigation. Jurisdiction fell on the Civil Aeronautics Administration, but a detailed examination of the wreckage could not take place until the following summer, once the seasonal thaw had passed. Much of the debris was already buried under several feet of snow, and one wing that was torn loose lay in a deep crevice on an inaccessible area of the mountain. Efforts concentrated instead on recovering the bodies before they became permanently entombed on the mountain.

By November 3 all the bodies had been found, but only a few had been successfully removed from the mountain. Over two dozen servicemen and several groups of civilians assisted with the recovery process, which involved carrying the bodies several miles through the rugged terrain to a mountain lake, where they could then be transported out by air.

Inclement weather continued to hamper the recovery efforts throughout the ordeal. Rainfall was almost continuous at the lower elevations, while fog and snow prevailed most of the day around the crash site. Six inches of snow fell on the mountain before the last body was finally removed.

Several days after the wreckage was found, a local paper reported that several pilots claimed the radio range station at Annette was fluctuating on the day of the crash, emitting an erroneous signal that brought airplanes into the airfield east of the actual instrument approach course. The paper went on to say the reports had been confirmed by several sources, but the Civil Aeronautics Administration

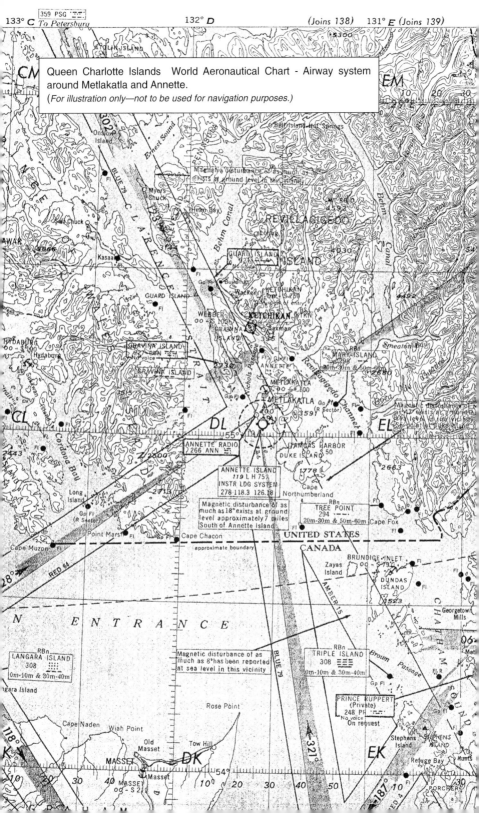

Queen Charlotte Islands World Aeronautical Chart - Airway system around Metlakatla and Annette.

(*For illustration only—not to be used for navigation purposes.*)

made no statement either supporting or denying the accusation. How the newspaper confirmed the reports was not explained in the article. The official Civil Aeronautics Board accident investigation report, released in March 1949, did not mention the newspaper account, nor did it give any evidence confirming the newspaper's statement. Even though a detailed investigation of the crash site was delayed until summer, the overall accident investigation still continued searching other sources for a possible cause of the crash. The flight crew's personal history and all company maintenance records dealing with the airplane were thoroughly checked. Transcripts of weather briefings and in-flight radio communications were studied for possible clues. Numerous personnel were interviewed and the navigation facilities used during the flight were checked for proper operation. Some minor discrepancies were uncovered with the navigation facility at Annette, but nothing significant that could explain why the aircraft was flying six miles east of the inbound course when it crashed.

It was determined that the experience level of the cockpit crew was well above normal and should not have been a factor in the accident. Captain Monsen had over 13,500 flight hours, with over 500 hours in DC-4 aircraft. The co-pilot, First Officer Foster, was almost as equally qualified with over 12,000 flight hours, of which over 350 were in DC-4s. He had been flying as an airline captain for years and was only serving as a first officer because of a temporary reduction in personnel by the company. Flight Engineer Dunwoody had over 2,000 hours and each of the crew had had forty-eight hours of rest prior to the flight.

Flight checks of the radio range station at Annette were conducted following the accident, as soon as the weather conditions permitted. A 3.5 ° error on the northwest course radial was found, which was 2° out of tolerance, but even with the error the inbound course would have kept the Pan American aircraft several miles west of where it was actually found. An interview with a military pilot who landed twenty-three minutes ahead of the Pan Am flight confirmed the radio range signal seemed to be operating normally during that period of time. Two airplanes that landed at Annette several hours after the DC-4's disappearance also reported nothing unusual with the transmission or reception of the radio range signal. The navigation facility at Annette was designed to be continuously monitored by a Civil Aeronautics Administration communications facility in Petersburg. Any changes in the signal strength, reception or abnormal operation of the radio range at Annette would have been observed by personnel at the monitoring station. According to the Civil Aeronautics Board accident report, all functions of the Annette Island system were normal during the time of the accident.

It was determined that there was an inaccuracy in the weather forecast the crew received before departing from Seattle, and that it failed to alert the crew to the more severe conditions that actually existed upon their arrival. Stronger winds around Annette below 7,000 feet were, at the time, causing severe turbulence, downdrafts and wind shears near mountainous terrain.

The company forecaster who issued the initial weather forecast did not anticipate the severity of the weather pattern approaching Annette, failing to predict the high wind conditions and increased turbulence the flight would encounter near their destination. An hour before the flight arrived at Annette, he did amend the original forecast, detailing the prevailing high wind conditions in the area, but the airplane did not receive the transmission.

A special surface observation at Annette was also taken an hour before the flight's arrival, reporting high winds and strong gusting conditions at the airfield. It was automatically broadcast and the inbound Pan American flight acknowledged its receipt.

The military pilot who landed shortly before the DC-4's scheduled arrival stated that he encountered light rime icing at 7,000 feet, with light to moderate rain during the descent and severe turbulence near the ground. His pilot report was not relayed to the DC-4.

The likelihood of severe icing or severe turbulence causing a loss of control and a subsequent crash of the Pan Am flight remained a possibility but still could not be substantiated.

Shortly after the accident, an Emergency Technical Order was supposedly issued to all military aviation units, requiring immediate inspection of all horizontal stabilizer bolts on their C-54 aircraft. A C-54 is a military version of the civilian DC-4. The Order stated that a significant number of corroded and broken bolts were being found during routine scheduled maintenance checks, and if not replaced, could potentially cause an in-flight separation of the horizontal stabilizer.

If an Emergency Technical Order was indeed issued to military aircraft, it would seem to indicate that a similar problem was just as likely to exist on the civilian version of the aircraft. There was no mention in the Civil Aeronautics Board accident investigation report of any such military Emergency Technical Order or a civilian Airworthiness Directive ever being issued.

A thorough examination of the Pan American wreckage was conducted by the Civil Aeronautics Administration in late August 1948. It was determined from the available evidence that the airplane had initially hit the rock face of the mountain fifty feet above the wreckage site in a 020° climb attitude. The flight path was approximately 145°, which was the approximate course for the outbound leg of the instrument approach at Annette. Why the aircraft was flying six miles east of the station when it impacted the mountain could not be explained.

Burn marks left on the slope showed that a flash fire had occurred immediately after the impact, but no evidence of a pre-crash fire was found. A fluxgate compass recovered from the wreckage verified that the fixed course at impact was the same as the flight path. Other aircraft instruments recovered were too badly damaged to be of any use. The extent of the damage in the cockpit and fuselage was so severe that the flaps and landing gear positions could not be determined. All four engines were found, however, and determined to be operating normally at the time of impact.

There was a possibility the airplane might have clipped some trees or the ground prior to impact, but an extensive search of the area did not find any evidence supporting that conclusion. No evidence of components coming loose from the aircraft before the crash was found either. There was no indication at all of any structural or mechanical failure prior to impact. From what could be determined from the wreckage, it appeared the airplane was in a normal, climbing profile when it hit at the 3,400-foot elevation of Tamgas Mountain.

The probable cause of the accident remained undetermined. Why the airplane impacted a mountain six miles east of the actual inbound instrument approach course is still a mystery. Nor can its continued flight path of 145°, at least five minutes after the pilot's last reported position over the radio range station, be explained.

Some sort of navigational error must have occurred. Whether it was mechanical or human error will never be known.

At that time it was the worst commercial air disaster in Alaskan aviation history. Even greater losses of life were soon to follow.

Final Approach

NOVEMBER 27, 1947

It should have been just another routine flight for the two experienced DC-3 pilots. Each was a World War II veteran with over 4,000 total flight hours, flying a familiar round-trip route between Alaska and Oregon for Columbia Air Cargo in Portland. The aircraft was a proven and dependable workhorse, ideal for transporting passengers and freight in all types of weather.

The round-trip flight originally departed from Portland during the early morning of November 25. There were no mechanical problems en route to Anchorage until the left engine experienced an overspeed condition during the landing approach at Merrill Field. A go-around was initiated as the pilots climbed to a safe altitude and tried restoring normal operation of the engine. The propeller was feathered as they circled for several minutes, then slowly restored to a normal pitch position as the pilot checked for a recurrence of the problem. It was verified as functioning correctly and they executed a normal approach.

After landing, maintenance personnel removed and cleaned the left engine governor, then bench-tested it for proper operation. They found nothing out of the ordinary and reinstalled the governor on the engine. The oil system sump and strainer were also examined and cleaned for possible obstructions. That evening the flight continued to Fairbanks and landed without any further difficulties.

After a twenty-four-hour crew-rest the pilots departed on the return flight to Portland, with intermediate stops scheduled at Anchorage and Yakutat. Seven passengers were on board. Severe turbulence and strong head winds battered the aircraft most of the way to Anchorage, but no other problems were encountered. The airplane was refueled and serviced at Anchorage for the next leg of flight, before reboarding the original seven plus an additional four passengers. No cargo other than personal baggage was being carried.

It was almost midnight before the Columbia Air Cargo DC-3 finally lifted off from Anchorage with two pilots and eleven passengers. Weather conditions remained severe until the aircraft passed through Portage Pass, then declined in intensity as the flight continued southeast toward Yakutat. Flying on instruments, the crew followed the Amber One airway past Cordova and Yakataga. At a cruising altitude of 6,000 feet, the flight conditions subsided to only occasional light to moderate turbulence and light to moderate icing, which was a welcome change from the previous conditions the flight encountered north of Anchorage. The decreased intensity allowed the passengers to relax and sleep a little before the next stop.

The flight reported passing Yakataga at 0138, with an estimated arrival time of 0220 given for Yakutat. Forty-six minutes later, the captain called Yakutat Radio, reporting they were leaving 6,000 feet for a straight-in approach to the airfield. The Civil Aeronautics Administration operator at Yakutat acknowledged the transmission, but did not question the captain's intent, even though a straight-in instrument approach was not an approved procedure for the airport. Current weather conditions at Yakutat were also passed to the flight by the Civil Aeronautics Administration operator, stating an indefinite ceiling with a 500-foot overcast, visibility of three miles in light drizzle, winds east/southeast at ten knots, and an altimeter of 30.17.

Straight-in instrument approaches along the northwest leg of the radio range were not authorized at Yakutat because there were no navigational aids in place that would allow an aircraft to positively identify its position far enough northwest of the station to begin a safe descent. All inbound aircraft were required to follow Amber One until passing over the radio range station, located a few miles northwest of the airport, then continue outbound a safe distance before executing a course reversal back toward the station. This allowed an aircraft to fix its location over the radio range before initiating the approach.

Once established over the radio range, an aircraft would proceed outbound on the reciprocal approach heading, no lower than 1,500 feet, then execute a procedure turn onto the inbound course. Only then could it descend out of the initial approach altitude of 1,500 feet, down to a minimum of 700 feet until passing the station. After station passage, a 32° right turn was required while continuing the approach to a minimum descent altitude of 500. If the airport were not in sight after the required inbound time to the missed approach point, the aircraft would initiate an immediate climb along the southeast leg of the radio range station.

Ten minutes after Yakutat Radio sent the current weather observation to the inbound DC-3, the operator asked the pilot to report the actual height of the ceiling once they broke through the overcast. The captain acknowledged the request and no further communication was received.

Shortly after the flight's last transmission, a local resident near the Yakutat Station, which was located approximately three miles from the runway, heard the flight fly overhead at a low altitude. Seconds later he heard a loud explosion and immediately contacted the Civil Aeronautics Administration office at the airfield. Several townspeople and Coast Guard personnel stationed at Yakutat, hiked to the crash location where they found the wreckage in a heavily wooded area one mile northeast of the radio station. By the time they arrived, a fire had already consumed the main cabin area, cockpit and most of the center section of the wings. There were no survivors.

The Civil Aeronautics Board began an accident investigation as soon as they received word of the crash. A ground team was dispatched the same day, arriving at the scene within twenty-four hours. They immediately began gathering evidence from the accident site.

It became apparent rather quickly that the aircraft had left a path of destruction through the trees as it crashed. The first point of contact was found to be a large spruce tree that had been hit with the left wing, over 700 feet from the wreckage, on an apparent heading of 070°. The top ten feet of the tree had been broken off by the impact, which also completely severed the wing outward from the engine.

As the aircraft plummeted from the air, it broke numerous trees and limbs along its flight path before impacting the ground on its

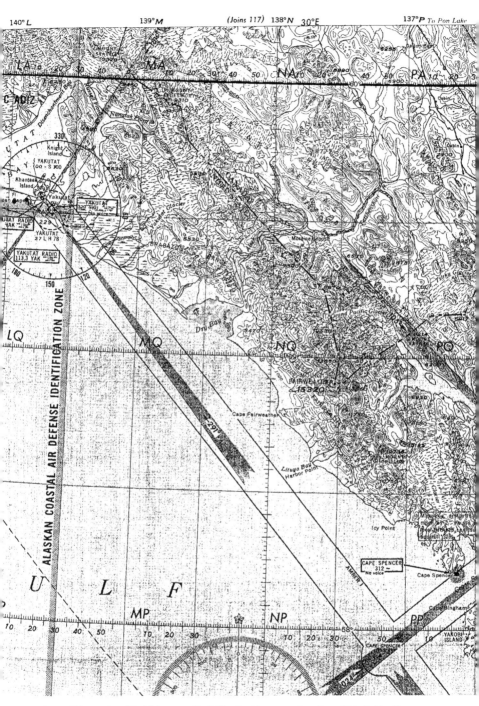

Mount Fairweather World Aeronautical Chart - Airway system from Yakutat to Cape Spencer.   (*For illustration only—not to be used for navigation purposes.*)

left side. The right wing was torn loose and thrown inverted near the fuselage. Flames erupted from the spilled fuel, spreading rapidly over the area and into the broken cabin. The heat was so intense it melted metal, completely destroying the center section of the aircraft. If anyone had survived the impact, they had no chance of escape in the ensuing fire.

From the evidence the accident team was able to examine at the scene, it was determined that the aircraft had been in a landing configuration with the gear extended and locked, and the flaps in an approximately three-quarters down position. No evidence of fatigue or structural failure was found in the wings, other than impact damage that occurred during the crash.

Both engines were also located in the fire area, excessively damaged by the flames. An analysis of the left engine revealed the propeller blades had been bent back along the contour of the cowling at a very slow rotational speed when the aircraft hit the ground, indicating the possibility of an engine failure prior to impact. It was also likely the engine malfunctioned after the left wing hit the first spruce tree, allowing the propeller to slow considerably during the few seconds before the crash.

Most of the accessory section of the right engine was found destroyed, but all three of the propeller blades were found in a low-pitch setting. Two of the left engine propeller blades were also discovered in a full, low pitch setting, and one in a 070°-080° high-pitch setting. The nose cone of the left engine was found cracked and two of the propeller segment gears broken.

A different pitch setting can only occur on individual blades of a propeller during a malfunction of the components or because of extreme impact forces being applied to the blades. During the approach for landing, the propellers would have been placed in a low-pitch setting, aligning all their blades at the same angle. Since one blade of the left propeller was found at a significantly different pitch setting than the other two, it had either slipped inside the gear housing in flight, which was possible during an overspeed, or had been knocked out of alignment in the gear housing by the severe impact.

Since the nose cone was also found broken, it indicated a possible result of the same overspeed or a pre-existing, weakened condition in the propeller housing. However, impact forces inflicted on

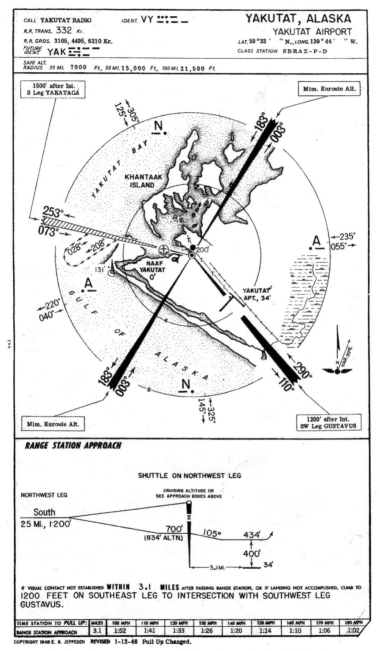

Jeppesen Standard Instrument Approach Procedure at Yakutat. Note the approach altitudes depicted are slightly different than the approach altitudes in effect at the time of the accident. *Excerpted from Jeppesen Airway Manual, Copyright 1948 E. B. Jeppesen* (*For illustration only—not to be used for navigation purposes.*)

the engine during the crash sequence would also explain the cracked nose cone and broken gears.

If the left engine had actually oversped or failed completely during the approach, it would probably have occurred at a low enough altitude where the pilot was unable to react quickly enough before descending and hitting the trees. Since the propeller was not found in a feathered position and the aircraft was perfectly capable of flying on one engine at its operational gross weight, that conclusion would seem to be a distinct possibility. In addition, no distress call was made before impact, which would suggest that the pilot did not have enough reaction time. Unfortunately, the extensive propeller damage found in the wreckage was reflective of severe impact forces as well as component failure. With no specific evidence pointing to either possibility, a conclusive determination could not be established.

In the accident board's opinion, there was no evidence of mechanical or structural failure prior to impact. The aircraft was determined to be flying too low during an unauthorized approach procedure, resulting in wing contact with a ground obstruction and subsequent separation. The board also mentioned a possibility that the crew had not adjusted the altimeter for the new setting at Yakutat, thus causing it to display an erroneous altitude during the approach. No evidence was found to verify that possibility. The cockpit altimeter had been severely damaged in the fire and no useful information could be retrieved from the component to establish its actual setting at the time of the crash. None of the possibilities can explain why the captain chose to ignore the standard instrument approach procedure and needlessly endanger thirteen lives.

An investigation of Columbia Air Cargo following the accident revealed that some of the maintenance records in the company were incomplete. No records had been kept confirming whether a pilot's maintenance repair requests had actually been completed, but no improper material or substandard work could be found on any of the company's aircraft either. The airline's Portland facility conducted all the major maintenance on their aircraft and was determined by the board to be thoroughly qualified to do so. Only emergency and turnaround maintenance was accomplished on aircraft when they were operating away from the main facility.

The DC-3 involved in the accident was manufactured in 1942.

It had a total of 3,756 hours on the airframe. The left engine had 700 accumulative hours and had never been overhauled. The right engine had 975 total hours and had also never been overhauled, although one was scheduled upon the aircraft's return to Portland.

Weather was not determined to be a factor in the accident. A ceiling of 500 feet and visibility of three miles existed at the time of the crash. All runway and airport lights were illuminated during the airplane's approach and clearly visible at the radio station three miles away. The pilot of a Northern Airlines airplane that landed slightly before the Columbia Air Cargo DC-3 stated that his flight did not encounter any severe weather conditions in the area and arrived without incident.

Official findings of the accident board determined Columbia Air Cargo, the accident aircraft and the crew to be properly certified. The probable cause was listed as a failure to follow the approved instrument approach procedure into Yakutat, resulting in a descent below an altitude sufficient to maintain obstacle clearance along the flight path.

Whether the captain's intentional violation of standard instrument procedures was derived from overconfidence and a perceived familiarity of the area, or some other factor, will never be known. Fatalities are always unfortunate when an error in judgment is a contributing cause to the aircraft accident, even more so when innocent passengers are involved.

Two days after the tragedy, all of the bodies were found and recovered from the crash site. Twelve of the thirteen bodies were flown to Portland for memorial services. The remaining victim was returned to Fairbanks for burial.

Impact on Mount Crillon

JANUARY 12, 1952

General Airways flight 785 was a DC-3C flying from Portland, Oregon to Anchorage, Alaska. There were no passengers aboard the cargo flight, which was carrying over 6,000 pounds of fresh produce, mostly crated eggs. The crew consisted of two pilots who had been flying the same coastal route together for several months and were experienced in DC-3 operations.

At 1147 Pacific Standard Time, the flight reported passing Cape Spencer Intersection at 9,000 feet. No further communication was received. When the aircraft failed to report passing the Yakutat Radio Range after its estimated time of arrival, an alert notice was issued to all stations along the flight route. Military aircraft were dispatched almost immediately and began a systematic search of the coastal area between Sitka and Yakutat. Wreckage was spotted the next afternoon at the 9,000-foot level of Mount Crillon, thirty miles off the instrument airway it had been tracking toward Yakutat. The aircraft had been severely damaged by the impact. There were no survivors.

Flight 785 originally departed from Portland at 0200 on January 12, before proceeding to Annette Island, south of Ketchikan, for refueling. The route was flown without incident and the airplane arrived at 0709 under overcast skies. A fuel truck was already standing by on the ramp as the DC-3 taxied off the runway.

After parking and shutting down the engines, the aircraft was fully serviced with Avgas and oil by ground personnel for the next leg of flight. While that was being done, the pilots updated the enroute and arrival weather for Anchorage at the nearby U.S.

Weather Bureau office. Conditions were forecast below approach minimums for their expected arrival time at Anchorage, so they decided to delay the takeoff until there was an improvement in the forecast. During the wait the airplane was towed inside a hangar to prevent any ice accumulation on the airframe from the freezing rain falling at the airfield.

Two hours after the flight arrived at Annette, the freezing rain turned to snow and the weather forecast for Anchorage improved. Both pilots reviewed the new flight information and were briefed on the latest enroute and destination weather before having the aircraft towed back outside in preparation for departure. Within a few minutes the engines were started, all systems were checked and chokes removed, before the DC-3 began moving along the taxiway for takeoff. It lifted off the runway at 0931, climbing northwest into the thick, gray clouds, before disappearing from view.

Forecast weather conditions for the flight route to Anchorage called for overcast skies and moderate winds, with a possibility of light icing. The airflow at cruising altitude was reported as stable, with only light turbulence along most of the route. Stronger winds were predicted over the high coastal mountains near Yakutat, but well off the airway. Winds aloft at 10,000 feet were estimated to be out of the southwest at forty-five knots between Annette and Sitka, then increasing to sixty-five knots north of that location. The 10,000-foot forecast was the closest flight level data available for their actual cruising altitude of 9,000 feet.

Air traffic control cleared flight 785 to proceed under instrument flight rules, direct from Annette to Sitka, then via the Amber One airway to Anchorage. The first flight segment to Sitka was authorized at variable altitudes above the cloud deck, based on the pilot's discretion, with instructions to climb and maintain a cruising altitude of 9,000 feet before intercepting the Amber One airway over the Sitka Radio Range.

Nine minutes after lifting off from Annette, flight 785 established contact with Annette Radio, estimating an arrival time over Sitka of 1050. At 1111 contact was again established with Sitka Radio while still southeast of the station. The captain advised the controller they were encountering strong head winds and were now estimating their arrival over the Sitka Radio Range in approximately five to ten minutes.

Their actual arrival over Sitka occurred two minutes later. The captain notified the controller that they were passing over the station at 1113, level at 9,000 feet and estimating passing over Cape Spencer Intersection, eighty-four miles to the northwest, at 1146. From Sitka, the flight would have tracked the Amber One airway by flying outbound on the northwest leg of the Sitka Radio Range. Once the aircraft arrived over Cape Spencer Intersection, which was fixed by cross-tuning and identifying the point where the southwest leg of the Gustavus Radio Range intercepted their course, the crew would change frequencies and track inbound on the southeast leg of the Yakutat Radio Range. A course change of 002° was required on the airway while changing between the outbound leg from Sitka and inbound leg to Yakutat.

Flight 785 seemed to proceed normally along the airway, and the crew certainly did not report any difficulties or concerns to air traffic control. At 1147, the captain notified air traffic control they were over Cape Spencer Intersection at 9,000 feet, estimating their arrival at Yakutat at 1245. It was the last radio transmission received from the flight.

The Yakutat Radio operator had no reason to assume anything was wrong until the flight failed to establish radio contact at the prescribed time. Numerous attempts at communication by the controller for an hour and a half past their estimated arrival time received no response. At 1414, a general alert was issued to all stations along the flight route, informing them of the missing aircraft. A short time later 10th Rescue Squadron aircraft from Elmendorf Air Force Base in Anchorage initiated a search. The Coast Guard also dispatched a surface vessel from Sitka to sweep the offshore waters near Yakutat.

Search efforts continued through the afternoon and early evening before halting that night, resuming again at first light on the 13th. Forty-foot seas and icing conditions stopped the cutter *Cahoone* from making it across the Gulf of Alaska from Sitka, forcing the ship to turn back towards port, but two search-equipped B-17s from Elmendorf flew into the area that morning. A Navy reconnaissance aircraft and Coast Guard patrol airplane were scheduled to fly from Kodiak that afternoon and assist in the search. High, gusty winds prevented many of the smaller civil aircraft in the area from getting off the ground and joining the effort.

Severe turbulence and extremely high winds over the coastal mountain range made it difficult to search all the peaks and glaciers in the area, but one of the B-17s located some wreckage at the 9,000-foot level of Mount Crillon that afternoon. After making several dangerously low passes over the site, the Air Force crew was able to confirm it was the missing DC-3. The word "General" was clearly observed in large letters on the left wing and a red stripe was visible running along the fuselage. One of the Air Force crew members was a former employee of General Airways and provided a positive identification. The crew took two photos of the wreckage, which were later confirmed as showing the missing aircraft.

Mount Crillon is the fourth highest peak in the range of coastal mountains between Yakutat and Juneau, rising to a height of 12,750 feet above sea level. It lies approximately eleven miles inland from the coast and forty-seven miles northwest of Cape Spencer Intersection. Numerous glaciers and steep, snow-covered pinnacles of rock and ice predominate the surrounding terrain.

The wreckage was located on the southwest slope of the peak, twenty-nine miles from the centerline of the Amber One airway. It was immediately evident to the B-17 search crew that no one could have survived the violent collision. The cockpit had been demolished as it was crushed and pushed back into the cabin area. Cargo and pieces of the airframe were scattered in a fifty-foot area around the site where the fuselage had broken open and turned completely around from the force of impact. The left wing and engine remained attached to the broken fuselage, but the right wing had been sheared off and lay behind the main area of wreckage. Only the tail section appeared relatively intact.

Another aircraft from the Civil Aeronautics Administration flew over Mount Crillon the next day, but could not locate any signs of the wreckage. Because the coastal range frequently experienced large accumulations of snow during the winter months, it was determined that either an avalanche or heavy snowfall the previous night had covered all evidence of the accident. Later flights by other aircraft also failed to sight any signs of the wreckage.

A debate ensued among government officials on whether to attempt a ground search of the area, but the option was soon dismissed as too dangerous. The high altitude and steep terrain prevented any access by helicopter or light airplane on the mountain,

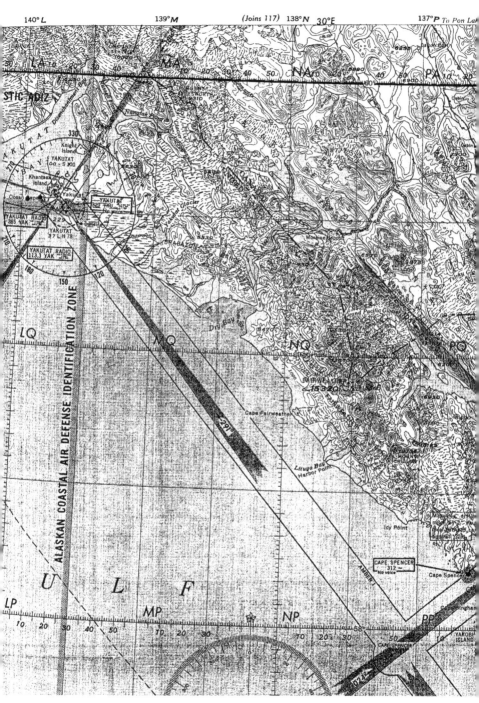

Mount Fairweather World Aeronautical Chart - Airway system from Yakutat to Cape Spencer.   (*For illustration only—not to be used for navigation purposes.*)

and landing on a glacier posed even more problems. Even bigger risks would be forced on any recovery team traversing the glacier and mountain by the extremely hazardous terrain. It was decided that it was not safe to attempt to reach the crash site, even in the spring, because of the increased potential for more fatalities. The deceased pilots of flight 785 would instead remain with their aircraft, encased in snow and ice somewhere on the rugged peak.

During the ensuing accident investigation, the Civil Aeronautics Board could not determine why the aircraft ended up so far off the airway. There were no apparent problems with the operation of the aircraft and the crew reported no difficulties with the navigation systems. All communications between the aircraft and air traffic control were normal throughout the flight.

Another aircraft, a southbound Pan American flight at 11,000 feet, had been in the vicinity of the General Airways airplane about the same time, and did not report any severe or extreme weather conditions. The captain of that flight reported over Gustavus, about sixty miles northeast of Cape Spencer, at 1141. He stated that his flight did not encounter any hazardous conditions until they were at Point Hugh Intersection, seventy-five miles east of Sitka on the Blue 8 airway. At that time, their flight winds increased to sixty knots from the west/southwest and light icing was observed. The pilot said a right drift correction of 014° had to be maintained from that point until they neared the town of Petersburg. Radio reception was reported as normal, with no unusual static conditions that might have interfered with air to ground communications. Only intermittent, light turbulence was experienced, even during periods of strong winds.

Analysis by the investigation team of the weather data that existed over the coastal region during the duration of the General Airways flight showed the actual conditions to be similar to those originally forecast. Instrument conditions were determined to be prevalent during the flight, with periods of light turbulence and a possibility of light icing. Turbulence was expected to have been severe over areas of high, rugged terrain near the crash site. The winds were believed to have been slightly stronger than forecast north of Sitka, from approximately 210° at eighty knots instead of the forecast 200° at sixty-five knots.

Monitor reports for the radio range stations at Sitka, Gustavus and Yakutat from January 12 did not reveal any discrepancies in signal transmission at the facilities. Flight checks of the Yakutat and Sitka Radio Ranges, conducted on the 14th and 15th, found them both operating normally as well. It was the accident board's contention that flight 785 should have been able to receive a good signal from Yakutat once it arrived over Cape Spencer Intersection, 126 miles away.

One interesting piece of information disclosed in the accident report, was the fact that when the General Airways crash occurred, the Civil Aeronautics Administration was conducting a study on a potential navigational problem with the airway between Sitka and Yakutat. The study had been initiated due to several unexplained accidents taking place in that area over the previous several years.

On July 29, 1950, a military C-54 transport crashed under very similar circumstances into Mount La Perouse, only seven miles southeast of Mount Crillon. The aircraft was also flying northbound at 9,000 feet on the same airway under instruments and, ironically, was also carrying a cargo of fresh produce. The bodies of the victims were never recovered due to the location of the wreckage in an extremely hazardous area.

The Civil Aeronautics Administration's investigation centered on the feasibility of a pilot mistakenly tuning the wrong radio range station after arriving over Cape Spencer Intersection. During this time frame, Sitka station was transmitting on a frequency of 323 kilocycles, while Yakutat transmitted on 332 kilocycles. A pilot flying on the northwest leg of the Sitka Range would usually stay on the right side of the on-course signal, or "N" signal, until cross-tuning to Gustavus Range to fix Cape Spencer Intersection. Once the intersection was reached, the aircraft's receiver would be re-tuned to the Yakutat frequency, thus enabling continued navigation inbound on the southeast leg of the Yakutat Radio Range. Due to the similarity between the Sitka and Yakutat frequencies, it was possible for a pilot to mistakenly tune in Sitka again, instead of Yakutat, after crossing the intersection. If that happened, a continued track along the "N" signal side of the course would take the aircraft off the Amber One airway to the north.

A similar error in frequencies could also occur while flying southbound, but would not be as critical, since the aircraft would proceed right of the course to the south, over open ocean. If the error

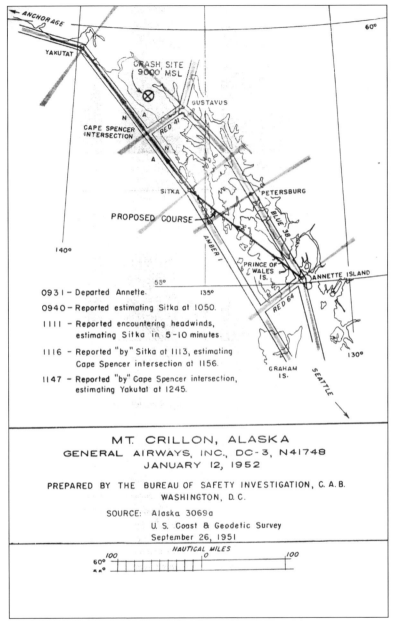

0931 – Departed Annette.

0940 – Reported estimating Sitka at 1050.

1111 – Reported encountering headwinds, estimating Sitka in 5-10 minutes.

1116 – Reported "by" Sitka at 1113, estimating Cape Spencer intersection at 1156.

1147 – Reported "by" Cape Spencer intersection, estimating Yakutat at 1245.

MT. CRILLON, ALASKA
GENERAL AIRWAYS, INC., DC-3, N41748
JANUARY 12, 1952

PREPARED BY THE BUREAU OF SAFETY INVESTIGATION, C. A. B.
WASHINGTON, D. C.

SOURCE: Alaska 3069a
U. S. Coast & Geodetic Survey
September 26, 1951

Image of Accident Report diagram. Excerpted from Civil Aeronautics Board Accident Investigation Report, File No. 1-0003, Attachment.
(*For illustration only—not to be used for navigation purposes.*)

occurred while flying north, the aircraft would eventually fly into the high mountain range bordering the Gulf of Alaska. In one fifty-mile stretch of land between Cape Spencer and Yakutat, there are fifteen mountains at least 9,000 feet in height within twenty miles of the coast. Numerous other peaks extend above 6,000 feet.

Although a mistake in navigation by tuning the wrong frequency was certainly possible while flying either north or south on the airway, it would only provide an error of a few degrees from the actual airway course. For flight 785 to hit Mount Crillon on a direct track from a point over Sitka station would have required a course error of 13°. If the airplane had been flying direct from a point over Cape Spencer Intersection to Mount Crillon, it would have required a 35° course error.

Another possible navigational error might have been due to the crew's failure in calculating an accurate wind correction to maintain the desired course track. Winds stronger than forecast from the west, as was the case for flight 785, would have increased the amount of course error, pushing the aircraft further off the airway to the right and into the mountains. That theory seems unlikely, however, since it would indicate that the crew was not monitoring either the radio beam's display indications in the cockpit or the audio signals being transmitted by the radio range station.

General Airways training policy was for the pilots to use the aircraft range receiver as the primary navigation system when flying instruments and the automatic direction finder receiver as a secondary system. A manual loop and marker beacon system were available on the aircraft for navigational purposes as well.

An investigation of the accident aircraft's maintenance records showed a past history of radio and instrument problems, although this by itself was not uncommon for cold weather operations in Alaska. In any case, all the discrepancies had been corrected before the flight left Portland. Two of the problems concerned a tube in the automatic direction finder receiver and the pilot's directional gyroscope, both of which were replaced the day prior to the flight. One of the maintenance write-ups mentioned a problem with the automatic pilot system, but the technician could not duplicate the malfunction and signed it off as working correctly. The captain of flight 785 was told of the previous fault with the automatic pilot system before they departed.

Weight and balance computations for the aircraft and the center of gravity were determined to be within allowable limits for the flight. No cargo was loaded or removed while on the ground at Annette, and the amount of fuel added was comparable to the original quantity on board upon departure from Portland.

An examination of both pilots' flight records found nothing unusual. The captain and first officer had flown together on several occasions during the previous six months, spending the majority of their time on the same Alaskan route. They had a combined total of over 9,000 flight hours, almost half of those hours in DC-3s. The captain had 1,000 hours of instrument flying and the first officer had 150 hours.

In its final analysis, the accident board could not determine the actual flight path of the aircraft before impact, nor the reason it diverted so far off course. Since the airplane hit the slope of Mount Crillon at its cruising altitude of 9,000 feet, neither a power loss nor crew incapacitation was considered a probability. From all indications, it was believed there were no malfunctions of the navigation systems or radio equipment, but that a navigation error of some type did occur.

The board concluded that the flight appeared to progress normally on the route from Annette, until diverting off the low-frequency airway somewhere between Sitka and Yakutat. Stronger than forecast winds did prevail at the time, possibly blowing the aircraft right of course. Actual winds were determined to be fifteen knots higher than predicted and at a 010° difference in direction. Since the flight's reported arrival times over Sitka and Cape Spencer did vary from the estimated arrival times, the winds must have been causing at least some minor difficulty.

In regard to the theory that the navigation frequencies might have been tuned incorrectly after crossing Cape Spencer Intersection, the board considered it a remote possibility because of the large difference in course track required for a relatively short distance of only fifty miles. The Civil Aeronautics Administration, however, did change the frequency at Yakutat to 385 kilocycles following the accident, alleviating any possible confusion with the Sitka frequency.

The Morse code station identifier for Sitka was also changed after the accident. Before the accident the Sitka identifier was SK, and at Yakutat it was VY. The difference in the sequence of dots and dashes was subtle enough that a person could easily confuse one with the other, especially if he was not listening carefully or was receiving any static interference over the radio at the same time. If a pilot mistakenly dialed in the wrong frequency after passing Cape Spencer Intersection, one identifier might have sounded similar enough to the other to not be noticed. The subsequent changes made by the Civil Aeronautics Administration after the accident were claimed to be only coincidental.

In conclusion, the Civil Aeronautics Board listed the probable cause of the accident as a deviation from the intended route because of improper, in-flight navigation.

Somewhere on Mount Crillon the General Airways DC-3 still lies hidden from view. Decades of falling snow and recurring avalanches have probably crushed what remained of the wreckage, sealing any evidence of what really happened in a tomb of ice. Perhaps some day pieces of the aircraft will be found, as has happened at other mountainous accident sites, but because of the remote and dangerous location it seems unlikely in the near future.

Disaster at 14,000 Feet

JUNE 3, 1963

After World War II, the military bases in Alaska continued to expand with the onset of the Cold War. Post housing, support services and recreation facilities became more common, allowing family members to accompany servicemen overseas on their tours of duty. With the increased numbers of soldiers and dependents traveling between military assignments, the Military Air Transport Service was expanded to accommodate the heightened volume of traffic. Contracts were established between the military and commercial air carriers for transporting Department of Defense personnel and their dependents on scheduled passenger flights. The contracted flights operated primarily between the United States and overseas locations, similar in many respects to normal commercial travel.

Elmendorf Air Force Base in Anchorage became a primary refueling hub for military and Military Air Transport Service aircraft en route to Japan and Korea, as well as the transition point for other bases in Alaska. On June 3, 1963, a Northwest Airlines Military Air Transport Service chartered DC-7 left McChord Air Force Base in Tacoma, Washington, bound for Elmendorf Air Force Base. On board the airplane were a total of 101 passengers and crew members. Approximately two and a half hours into the flight the aircraft crashed into the sea southwest of Annette Island, killing all the occupants.

It was by far the worst airline disaster in Alaska aviation history at the time, but unfortunately it was not the first Military Air Transport Service flight in Alaska that resulted in tragedy. In July

1951, a Canadian Pacific Airways DC-4 aircraft, carrying military personnel during the "Great Circle" airlift operation to Korea, disappeared along the coast near Yakutat. At the time it was en route to Elmendorf Air Force Base for a refueling stop. The airplane was never found.

Another Northwest Airlines Military Air Transport Service flight crashed just outside of Alaskan waters, near Sandspit, British Columbia in January 1952, killing thirty-six of the forty-three persons on board. A third aircraft involving a Military Air Transport Service contract flight occurred in July 1961, when an Alaska Airlines cargo DC-6 crashed at Shemya Air Base in the Aleutians. All six occupants were fatally injured during an approach in marginal weather. And in March 1962 a Lockheed Constellation belonging to the Flying Tiger Line impacted the ground short of the runway threshold at Adak. One crew member was killed during the post-crash fire, which completely destroyed the aircraft.

Just eight months before the June 1963 tragedy, a near disaster close to Sitka was narrowly avoided when another Military Air Transport Service DC-7 belonging to Northwest Airlines made an emergency landing in the ocean. All 102 occupants were successfully rescued with no serious injuries, thanks to the skill of the crew, the calm seas and the quick response of surface ships in the area.

In many ways the near disaster in October 1962 was a prelude to the tragedy on June 3, 1963. Both aircraft were Northwest Airline DC-7s under Military Air Transport Service contract, with over 100 personnel on board. Each was flying the identical instrument flight rules route from McChord Air Force Base in Washington to Elmendorf Air Force Base in Alaska, and both were in similar weather conditions.

The first DC-7 near Sitka had developed an in-flight emergency when power was lost to one of the engines after encountering icing conditions, resulting in partial engine disintegration. Prompt actions by the crew allowed a descent toward land where rescue vessels were standing by. Less than eight months later, the second DC-7 near Annette encountered icing and turbulence of its own. Whether those conditions contributed to a sudden and violent loss of control, resulting in the complete destruction of the aircraft as it impacted the ocean, is not known.

It was an early morning for the Northwest Airlines crew as they prepared the aircraft for flight at McChord Air Force Base. A separate aircrew had delivered the airplane a few hours before from Minneapolis, where it had just completed a 200-hour inspection. A Northwest Airline crew chief and an Air Force maintenance technician both conducted separate pre-flight inspections of the aircraft after its arrival, with neither finding any discrepancies. The passengers arrived at the terminal, checked their baggage, and were briefed by Air Force personnel before being moved into a holding area. While waiting to board, the airplane's fuel tanks and oil systems were serviced and the required over-water survival equipment was loaded on board. Blankets and pillows were placed on the seats for passenger comfort, while food and beverages were stored in the galley for later in-flight service.

As the flight crew arrived and began preliminary cockpit checks, the passenger baggage was brought out by truck and loaded in the cargo area. The cabin attendants finished preparing their areas then began greeting the passengers as they filed on board. There were expressions of anticipation from some at leaving for new assignments in Alaska, reluctance from others, and fatigue from most of the children at such an early departure. In all there were fifty-eight military personnel from the Air Force, Army and Coast Guard, along with twenty-two dependents. Some were traveling alone to join their family members already in Alaska. Fifteen Department of Defense civilians and their family members were also aboard. Many of the dependents on the flight were young children, flying for the first time.

Once everyone was seated, the cabin attendants conducted a passenger briefing covering the emergency exits and evacuation procedures. Shortly thereafter the airplane began taxiing for departure. At 0532 Alaska Time on June 3, it took off from the runway at McChord Air Force Base, climbing to meet the instrument airway south of Seattle before heading northwest over open water. Twenty minutes later it reached its cruising altitude of 14,000 feet between two solid cloud layers. Most of the passengers gratefully reclined their seats and settled in for a few hours of sleep.

Two weather forecasts for the route were received by the crew before departure at McChord, one from the Northwest Airlines dispatcher and another from the Air Force forecaster. Both were basically the same, calling for multiple cloud layers from 2,000 to

22,000 feet, with light to moderate icing in scattered rain showers and moderate turbulence near an occluded weather front in the vicinity of Annette Island. A 14,000-foot cruising altitude was selected to allow the aircraft to remain in calmer weather conditions between the two predominate cloud layers along the route. Enroute time to Anchorage was estimated at approximately five and a half hours. There was nearly eight hours worth of fuel on board.

The flight progressed normally along the instrument flight rules route until reporting over Domestic Annette Intersection, two and a half hours after takeoff. The intersection was located eighty-seven nautical miles southwest of Annette Island. The crew transmitted a request for a change in altitude to 18,000 feet at that time, but gave no explanation for the request. Air traffic control at a facility in Sandspit, Canada, acknowledged the message, but told the flight they could not issue the clearance because of conflicting traffic. A Pacific Northern Airlines aircraft was already at 18,000 feet, only one minute behind the Northwest Airlines DC-7. The Northwest crew did not acknowledge receipt of the transmission, and two minutes later the controller tried contacting them again, advising the flight they were cleared to 16,000 feet instead. When there was still no response, air traffic control asked the other flight to attempt contact, with no success.

Normal procedures required air traffic control to issue an alert notice any time an aircraft operating under instrument flight rules did not establish contact within a certain time period after its estimated arrival time over a specified or compulsory reporting point. Since the Northwest flight had already called passing over Domestic Annette Intersection, mandatory communication was not required again until reaching the next reporting point at Domestic Sitka. At 0916, when the specified time interval had passed from the flight's estimated arrival over Sitka, Anchorage Center could not establish contact and issued an alert notice to all stations. All communication attempts failed in locating the overdue aircraft. An emergency was declared at 0935, initiating search and rescue procedures along the route of flight.

The Coast Guard in southeast Alaska was one of the first units to respond, dispatching two aircraft and four fast ocean cutters from their coastal ports at Ketchikan, Sitka and Juneau. Military aircraft from Elmendorf and Eielson Air Force bases and the Royal

116

Canadian Air Force quickly joined the effort to assist. A military transport en route from McChord Air Force Base was directed over the last known area of the missing airliner, and the strategic airlift command diverted two KC-135 refueling aircraft to assist the searching airplanes. All ships and fishing boats in the area were also alerted.

Since contact with the missing airplane was lost after it reached the Domestic Annette reporting point, the search concentrated around that area. Nine hours after the Northwest Airline flight disappeared, a search airplane from the Royal Canadian Air Force spotted wreckage thirty-five miles west of the DC-7's last known position. No survivors could be seen in the debris scattered over the ocean surface. Hundreds of small pieces of flotsam and an oil slick were all that remained. It was readily apparent that the impact with the water had been at an extreme velocity, completely destroying the aircraft.

A Japanese vessel was the first surface ship to reach the area and confirmed there were no signs of survivors or floating bodies. The Coast Guard cutter *Sorrel* and commercial freighter *Chena* arrived a short time later. It was obvious no one could have survived the impact. Collecting the wreckage for future analysis began immediately. All recovered items were then transported to Annette Island where federal investigators could examine the evidence.

Approximately 1,500 pounds of wreckage was retrieved from the ocean surface before the search was terminated on June 6. Most of the debris consisted of uninflated life rafts and flotation devices, clothing, personal baggage, pieces of the interior cabin structure, blankets, pillows, numerous seat cushions with portions of the aluminum frame still attached, a few twisted and broken structural sections, and a small amount of human remains. A water depth of 8,000 feet at the point of impact precluded the recovery of any additional components from the ocean floor.

Officials from the Civil Aeronautics Board, Federal Aviation Administration, Air Force, Army, Coast Guard and the FBI took part in the investigation. They analyzed every piece of debris, investigated crew and passenger backgrounds, examined maintenance and flight records, interviewed service personnel, dispatchers and air traffic controllers, and studied in-flight weather data for any anomalies. After a lengthy investigation, no evidence of in-flight fire or explosion was found and no conclusive explanation of why the aircraft plunged into the sea could be determined.

By having the U.S. Navy Oceanographic Office compute the drift of the debris from existing ocean currents and surface wind at the time of the accident, it was determined that the impact point was approximately eight miles southwest of where the wreckage was found. The impact location suggested the aircraft had maintained its flight path for an additional five to nine minutes after the last communication over Domestic Annette.

Structural pieces of the aircraft recovered from the surface indicated the airplane was inverted when it impacted the water. The congregation of debris in only one area also indicated that the airplane was intact as it plunged into the sea. The number of life vests found still in their containers suggested the passengers had had insufficient time to prepare for the emergency, or were at least inhibited from doing so by the aircraft's sudden change in attitude. The accident board concluded that the crew probably experienced the emergency shortly after radioing their position over Domestic Annette, since attempted contact from the Sandspit controller a few minutes later was in vain. The captain of the Pacific Northern airliner near the Northwest flight did state that there was heavy radio interference in the area, however, which could possibly have blocked communication.

Analysis of the in-flight weather data did not suggest the possibility of a loss of aircraft control from icing or turbulence, even with moderate icing and moderate turbulence forecast near the occluded weather front in the vicinity of their last radio contact. The Pacific Northern Airlines flight at 18,000 feet encountered only light icing and light turbulence in the area, neither of which should have posed a problem for the Northwest DC-7.

It was possible the crew might have requested a change in altitude to exit any turbulence they were encountering for the comfort of the passengers. This would have been standard procedure when the passengers were receiving an in-flight meal, which was probably happening at that time. Icing would not have been a concern unless the aircraft's anti-icing systems failed. The previous accident of another DC-7 near Sitka in 1962, certainly demonstrated the potential for a loss of engine power from such an occurrence.

A subsequent investigation into all the crew members determined they were properly trained and qualified. Each was experienced with DC-7 operations and had flown the same route on previous occasions. Captain Olsen had over 15,000 flight hours, First Officer Wenger over 11,000 hours, and Flight Engineer Larson over 7,000 total hours.

No discrepancies were found in the aircraft's maintenance records. It had been properly serviced before departure and had just completed a maintenance inspection the previous day. The crew who delivered the aircraft from Minneapolis reported all systems to be operating normally.

Fuel analysis of the refueling truck at McChord Air Force Base revealed no evidence of contamination. The gross weight of the aircraft was below the maximum allowable range and the loading limits were within normal parameters. No cargo other than personal baggage was on board. By all accounts the aircraft in question was completely airworthy and capable of flight for the forecast weather conditions. Due to a lack of evidence, the investigation board could not determine the probable cause of the accident.

Many of the 101 people who lost their lives on that fatal flight were young servicemen on their first assignment to Alaska. Included in the total number of servicemen and dependents were several family groups of five people. Most of the remaining servicemen were accompanied by at least one dependent. The human remains recovered after the disaster were very limited and proved insufficient to allow proper identification of any individual victim.

Memorial services were conducted at the respective military bases in Alaska and individual hometowns in the days following the accident, but none was more fitting than that given by the Coast Guard Cutter *Sorrel*. Its crew had been at the scene since shortly after the wreckage was first located, and more than anyone they felt an emotional link with the victims. When the recovery operation was finally completed, the men stood on deck with their heads bowed as the ship's flag was lowered to half-mast. A twenty-one-gun salute was rendered, then the ship slowly turned her bow away toward the distant coastal islands, still invisible on the horizon.

Unfortunately, the crash of the Northwest Airlines DC-7 on June 3, 1963 was not the last disaster involving an aircraft under military contract in Alaska. While transporting military personnel to Vietnam on November 27, 1970, a Douglas DC-8 of Capital

119

International Airways crashed during takeoff from Anchorage, killing forty-seven of the 229 people on board. Another DC-8 crashed near King Cove in September 1973, while operating under instrument flight rules. That cargo airplane was completely destroyed, fatally injuring all six occupants.

Tragedy near Juneau

SEPTEMBER 4, 1971

A solid overcast below the Boeing 727's flight path obscured any visual references with the ground as the aircraft descended on the instrument approach into Juneau, Alaska. High peaks on the nearby islands and coastal mountains also remained hidden behind multiple layers of clouds. Light rain pelted the cockpit windows as the Alaska Airlines pilots tracked the localizer course inbound to the airport. The landing gear was lowered when they were cleared by air traffic control for the approach. As the jet passed through 4,000 feet a few minutes later, the captain contacted Juneau Tower and reported over Barlow Intersection, only ten miles from the runway. Both pilots watched the flight instruments and stole an occasional glance outside, thinking they would be safely on the ground in a matter of minutes. It was not to be.

The aircraft established no further communication. Fourteen minutes after the last transmission the control tower notified search and rescue facilities of a possible mishap. After several hours, the aircraft wreckage was found on a snow-covered slope in the Chilkat Mountain Range, one mile east of Teardrop Lake and 18.5 miles west of the Juneau airport. Debris was scattered over a wide area where the airplane had almost disintegrated on impact. A few minor post-crash fires blackened some of the wreckage, but the major portions lay untouched along the edge of a ridge and adjoining canyon. The point of impact was at the 2,500-foot level, in approximate alignment with the inbound localizer course to the Juneau airport. It was the worst air disaster in U.S. history at that time, taking the lives of 104 passengers and seven crew members. There were no survivors.

At the time, the Juneau Airport did not have a precision landing system in place. All instrument approaches at the airfield were without a glide slope, which allows an aircraft to descend along a precise track while aligned with the runway on the inbound course. Two non-precision approaches were available, both making use of a localizer at the airfield and VHF omni-directional range and nondirectional beacon navigational aids away from the airfield for fixing points along the inbound course. The mountains around Juneau required an approaching aircraft to make a final turn to the runway only three miles from the airport.

Alaska Airlines flight 1866, referred to as AS66, was a daily scheduled passenger flight from Anchorage to Seattle, with intermediate stops at Cordova, Yakutat, Juneau and Sitka. The flight was operating under instrument flight rules, as required by federal and Alaska Airline regulations. No navigational problems were encountered for the majority of the flight after takeoff from Anchorage, at 0913 that morning. It landed at Cordova around 0942, departing again at 1034 for Yakutat. The flight arrived at Yakutat at 1107, and after a brief turnaround left for Juneau at 1135. While on the ground at Yakutat, a clearance was issued by air traffic control for the next instrument flight to Juneau. Approximately thirty-five minutes after departure from Yakutat, the Boeing 727 impacted the western side of a barren slope in the coastal range of the Chilkat Mountains.

From air traffic control and cockpit voice recordings analyzed after the accident, it was determined that AS66 progressed normally after departure from Yakutat until reaching Pleasant Intersection, thirty-eight miles west of Juneau. The instrument flight rules clearance received from air traffic control while on the ground at Yakutat authorized the flight to proceed to the Juneau airport via the J-507 airway to Pleasant Intersection, then direct to Juneau. The pilots were instructed to remain on course at 9,000 feet or below until fifteen miles southeast of Yakutat, then to climb and maintain flight level 230 (23,000 feet). The flight reported reaching flight level 230 at 1146, sixty-five miles east of Yakutat.

At that time, Anchorage Center further cleared the flight to descend at the pilot's discretion, so as to cross Pleasant Intersection at 10,000 feet. A clearance limit to Howard Intersection was also given and they were told to report when descending through 11,000 feet. A current altimeter setting for the Juneau airport was also passed at that time.

AS66 reported leaving flight level 230 at 1151. Three minutes later the controller instructed the flight to maintain 12,000 feet, and changed the clearance limit to Pleasant Intersection, due to concern about another aircraft in the area. Air traffic control explained that a Piper Apache on an instrument departure from Juneau was not following the clearance it had been given and its exact position could not be confirmed. Apparently the Piper's pilot did not have a current instrument flight rules chart and was flying off outdated information that had been subsequently changed. Radio contact between the Piper and air traffic control was also hindered by a weak radio aboard the small airplane.

At 1158, AS66 reported entering a holding pattern over Pleasant Intersection. Cockpit coordination between the crew seemed to be distracted at that time by the Piper Apache's ongoing situation with air traffic control. The captain voiced obvious concern about the other aircraft to the first officer and spent several minutes acting as a radio relay between the smaller aircraft and air traffic control.

Once the Alaska Airlines flight reported holding at Pleasant Intersection, the controller cleared the flight to continue inbound to Howard Intersection while maintaining 12,000 feet, then to enter holding with an expected approach time of 1210. At 1201, only a minute after receiving the clearance, the captain of flight AS66 reported their arrival over Howard Intersection, even though their actual position was still nine miles to the west. The distance between the two intersections was 21.5 miles and should have taken approximately five minutes of flight time. Since Pleasant Intersection was reported at 1158, arrival over Howard Intersection should not have occurred until at least 1203, but none of the crew noticed the discrepancy. Continued concern over the Piper Apache's location distracted the cockpit crew until at least 1205.

Falsely assuming they were at Howard Intersection, the crew entered a holding pattern using right-hand turns at 1201. Five minutes later, during the first turn inbound on the localizer course, the controller asked the flight's position in holding. When the captain confirmed that the flight was on the inbound track of the holding pattern, the controller cleared the flight for the straight in localizer approach to Juneau, with further instructions to cross Howard

Intersection at or below 9,000 feet. The captain acknowledged and reported leaving 12,000 feet at that time, subsequently activating the landing gear mechanism a few seconds later.

The next intersection fix after Howard Intersection was Rockledge, 3.2 miles farther along the inbound course. The crew confirmed they were over Rockledge at 1208, now flying at approximately 220 knots in a descent of 4,000 feet per minute. Their actual position was still over nine miles west, near Excursion Intersection. The minimum altitude for the approach at their actual position on the inbound course was 6,500 feet, but they continued to descend through 4,500 feet, unaware of the navigational error. At that time, however, cockpit voice recordings of the first officer seemed to reflect an uncertainty with the indications he was receiving on his course display.

At 1208:43 the controller instructed AS66 to contact Juneau Tower. A few seconds later the captain established contact with the tower, reporting inbound from Barlow Intersection, which was only a short distance west of the Juneau airport. Their actual location was still well short of Howard Intersection and west of the Chilkat Mountains lying directly in their flight path. The tower controller responded at 1209:04 with current runway information at the airport. No acknowledgment was received from the flight. Approximately ten seconds after the tower's last transmission, the aircraft impacted the mountain slope.

When search crews located the wreckage in the Chilkat Mountains a few hours later, the catastrophic impact was immediately obvious. Pieces of every size littered the terrain, from small, indiscernible shreds of debris, to more recognizable sections of the cockpit and forward fuselage. Some of the aircraft components, including the three demolished engines, which came to rest at the bottom of a small gully, had tumbled or been flung down the slope by the force of impact. Everywhere along the path of destruction were torn pieces of luggage, exposing clothing and personal effects that lay scattered across the snow. Mangled body parts and corpses were also strewn throughout the wreckage, adding gruesome evidence to the full extent of the tragedy.

Rain and overcast skies were still prevalent at the crash site the first evening, when five Alaska State Troopers arrived on the mountain to secure the area. They remained throughout the night, until replaced by twenty-three National Guardsmen and local mountain climbers the next morning. Officials from the National Transportation Safety Board and FBI also arrived to begin a preliminary investigation of the disaster. The entire area was sealed off while workers began locating and marking every piece of the aircraft, as well as finding and retrieving the bodies from the wreckage. It was a somber task, especially when removing the dead from the debris. Securing the bodies was made somewhat easier with the arrival of several local helicopters, which assisted in lifting the remains to a base camp further up the mountain. From there they were loaded onto a much larger Coast Guard helicopter for transport to Juneau.

By the evening of the third day following the tragedy, fifty-six of the 111 bodies and both cockpit recorders had been recovered. Bad weather continued to hinder much of the recovery process with persistent rain and high winds. By September 8, almost all the bodies had been found at the crash site, but only eighty-nine had been removed from the mountain. Of those, only seventeen were positively identified by an FBI disaster team working out of a temporary morgue in Juneau. It would be several more days before all the bodies could be transported to Juneau and identified, and months before aircraft components from the wreckage could be tested and analyzed.

Thirteen months later, on October 13, 1972, the National Transportation Safety Board released the official Aircraft Accident Report. Findings of the investigation revealed no evidence of any structural failure, fire, or explosion that could have caused the crash. The aircraft was determined to be fully airworthy on the day of the flight and maintained in accordance with requirements. The crew was also properly qualified and certified for flight operations, and post-mortem analysis of the bodies could find nothing that might have interfered with the crew's physical ability to carry out their duties.

All of the cockpit crew members had extensive flight experience and were familiar with flight operations in and out of the Juneau area. Captain Richard Adams had been employed by Alaska Airlines since June 1955 and had almost 14,000 flight hours, of which 2,600 were in Boeing 727s. First Officer Leonard Beach had been employed by Alaska Airlines since February 1966 and had a total of 5,000 flight hours, 2,100 of those in 727 aircraft. The flight engineer, Second Officer James Carson, had been hired in June 1966 and had flown almost all of his 2,600 hours in 727s. They had all had adequate crew rest prior to the flight, and at the time of the accident they had been on duty for a little over four hours.

The probable cause of the accident was determined to be misleading navigational information received inside the cockpit, resulting in the aircraft descending below the minimum approach altitude. What exactly the misleading navigational information was could not be determined, but the cockpit voice recordings established that the flight crew thought they were much closer to Juneau then they actually were. The navigational error first occurred as the flight was established inbound on the instrument approach, prior to arrival over Howard Intersection. In the aftermath of the tragedy it was also pointed out that there were other navigational aids that could have been used by the crew to verify their position along the approach course, but it was not mandatory for them to do so.

Immediately following the accident, the primary focus of the National Transportation Safety Board was on determining how and why the fatal crash occurred. Since there was no indication of a fire, explosion or structural failure prior to impact, attention centered on several other factors that could have caused the mishap. A malfunction in the operation of the navigational aid facility at Sisters Island, which was a VHF omni-directional range station used to fix the intersections along the localizer course to Juneau, was a possibility. Other potential problems were a mechanical malfunction of the aircraft's navigation equipment, pilot error from wrongly interpreting navigational information inside the cockpit, or signal interference from some outside source. Each possibility was thoroughly investigated during months of analysis and testing, with no conclusive results obtained.

There was extensive discussion on the likelihood of a system error in the Sisters Island VHF omni-directional range, which could have sent false signal information to a receiving aircraft. Since AS66 was using the VHF omni-directional range station to fix the intersections along the inbound course, an error in signal transmission might explain how the crew thought they were further east of their actual location. No discrepancies were found during the investigation, however, and no other aircraft reported any problems with the VHF omni-directional range reception prior to the accident. One aircraft was even tracking outbound from the Sisters Island VHF omni-directional range to another station at the time of the incident, and experienced no navigational problems.

Only limited information was obtained from the recovered navigation equipment aboard the aircraft because of the extensive crash damage, but bench tests conducted on identical types of equipment could find no conclusive errors or failures that might have contributed to the accident. All the ground navigation stations used by the flight were also found to be operating correctly, verified by extensive ground and air checks of the operational systems. Several post-accident test flights were also flown along the same localizer course as AS66, showing completely normal indications from all the facilities used during the inbound approach. All available evidence revealed that the flight progressed routinely along the J-507 airway until it was established inbound on the Juneau LDA NDB-2 localizer approach.

There was no military or civilian electronic activity in the area at the time of the accident that might have interfered with signal reception on board the aircraft, nor were there any unusual meteorological influences. Flight tests were even conducted under similar tidal conditions from the time of the accident, to see if they adversely affected the VHF omni-directional range receiver. Nothing out of the ordinary was observed.

Human error could not be identified with any certainty as the cause of the accident, but several factors could have contributed to the misinterpretation of navigational information by the crew. Once the flight neared Pleasant Intersection, the first officer changed his navigation receiver to the localizer frequency at Juneau for tracking the inbound course. The captain was requested to tune the other navigation receiver to the Sisters Island VHF omni-directional range in order to fix the correct step-down points along the approach. From post-crash analysis of the cockpit voice recordings, it seems likely the captain did not comply with the request and instead left his navigation receiver tuned to the same localizer frequency as the first officer.

Proper execution of the approach required that two components be used in conjunction with each other to identify correct intersection radials along the inbound course. First, the VHF omni-directional range navigation receiver had to be tuned to the correct station, and second, the course indicator had to be set on the correct radial from the station. If this was not done correctly, intersection fixes along the approach course would be inaccurate. During the time the first officer initially requested the VHF omni-directional range be tuned and identified to Sisters Island, the captain was involved in a three-way conversation between the Piper Apache and air traffic control.

Minor concern over the other aircraft continued to partially distract the attention of all three crew members for another eleven minutes of the approach, causing significant concern for a period of five minutes during their final descent for landing. Only after the first officer had asked the captain a second time to set his course indicator on the correct intersection radial, did he respond vocally, but at no time did he actually confirm that the VHF omni-directional range navigation receiver had been tuned correctly. Without the VHF omni-directional range receiver tuned to the correct station, the captain's course indicator deviation bar would have shown an incorrect position on the inbound course, relative to the aircraft's actual location. The erroneous display on his flight instruments should have been recognized, but tragically it was not.

Irritation over the other aircraft seemed to have distracted the captain's attention from the navigation instruments during the approach. However, it would seem unlikely that all the cockpit crew members would be simultaneously negligent in noticing any discrepancies with the instruments over a span of several minutes. Even so, the other aircraft continued to be a concern until less than two minutes before impact, when the last comment concerning the Piper Apache was voiced by the first officer.

The accident board concluded that there was insufficient evidence to explain how the misleading navigational information was displayed inside the cockpit. Because of the obvious hazards imposed by the terrain, the board did determine that the Federal Aviation Administration should have required the use of other available navigational aids in the area when aircraft were executing the localizer approach. It was further recommended that distance measuring equipment be installed at the Juneau airport, allowing future aircraft to accurately verify their position and the location of the inbound fixes along the localizer course.

Merrill's Travelair 7000 on Wheels.
Photo: Anchorage Museum of History and Art, Aeronautics-Anchorage Collection

Hamilton Metalplane in which Eielson and Borland were killed.
Photo: The Maas-Wheeler-Clifton Collection, photo 1975-0111-01246, University of Alaska Fairbanks, Alaska and Polar Regions Archives

Above: Junkers F-13, similar to Paddy Burke's.
Photo: The George King Collection, photo 1988-0164-00024, University of Alaska Fairbanks, Alaska and Polar Regions Archives

Left: Post-Rogers Lockheed Orion on the Chena River in Fairbanks the day before the accident.
Photo: The George King Collection, photo 1988-0164-00067, University of Alaska Fairbanks, Alaska and Polar Regions Archives

Below: Post-Rogers Lockheed Orion wreck near Barrow.
Photo: The Day Dennedy Aviation Collection, photo 1991-0098-01251, University of Alaska Fairbanks, Alaska and Polar Regions Archives

130

Above: Pacific Alaska Airways Lockheed 10-A, similar to Gillam's plane.
Photo: The George E. Young Collection, photo 1981-0024-00170, University of Alaska Fairbanks, Alaska and Polar Regions Archives

Below: Canadian Pacific DC-3, similar to a Pacific Alaska Air Express DC-3 lost near Yakutat on November 4, 1948, Columbia Air Cargo DC-3 on November 27, 1947 and General Airways DC-3C on January 12, 1952.
Photo: From 1000aircraftphotos.com, Web Site by Ron Dupas

Above: Swiss Air DC-4, similar to Canadian Pacific DC-4 lost on July 20, 1951 and Reeve Aleutian C-54 on September 24, 1959.
Photo: Ralph Kunadt at airlinephotos.com

Below: Cessna 310 similar to Pan-Alaska Airways plane lost with Congressmen Boggs and Begich.
Photo: Courtesy of Ron Dupas at 1000aircraftphotos.com

Above: Grumman "Goose," similar to Webber Airlines accident aircraft on August 25, 1978, taking off from Wrangell Harbor.

Photo: The Machetanz Collection, photo 1973-0075-00661, University of Alaska Fairbanks, Alaska and Polar Regions Archives

Right: Pan American DC-4, similar to accident aircraft on October 26, 1947.

Photo: Courtesy of Ron Dupas at 1000aircraftphotos.com

Above: Alaska Airlines Boeing 727, similar to accident aircraft on September 4, 1971.
Photo: George Young Collection, photo 1981-0024-00175, University of Alaska Fairbanks, Alaska and Polar Regions Archives

Below: Northwest Airlines DC-4, similar to the accident aircraft on March 12, 1948.
Photo: Ron Dupas

Above: Canadian Pacific DC-6, similar to accident aircraft on August 29,1956.
Photo: Ron Dupas at 1000aircraftphotos.com

*Above:*Alaska Airlines DC-6, similar to accident aircraft on July 21, 1961.
Photo: Ron Dupas at 1000aircraftphotos.com

Below: Northern Consolidated Airlines Fairchild F-27B, similar to Wien Consolidated Airlines
F-27B on December 2, 1968.
Photo: Anchorage Museum of History and Art

Above: World Airways DC-8, similar to accident aircraft on September 8, 1973.
Photo: William Sierra

Below: Air Inuit DHC-6 Twin Otter, similar to Alaska Aeronautical Industries DHC-6 on September 6, 1977.
Photo: Moritz Herrmann

11,000 ft

9,000 ft.

Left: Crash area of Northwest Airlines DC-4 on Mt. Sanford, March 12, 1948.
Photo: Anchorage Museum of History and Art

Below: Alaska Airlines DC-3, similar to accident aircraft on January 20, 1949.
Photo: Richard Silagi

Bottom: MATS Lockheed L-749A Constellation, similar to Pacific Northern Airlines Constellation on June 14, 1960.
Photo: Ralph Kunadt

Above: Capiton International DC-8, similar to accident aircraft on November 27, 1970.
Photo: Eduard Marmet

Below: Falcon Express Cargo Beech 1900C, similar to Ryan Air Service 1900C on November 23, 1987.
Photo: Nobuhiro Horimoto

Above: Japan Airlines DC-8, similar to accident aircraft on January 13, 1977.
Photo: Yosuke Kinoshita

Above: Pilgrim 100B, similar to Pan American 100B on April 6, 1944.
Photo: William Drawbaugh Collection, photo 1991-0201-00011, University of Alaska Fairbanks, Alaska and Polar Regions Archives

Above: Everts Air Fuel C-46, similar to Transocean Airlines C-46 on December 30,1951.
Photo: Ralph Kunadt at airlinerphotos.com

Below: Wien Alaska Airlines Fairchild F-27B, similar to accident aircraft on August 30, 1975.
Photo: Ron Dupas at 1000aircraftphotos.com

Above: Northern Air Cargo DC-6, similar to accident aircraft on July 20, 1996.
Photo: Ralph Kunadt

Below: Lockheed Vega, similar to Pat Renahan's lost on October 28, 1930.
Photo: Kay Kennedy Aviation Collection, Photo 1991-0098-00451, University of Alaska Fairbanks, Alaska and Polar Regions Archives

Above: T & G Aviation DC-7, similar to Northwest Airlines DC-7 lost on June 3, 1963.
Photo: Ralph Kunadt

Right: DC-8 crash site in Anchorage on November 27, 1970.
Photo: Excerpted from Aircraft Accident Report, File No. 1-0025, and National Transportation Safety Board, Report Number: NTSB-AAR-72-12

During the accident investigation, it was revealed that possible fluctuations could be occurring in the signal transmission from the Sisters Island VHF omni-directional range and similar VHF omni-directional range facilities. In fact, several months after the accident, a significant navigational error was reported at another VHF omni-directional range station, 224 miles southeast of the Sisters Island VHF omni-directional range. Attempts to duplicate the error were unsuccessful, however. Even though tests conducted on VHF omni-directional range navigation facilities did not uncover any positive confirmation of signal fluctuations, the board did recommend that the Federal Aviation Administration continue testing and researching the potential problem.

A few years after the crash of AS66, the Federal Aviation Administration accepted partial blame for the navigational error when it was determined that the VHF omni-directional range signal had malfunctioned by transmitting a directional error of 35° to 40°. In a court settlement, the Federal Aviation Administration agreed to pay $4.5 million of the $15 million damage claim awarded to plaintiffs in the case. As part of the settlement, new navigation facilities were installed at Juneau.

Incidents of possible navigation errors continued to occur for many years following the accident. In late 1972, another commercial airliner experienced a similar course error of 40° while on an instrument approach to Sitka. The plane's captain and a Federal Aviation Administration inspector, who was also in the cockpit at the time, both observed the error. Furthermore, the captain stated that, after the incident, two Alaska Airline pilots told him they too had experienced previous navigational display errors in the area, which showed their location as east of their actual position. Apparently the pilots were able to verify their true position by using visual references off the ground.

Another accident involving a navigational error in the Juneau area occurred on October 22, 1985, when a Learjet on an instrument approach crashed in the same approximate location as the Alaska Airlines 727. As in the previous accident, the Learjet pilot apparently thought his airplane's position was nine miles further east on the inbound course. The last radio transmission reported their location as near Gustavus, still west of the Chilkat Range. All four occupants were killed on impact.

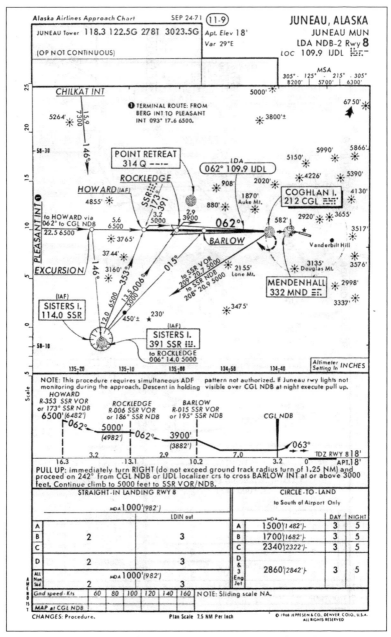

Image of Accident Report Standard Instrument Approach Procedure at Juneau. Excerpted from Aircraft Accident Report, File No. 1-0008, and National Transportation Safety Board, Report Number: NTSB-AAR-72-28

(*For illustration only—not to be used for navigation purposes.*)

146

Tragedy struck again on November 12, 1992. A C-12 aircraft belonging to the Alaska Army National Guard was flying an instrument approach into Juneau when it impacted a mountain slope near the other two previous accident sites in the Chilkat Mountains. As in the other incidents, the C-12's crew apparently received erroneous navigational information that showed their location as ten miles east of their actual position. There were no survivors.

If nothing else, the terrible accident of Alaska Airlines flight 1866 serves as a reminder to all pilots that proper cockpit coordination is vital to the safe operation of an aircraft. It is also an excellent example of why additional navigation systems aboard the aircraft should always be used as a backup to the primary systems during an instrument approach, whether or not they are mandatory. By simply tuning either of the automatic direction finder receivers in the cockpit to one of several nondirectional beacons in the area, the pilots could easily have verified any erroneous information they were receiving from the other systems.

Following the findings of the accident board, the localizer approach at Juneau was upgraded with distance measuring equipment. Except for a few other minor changes over the years, the localizer runway 8 approach procedure remains basically the same today.

Wreckage in Sumner Strait

AUGUST 25, 1978

Low areas of stratus clouds and fog prevailed over the coastal waters around Prince of Wales Island on August 25, 1978. Intermittent rain showers pelted the otherwise calm seas. It was a typical day for the Southeastern Panhandle of Alaska, where weeks of continuous drizzle were not uncommon. After a time, the dreary conditions would be interrupted by patches of sunshine breaking through the clouds, or a few days of perfectly blue skies that somehow made the other weather insignificant.

For the most part, the economy of the region is based on logging and fishing, both of which have flourished on the islands and surrounding waters since the early 1900s. Thousands of commercial fishing vessels labor to fill their holds with halibut and salmon during the summer months, while the many logging camps work equally hard felling and transporting valuable timber when not hindered by federal mandates. The abundant harvests are then taken to the larger coastal towns for processing in the canneries and mills, before being shipped out to distribution points in the United States or overseas.

Some of the smaller communities that service the fishing and logging operations are linked by a few miles of rough road, but most are isolated in remote bays on a number of different islands along the coast. Transportation is limited to either sea or air travel, with aircraft obviously the quickest method. Airplane and helicopter operations are a common occurrence and are an extremely valuable commodity, not only to the inhabitants, but also to private companies and government agencies operating in the region. Aviation had itself become a productive industry, thriving on the needs of an expanding Alaska.

Webber Airlines, Inc., based in Ketchikan, had been flying in southeast Alaska since the early 1970s as a local passenger and cargo air-taxi operation. It owned several types of float-equipped aircraft, including a Grumman Goose G-21A amphibian that conducted daily scheduled and non-scheduled flights in the area. Due to a lack of navigational aids and airport facilities at most of the destinations, visual flight rules were normally followed on the routes. Occasionally a flight would be delayed or even canceled because of inclement weather conditions, but whenever possible the pilots tried meeting the obligations of the company as best they could.

On the morning of August 25, one of the company aircraft on the scheduled flight from Ketchikan was unable to reach the western side of Prince of Wales Island because of adverse weather blocking the overland passes. The pilot returned to Ketchikan to await improved conditions, hopeful of making it through the pass in time for the next scheduled pick-up that afternoon. Instead, the company's owner, Jack Swaim, decided to take the flight himself in the larger Grumman Goose, as it could accommodate both groups of passengers from the morning and afternoon flights without the need to dispatch a second aircraft. He also wanted to ensure that a passenger waiting at the first destination made it back to Ketchikan in time for a connecting flight on Alaska Airlines. After having the aircraft refueled at the company dock and receiving reports of better weather conditions from the logging camps along the route of flight, Swaim prepared the twin-engine amphibian for departure. The airplane was untied then pushed away from the dock as the piston engines turned over and caught easily. A small puff of exhaust was quickly left behind as it taxied out into Tongass Narrows in front of town and turned into the wind for departure. The sound of the engines echoed across the water as the throttles were pushed full open, thrusting the airplane forward in increased speed until it lifted off the calm surface a few seconds later.

Swaim reported off at 1300 with the company flight operations without bothering to file a Federal Aviation Administration flight plan. Instead he used a company flight plan left with the dispatcher, who was well aware of the intended route. He did not receive an official weather briefing either, deciding to rely on his own judgment, his familiarity with the area and weather observations from local logging camps. Shortly after departure he did contact Ketchikan Radio for local traffic advisories.

A thick overcast lay over the area as the Grumman Goose climbed northwest into Clarence Strait. An occasional rain shower reduced the visibility down to a few miles, but the weather was an improvement over the earlier conditions. A mild breeze barely disturbed the glassy water below, which was more affected by the wake of a passing boat than by any intensity from the wind.

Swaim continued up the strait past Myers Chuck and Ratz Harbor, then turned inland over Prince of Wales Island after passing Coffman Cove. Following Sweetwater Lake, he proceeded southwest around the higher hills, staying just below the clouds hanging in the pass until turning west again into Tuxekan Passage. After crossing the narrow expanse of water, Swaim touched down smoothly in Nichen Cove at 1345 on the east side of Tuxekan Island, then taxied to the dock at Naukati where the passengers were already waiting.

Both groups of passengers from the 1215 and 1430 scheduled flights were loaded, as well a large amount of baggage and cargo. Two additional passengers that were not on the manifest, but who had requested transportation to Labouchere Bay, were forced to remain at Naukati for a later flight that evening. Swaim was already irritated because of the weather delay and became more agitated over the discussion concerning the other passengers. He was in such a hurry after loading the cargo that the eight passengers he did take were barely seated before the aircraft was pushed away from the dock and the engines started. The airplane was only certified for ten total passengers and the extra space in the back of the airplane was filled with additional food supplies and equipment belonging to several of the passengers flying to Labouchere Bay.

Shortly after departure from Nichen Cove, Swaim radioed his company operations he was en route to the next destination. Flying north through El Capitan Pass, he followed the water route into Shakan Bay and past Hole-in-the-Wall on the northwest corner of Prince of Wales Island, arriving at the logging operation on the edge of Labouchere Bay at approximately 1420. The camp radio operator met the airplane as it pulled alongside the dock.

Four of the passengers and most of the cargo were unloaded

quickly by the pilot, then a heated discussion developed over one of the passengers waiting to board for the flight to Ketchikan. Apparently she had been scheduled on the flight without Swaim's knowledge after he left Ketchikan. He became even more irritated as the conversation continued, but he did allow her to board the aircraft with the other passengers who had been waiting. The airplane now held a total of eleven passengers, one more than the allowable limit.

Once again Swaim was in such a hurry that some of the arriving passenger baggage was not off-loaded, and other pieces being on-loaded were hastily thrown into the aircraft. After loudly slamming the rear entry door, he quickly jumped behind the controls and taxied the Grumman amphibian out into the bay for departure. It lifted off at approximately 1435, turned north into Sumner Strait, then disappeared from view behind a point of land in front of the bay. A short time later Swaim reported to the company radio operator at Ketchikan that they were airborne.

Nothing further was heard from the flight and the only other person who reported seeing the aircraft was a truck driver parked on a logging road near the small fishing community of Point Baker, three and a half miles north of Labouchere Bay. The airplane was observed flying a few hundred feet above the water as it passed the tip of the island in relatively good weather conditions. It appeared to be proceeding normally at that time on a northeasterly heading. After less than a minute, the driver's line of sight was obstructed by a nearby hill.

Exactly what happened to the aircraft over the next several minutes is a matter of speculation, but from the limited debris found in the water almost two hours later, it can be assumed that the airplane hit the surface with extreme force before breaking open and sinking. Whether the accident was caused by pilot error, weather or mechanical failure, was never determined, since the aircraft was never recovered.

At first the flight was only listed as overdue back in Ketchikan, but when two halibut boats from Wrangell reported finding an oil slick, pieces of flotsam and a body near Point Baker, the Coast Guard assumed it was the missing aircraft. A helicopter was dispatched to search for possible survivors, while the halibut boats *Unimak* and *Arliss* remained on site until it arrived. The wreckage was positively identified a short time later as being from the overdue flight when they found pieces of personal baggage belonging to one of the eleven passengers.

With confirmation that the aircraft had crashed in Sumner Strait, the Coast Guard cutters *Elderberry* and *Cape Romain* were dispatched from their respective ports in Petersburg and Ketchikan to assist in the search and recovery. A second Coast Guard helicopter also joined the effort, which by then included several civilian aircraft and numerous private vessels.

An intensive sweep of the Sumner Strait area around the impact site was conducted throughout the evening, but only four bodies were found floating on the surface among smaller pieces of debris. The largest section of aircraft structure recovered was a flap vacuum tank that had been installed in the nose compartment. Most of the recovered items consisted of personal baggage, flotation devices and small pieces of insulation and wood from the cabin interior. A large oil slick a mile long and a half mile wide covered the area, which was located about two miles north of Point Baker. The other eight occupants of the aircraft were never found.

Because of the wreckage location in proximity to Point Baker, it was determined the aircraft probably crashed around 1445, only minutes after last being seen by the logging truck operator. During the ensuing investigation no known cause of the accident could be found, although a mechanical malfunction or unexpected weather conditions might have been contributing factors.

The aircraft had over 9,400 hours on the airframe, with the last major overhaul completed in 1967. A 100-hour inspection was performed only three days before the accident, and some structural and mechanical repairs were carried out in 1977 after a hard landing had damaged several components. It was revealed that the repair of some of the faults annotated during the recent 100-hour inspection had been deferred until a later date because of the unavailability of parts. The faults included fabric work on some of the control surfaces, replacement of several structural and engine components due to corrosion, replacement of two oil lines that were frayed, replacement of a cracked spinner assembly and propeller bulkhead, and small holes in the heater ducts.

The aircraft was flying under a special operating limitation that specified a maximum gross weight of 8,920 pounds, based on single-engine capability. Gross weight at takeoff from Labouchere Bay was determined by the accident investigator to be at a minimum of 400 pounds above maximum, and possibly more. In addition, the aircraft was only certified to carry eleven occupants, including the pilot. Twelve people were on board. This was not the first time Webber Airlines had exceeded the requirement. One of the passengers that got off the airplane at Labouchere Bay also claimed he did not have a seat belt during the flight from Nichen Cove.

Weather conditions at the time of the accident were forecast as marginal, with diminished visibility in rain and low clouds. Ceilings as low as 400 feet and intermittent rain showers were present along the route before the accident. Other pilots in the area reported occasional clouds extending down to 200 feet in the heavier rain showers, with visibility as low as a quarter mile. Winds were calm over the area, with a smooth, glassy surface on the water. Only an hour after the accident, a thick fog layer in the vicinity of the crash site extended seven miles across Sumner Strait, but outside the fog the ceiling and visibility were 2,000 feet and ten miles.

Pilot and owner Jack Swaim had logged over 5,700 hours during his flying career, 684 of which were in the Grumman G-21A. He held an aircraft rating for single and multi-engine land and sea operations, but he was not instrument certified. There was also no evidence of Swaim receiving the required annual recurrent training in the Grumman amphibian, as specified in his company's operations manual.

It was believed that all four bodies recovered from the accident site had been seated in the aft cabin area of the aircraft, since three of the four had boarded during the last stop at Labouchere Bay. Autopsies confirmed the fatal injuries to be a result of severe impact forces sustained when the airplane hit the surface. Because of the water depth and strong tides in the strait, no recovery of the other bodies or the aircraft has been attempted.

Circling Approach at Cold Bay

August 29, 1956

Captain Thornton Tweed was a senior DC-6 pilot on the Vancouver to Hong Kong route for Canadian Pacific Airlines. In addition to his normal captain duties on the August 29th flight, he was also supervising another pilot in preparation for an upcoming evaluation. The other pilot was Phillip Iverson, a qualified captain on domestic routes who was being trained as a captain for the airline's overseas flights. Together they had over 22,000 total hours in different aircraft, with Captain Tweed by far the most experienced in DC-6s.

Accompanying them on the round-trip flight were First Officer Love, navigators Hunter and Short, and flight attendant Lee, Wong and Jordan. The first scheduled stop would be in Cold Bay for refueling, then onto Hong Kong, with an intermediate stop in Tokyo, Japan. The additional crew members not initially involved in the flight were allowed to rest in the sleeping compartment until called for duty.

Referred to as flight 307, the DC-6 departed from Vancouver, British Columbia, at 1347 with fourteen passengers. A detailed weather briefing had been obtained prior to departure, forecasting no significant enroute weather hazards and a ceiling of 1,200 feet upon arrival at Cold Bay. Moderate winds and seven miles of visibility were expected at ground level. The flight was cleared as filed on an instrument flight plan from Vancouver to Cold Bay, via the Green 10 airway, Amber 1 airway and Great Circle route, with an estimated flight time of slightly over seven hours.

Flight 307 proceeded normally, transmitting routine position reports as it flew at its assigned cruising altitude, which varied from

10,000 to 12,000 feet. At 2011, six and a half hours after takeoff, the flight reported 100 miles from Cold Bay, estimating their arrival over the station at 2036. Then at 2024 the company dispatcher at Cold Bay passed the latest weather observation at the airfield, reporting a ceiling of 500 feet with one and a half miles of visibility, light drizzle and fog, and winds from the northwest at twenty-one knots. The flight acknowledged receipt of the message.

When flight 307 arrived over the low-frequency radio range station, located 2.2 miles northwest of the airport, the captain turned outbound on the published instrument approach, requiring a course reversal back inbound to the airfield. A few minutes later at 2042, the flight completed the procedure turn and reported established on the inbound course to runway 14. That was the final communication from the aircraft.

Several people on the ground stated they observed the DC-6 descend through the overcast and pass over the runway at a low altitude around 2045. The landing gear was down and landing lights were on. One of the witnesses was the company dispatcher, standing on the airport ramp as the airplane came in for the approach. He reported that the aircraft was descending toward runway 14 when it suddenly applied power and turned over the airfield to the southeast. The airplane passed his viewpoint at less than 100 feet above the ground, before banking away in a slight climb. It disappeared from view and a few moments later observers saw a fire on the ground in the same direction.

Even though there was a quartering tailwind of 20 knots during the aircraft's descent to runway 14, it was believed the captain's initial intention was to execute a straight-in approach. Because of excessive airspeed, too steep an approach angle or possibly both, the decision was changed at the last minute to execute a circling approach to runway 26 instead. The captain's actual intention could never be positively determined, however, because the aircraft crashed moments later while in a shallow descent, only a mile southeast of the airfield, killing fifteen of the twenty-two people on board.

The control tower was not operational at the time of the accident and no Civil Aeronautics Administration facility existed at the airfield, so the flight's landing intentions were never communicated. Two private communication facilities were in operation at the air-

155

field, one belonging to Reeves Aleutian Airways and the other to Northwest Orient Airlines. The private stations were used primarily to relay position reports and clearances between air traffic control and company aircraft. Canadian Pacific Airlines used the Northwest Orient communication facilities on their Alaska routes and also had their own dispatcher stationed at Cold Bay.

As the airplane turned for a circling approach back to the airfield, it began losing altitude in a slight nose low descent. Less than a minute later it hit the ground in a shallow left turn, shearing both wings and breaking open the fuselage, scattering wreckage over a quarter-mile area of coastal tidal flats. Ruptured fuel tanks in the wings immediately burst into flames. Most of the aircraft was completely destroyed by the impact and resulting fire.

Three passengers and a flight attendant near the center and back of the airplane managed to escape through a break in the cabin after the impact, and the other three surviving crew members were either thrown clear of the aircraft during impact or escaped by crawling away from the wreckage before it was consumed by flames. All the remaining occupants were killed during the crash, with many thrown violently outside the fuselage by the force of impact. Some of the victims were not located until several days after the accident.

Among the survivors was Captain Tweed, who had occupied the right pilot's seat and received extensive head injuries during the crash. Another was Bill Short, the duty navigator, who sustained numerous injuries of his own. At the time of impact he was in the navigator station behind the pilot seats, separated from the cockpit area by a blackout curtain that prevented any visual contact with the cockpit or any outside references. First Officer Love, who was resting in a crew sleeping compartment, also survived, but received serious internal injuries when he was thrown out of his bunk by the force of impact. Dolores Jordan, the only surviving flight attendant, sustained a painful back injury, but still managed to help two children exit the airplane safely. The third surviving passenger was able to get out on his own. Miraculously, none of the surviving passengers were seriously injured.

Following the crash of flight 307, the Coast Guard and Navy dispatched several aircraft with medical personnel and supplies to assist the survivors. Two vessels were also sent to search the nearby waters for three of the missing bodies, presumed to have been car-

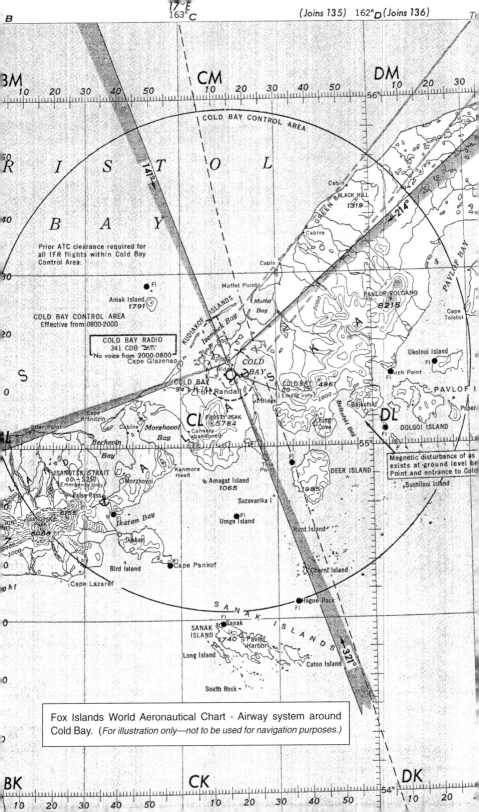

Fox Islands World Aeronautical Chart - Airway system around Cold Bay. (For illustration only—not to be used for navigation purposes.)

ried away by the outgoing tide. All seven survivors, with the exception of Captain Tweed, were flown to Elmendorf Air Force Base in Anchorage the following day, before continuing onto Vancouver the next morning.. Tweed remained in Anchorage in intensive care and never recovered enough from his injuries to give an accurate account of the tragedy.

Inclement weather at the crash site and around Cold Bay hampered the search efforts as much as the daily high tides, which partially covered the wreckage for a few hours before receding again. Eventually two of the missing bodies were located and transported with the others back to Vancouver for burial. Only an eight-month-old baby remained unaccounted for by the following week. The mother had died in the crash.

A four-member accident investigation team from the Civil Aeronautics Board arrived at the crash site two days after the crash, accompanied by officials from the Canadian Department Of Transport. Only after an extensive investigation of all available evidence obtained from the aircraft wreckage, survivors, witnesses, flight and maintenance records, operating procedures, weather data and navigation facilities was an official accident report released in May 1957.

It was determined that the DC-6 had been in a landing configuration with the landing gear and flaps extended as it approached runway 14. The aircraft then applied power while over the runway to execute either a missed approach or circling approach, and turned southeast away from the airfield. Shortly thereafter the gear was retracted, as would be expected, but for some reason the flaps were also fully retracted without any corrective increase in power or change in flight attitude being applied. A decrease in lift and corresponding loss of altitude resulted, placing the aircraft in a nose low descent. While still in a descending turn, the airplane impacted the tidal flats on an approximate heading of 040° and an airspeed of 186 knots.

All four engines and propellers were found to be operating normally prior to the crash, although at a lesser power setting than was required to execute a missed approach. When executing missed approach procedures, Canadian Pacific Airlines required their pilots to apply maximum except takeoff power, retract the landing gear and place the wing flaps at a setting of 020°. For some reason that was not done. Instead, an insufficient power setting was applied and the flaps were placed in a zero degree position. The area of the crash had very few references, especially at night, and it is likely the crew was unaware of their decreasing height above the ground as they continued turning downwind and retracted the flaps.

From eyewitness accounts it seemed likely the pilot decided to attempt a circling approach to runway 26 after overflying runway 14, instead of executing the published missed approach procedure, which required an aircraft to fly outbound on the north leg of the radio range station while climbing to 2,700 feet. A circling approach could only be accomplished below the 500-foot overcast and while maintaining visual contact during the turn back to the airfield, which is what the pilot was apparently doing.

None of the surviving crew members recalled any problems with the aircraft or crew during the flight, although the navigator heard Captain Tweed express disagreement as Captain Iverson applied power during the landing approach to runway 14. This would seem to indicate some confusion at that time on how the approach was being flown.

First Officer Love had been in the sleeping compartment during the crash and remembered the pilots making several power changes during the initial approach. It seemed unusual to him at the time, although any turbulence during the descent could have forced the crew to maintain their approach angle with appropriate power applications. He also stated that the power increase applied during the missed approach seemed insufficient and the aircraft experienced a sinking effect just seconds before the crash. This feeling would be expected had the flaps been fully retracted at that time.

The accident board found that the high intensity approach and runway lights for runway 14 had been activated for flight 307's arrival, and all were in normal operating condition. A flight check of the radio range station at Cold Bay was also conducted following the accident and was found to be functioning correctly.

Enroute and arrival weather for the flight was basically the same as initially forecast, except for a lower ceiling and visibility at Cold Bay, which was reported to the crew before the approach. A post-crash analysis of the weather data also determined that light to moderate turbulence was likely below 2,000 feet during the time of the accident.

Landing minimums at Cold Bay for Canadian Pacific Airlines DC-6s established a minimum of 400 feet and one mile of visibility for straight-in-approaches at night, and a 500-foot ceiling and one and a half miles of visibility for circling approaches. Both approaches were at or above minimums at the time of the accident. There were no mechanical malfunctions or structural failures of the aircraft that could be determined prior to impact. The airplane was airworthy, loaded within the allowable weight and balance limits, and had a total time on the airframe of 10,507 hours. All four engines had between 600 and 1,200 hours at the time of the accident, well below the total hours required for a mandatory overhaul.

Each crew member was found to be properly certified and trained for flight operations. Captain Tweed had flown sixty hours in the previous thirty-day period. He had been employed by the airline since 1942 and had over 9,500 flight hours, 2,900 of which were in DC-6 aircraft. Captain Iverson had flown 75 hours in the previous thirty-day period, had also been employed as a pilot by the airline since 1942 and had flown over 12,700 total hours, including 465 hours in DC-6s.

No explanation could be determined as to why the pilots prematurely retracted the wing flaps during a circling approach back to the airfield, but that action caused the subsequent loss of lift and altitude, resulting in contact with the ground. A twenty-knot quartering tailwind also prevailed during the turn, increasing the ground speed of the aircraft prior to impact.

In many accident investigations where the evidence points to pilot error, and there are no surviving crew members, the official report will often state the probable cause without an authentic explanation for the actions of the pilot. Even with the improved analysis capabilities available today, determining the cause of an accident can still be based on limited information. Since the installation of flight data recorders and cockpit voice recorders on commercial airliners, crew conversations and aircraft flight data can now be recorded and hopefully retrieved in the aftermath of a crash. Unfortunately, the thought process of the crew members will still be a matter of speculation in the event of their death. When crew members do survive, however, their accounts of the accident can be extremely helpful in filling in the missing details. In the case of the Canadian Pacific Airlines DC-6, unfortunately, even the surviving

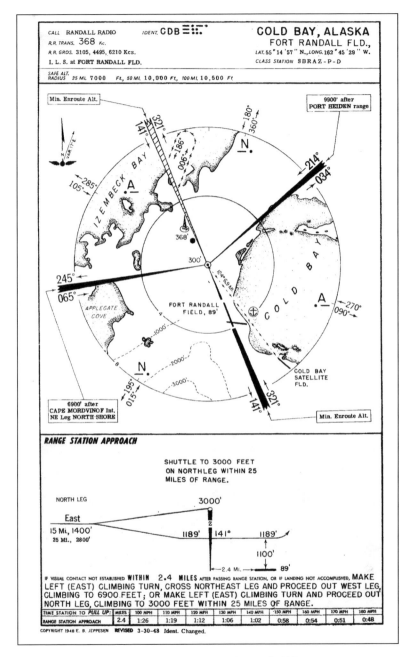

Jeppesen Standard Instrument Approach Procedure at Cold Bay.
Excerpted from Jeppesen Airway Manual, Copyright 1948 E. B. Jeppesen
(For illustration only—not to be used for navigation purposes.)

161

crew members could not provide much useful information, leaving several important details unexplained.

The probable cause for the fatal crash of Canadian Pacific Airlines flight 307 was determined to be the full retraction of the wing flaps during a circling approach without corrective action being applied to maintain the aircraft's flight altitude. Why two experienced pilots simply allowed the DC-6 to fly into the ground, without being aware of their actions, will never be known.

Great Sitkin Island

SEPTEMBER 24, 1959

Reeve Aleutian Airways flight 03 departed from Anchorage shortly after 1000 in the morning on a scheduled weekly flight to Cold Bay, Adak and Shemya in the Aleutians. The aircraft and crew would remain overnight at Adak then continue onto Shemya the next morning before returning to Anchorage. After departure and climbing to an assigned cruising altitude of 8,000 feet, the C-54B proceeded on course, flying the route filed on their instrument flight plan.

On board were five crew members, including the captain, first officer, flight engineer, two flight attendants and twenty-two passengers. The captain was a very experienced pilot with almost 13,000 total flight hours, who had been flying the same Aleutian route for several years. He was also Reeve Aleutian Airways senior pilot. As such, Captain Strouse was responsible for training and evaluating the other company pilots, administering proficiency flight checks, and maintaining all aircrew flight records.

Prior to departure from Anchorage, a detailed weather briefing for the route and destinations was received by Captain Strouse, showing various scattered to overcast cloud layers from 1,000 to 10,000 feet. Occasional light rain and moderate turbulence were also expected, with ten- to twenty-knot winds at their flight altitude from the northwest. Hourly weather updates were passed to the crew from the company dispatcher once the flight was airborne.

No problems were encountered on the first three-and-a-half-hour flight to Cold Bay. After off-loading eleven passengers and their baggage, the airplane was refueled for the final three-hour leg to Adak. The remaining passengers included two civilians, seven military personnel from the Air Force and one each from the Army and Navy.

While on the ground a second instrument flight plan was filed, with a request to fly visual flight rules on top (VFR on top) once the flight reached cruising altitude. VFR on top is an instrument flight rules (IFR) clearance that allows aircraft to operate at different altitudes while flying in visual conditions along the specified route. Air Traffic Control granted the request and cleared the flight to continue to the Mordvinof Intersection, then to proceed VFR on top from there to Adak.

At 1419, the C-54 departed from Cold Bay and turned southwest over the low-frequency range a minute later. The captain advised air traffic control that the cloud tops were at 1,200 to 1,600 feet and they were continuing a climb to 4,500 feet. Their arrival time over Mordvinof was estimated at 1445. Air traffic control acknowledged and advised the flight to pass all further enroute position reports directly through the Reeve Airways radio dispatcher.

After climbing through the lower cloud decks, the crew had unlimited visibility and a clear blue sky above them. A white blanket covered the ocean below, except where an occasional break revealed a patch of dark sea. The chain of Aleutian islands stretched on a parallel course out their left window, masked from view by the clouds until curving back northwest across their flight path at Adak, over 500 miles away. From there the islands continued for another 350 miles to Attu, before eventually crossing the International Date Line into Russian-controlled waters off the Kamchatka Peninsula.

Captain Strouse reported arriving over Mordvinof Intersection on schedule at 1445, still visual flight rules on top at 4,500 feet and estimating the next reporting point at 1458. Thirteen minutes later, the radio operator at Reeve Aleutian Airways received a transmission the flight was passing the Akutan reporting point and estimating passing Easy I at 1524. The next three reporting points were crossed within three minutes of the estimated times, the last one at 1650, only 100 miles from Adak. All the position reports confirmed the flight was maintaining VFR on top at 4,500 feet. Arrival over the radio range station at Adak was estimated as 1725.

After the flight reported 100 miles from Adak, the company radio operator advised the captain they were cleared by air traffic control to continue visual flight rules on top and to contact approach control for landing instructions when thirty miles out from Adak. A current altimeter setting at the airfield was also given.

No further communication was received until 1715 when the flight advised the radio operator it was canceling the instrument clearance and proceeding visually into Adak. Two minutes later the flight made its initial call to Adak approach control. The controller responded almost immediately, but no further contact could be established with the aircraft. Numerous attempts were made over the next twenty-three minutes before search and rescue facilities were notified by air traffic control.

An hour after the aircraft was reported missing, a Navy search aircraft reported spotting a fire on the northeast side of Great Sitkin Island, approximately twenty-two miles from Adak. After an over-flight of the area, wreckage was observed at the 2,100-foot level of the island on the eastern slope of the mountain. Only the tail section appeared to be intact, where it had apparently broken away from the fuselage during the impact. The remaining wreckage was scattered over a 100-yard area, with the forward cabin section and cockpit completely destroyed by the resulting fire. There were no signs of survivors.

Great Sitkin Island is located northeast of Adak, slightly south of the airway centerline leading to the low-frequency radio range station. The island is nearly circular in shape and approximately ten miles across at its widest point. Similar to the other islands in the Aleutian chain, it is principally volcanic rock covered with a thin layer of topsoil. Although small compared to other islands in the Aleutians, the dormant volcano near the center of Great Sitkin Island is one of the highest mountains in the Aleutian chain, rising to a height of 5,710 feet.

A military rescue team comprising twenty-five Marines and six Navy medical personnel reached the crash site the morning after the accident. Vessels from the Navy and Coast Guard assisted by trans-porting the men from Adak to the shore of the island, where they then hiked up the lava rocked slope in the hope of finding survivors. Unfortunately, after arriving at the site and conducting a search, it became apparent that all the occupants of the aircraft had perished. Work therefore began to locate the bodies and recoverable pieces of wreckage for the accident team, who arrived the following day.

They found the bodies of the sixteen victims and moved them off the mountain by helicopter on the 27th, then few them to Elmendorf Air Force Base in Anchorage for identification. Examination of the accident site by a Civil Aeronautics Board investigation team began once they arrived on the 26th. It was determined that the aircraft first contacted the ground with its left wing while in a climbing turn and on an approximate heading of 285°, indicating that the crew had probably seen the terrain just before impact and tried to recover. The tail section had separated from the rest of the airplane on contact, remaining relatively in place as the fuselage was carried forward by the momentum and torn apart on the slope. The force of the collision hurled two of the four engines into a gully over 400 feet from the main wreckage. Most of the remaining aircraft not already destroyed by the impact was consumed in the subsequent fire.

Because of the extent of the damage inflicted by the impact, all the cockpit instruments were found to be completely unreadable. From the other limited wreckage that could be examined, it was determined the landing gear had been fully retracted at the time of the accident and there were no indications of explosion or fire before the crash. Analysis of the engines and other mechanical components showed them to be operating normally before impact. Only two of the four propeller assemblies were in a recoverable condition for examination and both were found set in low pitch positions, indicating they were developing power.

Company maintenance records on the aircraft were also examined for possible errors, but they showed no discrepancies or potential problems that might have contributed to the accident. In addition, no radio communications during the flight revealed any crew concern or problems with the aircraft.

A study of the weather patterns encountered while en route from Cold Bay and over Great Sitkin Island, revealed nothing unusual. Flight conditions were determined to be as forecast and briefed to the airplane's captain. A 1645 surface observation at Adak, reported 1,500 feet broken and 7,000 feet broken, with seven miles of visibility and winds out of the west at eleven knots. Just prior to the accident, a Navy pilot inbound to Adak observed a solid overcast at 7,000 feet over the area, with clear skies and unlimited visibility above the clouds. He stated that he could not see Great Sitkin Island.

After the accident, another Navy pilot in the vicinity reported a lower broken layer at 2,000 feet over the island.

No possible cause of the accident could be found until members of the investigation team examined Captain Strouse's flight records. It was revealed that in addition to not having received a current annual flight evaluation, as required by regulation, Strouse had also apparently falsified the mandatory medical currency information kept on file at the company. As a captain with an airline transport pilot rating, Strouse was required to receive a medical examination every six months in order to maintain a valid Class I medical authorization. Although his flight records indicated he had properly met those requirements, Federal Aviation Administration records disclosed that his last official medical certification was actually three-and-a-half years old. Further inquiries were conducted to alleviate the possibility of a paper error causing the discrepancy, but only substantiated the initial findings and confirmed the Federal Aviation Administration records as being correct.

The reason for Captain Strouse's deception became apparent a short time later, once the doctor who had examined him after his last medical certification in March 1956 was located. It turned out that Strouse had been diagnosed with glaucoma and cerebrovascular disease, which would prevent him from performing further commercial pilot duties. The evidence of cerebrovascular disease was especially significant, because it affects the blood supply to the brain, resulting in symptoms of possible memory loss, alteration of judgment and reasoning, and even paralysis. Whether the disease contributed to the accident, or to what level it had progressed in his body, could not be determined.

Captain Strouse's actions during the flight seem to indicate his judgment may have been distorted by the fact he canceled the instrument flight rules clearance and deliberately descended into a solid cloud layer without any visual references. At the time, the flight was only thirty-five miles from Adak and continuing under instrument flight rules would have added only a few more minutes to their arrival time.

The investigation board concluded that Captain Strouse was unaware of his exact position when he began the descent, erroneously assuming he was either at a point beyond Great Sitkin Island or well abeam the inbound course. But this does not explain the fact that he should have known the island was near their flight path, whether it was obscured by clouds or not. He was, after all, familiar with the Aleutian route and approach into Adak after years of flying with Reeve Aleutian Airways as a captain and senior check pilot. In addition, the aircraft's position in relation to the island should have been obvious from the time that had elapsed since crossing the last reporting point. Even if for some reason he mistakenly thought they had already passed the island, it still could not explain why he allowed the aircraft to descend into a thick cloud mass that was obscuring any visual contact with the surface.

The accident investigation board did determine that Great Sitkin Island was obscured by two different cloud layers, with bases at 1,500 and 7,000 feet at the time of the accident. But fog, precipitation and turbulence were not found to be contributing factors. The board concluded that the captain's failure to properly maintain visual flight over hazardous terrain was not reflective of the competence expected from an airline pilot and was the probable cause of the accident.

Following the accident and the findings of the accident board, Reeve Aleutian Airways initiated changes in both their aircraft approach requirements at Adak and the maintenance of individual flight records. All future approaches would be conducted only under instrument flight rules and a copy of each crew member's actual medical certificate was subsequently required to be kept on file at the company.

Captain Strouse concealed his medical condition for over three years and managed to continue flying safely until September 24, 1959. Only his position as the company's chief pilot allowed him to continue his deception for so long. During the three years following his last medical certification, he still performed adequately during required proficiency evaluations with other check pilots, since no apparent previous lapses in judgment or skill were uncovered by the investigation board. Unfortunately, as has been shown in all too many accidents, just one moment of indecision or improper action is enough to result in tragedy.

It is possible Captain Strouse's cerebrovascular disease had nothing to do with the accident. After all, why did an experienced first officer allow the aircraft to be placed in a dangerous situation, regardless of the mental state being exhibited by the captain. Was it overconfidence in the captain's ability by the first officer, a reluctance to express any disagreement or concern with the senior pilot who could influence his future advancement in the company, or a simple navigation error, amplified by a break in the overcast that persuaded the crew to cancel their instrument flight rules clearance and descend visually?

In December 1973 a Navy DC-6, known as a C-118A, also crashed into the mountain on Great Sitkin Island while on approach into Adak, killing all ten aboard. The aircraft was scheduled to transport servicemen home for the Christmas holiday.

Below the Glide Path

JULY 21, 1961

Alaska Airlines flight CKA779, a DC-6A under government contract with the Military Air Transport Service, was on an instrument approach into Shemya, Alaska for a refueling stop before continuing onto Tachikawa Air Force Base in Japan. Six crew members were aboard, along with 26,000 pounds of cargo.

It was 0200 on an unusually dark night for a summer month in the Aleutians. The moon was below the horizon and no ambient starlight filtered through a thick overcast that stretched east of the island for hundreds of miles. Minimum approach weather conditions were prevalent over the airfield, with only a 200-foot ceiling and visibility of one mile being reported.

As the aircraft flew inbound on the precision radar approach, it dropped below the glide slope and hit the ground 200 feet short of the runway threshold in a level attitude. The impact broke the fuselage in half as it slid forward, wrenching the engines and heavier cargo from their mounts and onto the runway. Fire erupted almost immediately, burning the airframe to a blackened hulk. All six occupants were killed.

The four-engine transport had originally departed from Everett, Washington on July 20 for Travis Air Force Base in California. Upon arrival, thirteen tons of military cargo were loaded on board and secured under the supervision of the airplane's flight engineer. After the airplane was refueled and serviced for the next leg of the flight to Anchorage, it was restarted and taxied into position for takeoff. A short time later the large DC-6 departed without incident, proceeding normally for the duration of the nine-hour flight. At some point the off-duty crew who had been resting in the cabin, switched with the other crew members, ensuring no one became fatigued and everyone stayed adequately rested for various shift changes during later flights to Shemya and Japan.

Arrival at the Anchorage Airport that evening was without incident. A little over an hour was spent on the ground servicing the aircraft before it was again ready for takeoff. A navigator who was familiar with the international routes that lay ahead also joined the crew in Anchorage. Once weather and NOTAMS (notice to airmen) were checked for the next leg to Shemya, an instrument flight rules flight plan was filed over the appropriate route, estimating an enroute time of six hours and forty minutes. Conditions along the Aleutian Islands called for low overcast conditions of fog and stratus with moderate winds out of the southeast near the surface.

Departure from Anchorage at 1940 was routine. Five hours later CKA779 established contact with Shemya Radio, giving a position approximately 300 miles northeast of the airfield. The flight continued inbound at flight level 100 (10,000 feet) and sent another position report at 0123, estimating their arrival at Shemya at 0155. Shemya Radio acknowledged, advising the flight that there was no other traffic in the area and to descend and maintain 5,500 feet until contacting ground controlled approach (GCA) for further instruction.

All details of the conversations between the aircraft and the ground controlled approach controller were based on official statements given by the controller to the Civil Aeronautics Board following the accident. No radio communications were recorded during the approach, a violation of policy established by Northwest Airlines. The airline was the private owner and operator of the Shemya ground controlled approach facility, and as such it was not under the normal jurisdiction of the Federal Aviation Administration.

The Shemya ground controlled approach facility was the only privately owned and operated system of its kind in the United States serving civil air carriers. As such, the instrument approach equipment did not require Federal Aviation Administration approval, and the controller was not required to meet any of the Federal Aviation Administration's requirements for certification, training, or proficiency.

171

Twenty-two minutes later the crew radioed the Shemya ground controlled approach controller, verifying they were inbound at 5,500 feet. The controller established radar contact and confirmed their location as eighteen miles northeast of the airfield. At that time the controller also advised the flight to expect possible downdrafts within a mile of the runway. The current weather conditions at Shemya were reported to the flight as an indefinite ceiling of 200 feet, with the sky obscured and one mile of visibility in fog.

Instructions were given aligning the aircraft with the inbound course to runway 10 and establishing its descent on the glide slope. According to the controller, the flight followed the correct course inbound for the extent of the approach. As the aircraft neared the runway, however, it gradually descended below the glide slope. At a distance of two miles it was ten to fifteen feet below the glide path, then thirty to forty feet below at one mile. During the continuing radio transmissions, the controller advised the flight they were below the glide slope, but he did not observe any apparent corrections on the radar screen.

The flight remained thirty to forty feet below the glide path until it was over the approach lights, 1,460 feet from the threshold. Even though the flight was being continually advised by the controller that they were low, he stated he was not overly concerned about the lack of correction, because thirty to forty feet below the glide slope was still within the allowable safety zone. A moment later the aircraft began a much steeper descent, taking it further below the glide path, but the controller assumed the pilot was then initiating a visual approach to the runway. Because of that assumption, he did not advise the flight that it was now well below the glide path and exceeding the established safety limits for the approach. Had he done so, the pilot would have been required to execute a missed approach.

As the controller watched the aircraft's position on the radar screen, its forward progress suddenly stopped at the end of the runway. He stated that he knew the airplane had crashed at that time because the radar target did not continue moving further down the screen, as would normally happen. The time was noted as 0211 and a crash notification was immediately sent to the fire-rescue service on the airfield.

After being notified within a minute following the accident, the

Shemya weather observer made a special weather observation that measured a 100- to 300-foot variable ceiling at the airfield, with visibility varying from a half to one mile in fog. A variable ceiling of 100 to 300 feet would normally be reported as 200 feet for approach purposes. Winds were noted from the southeast at eight knots on the surface and out of the south at twenty knots above 500 feet. The published GCA weather minimums for Alaska Airlines at Shemya were a 200-foot ceiling and half a mile of visibility.

An examination of the crash site by the accident investigation team later that day revealed all the wreckage to be either in the specific area of impact or forward of that position in the direction of flight. There was no evidence of a collision with the approach lights or other objects prior to impact with the ground.

The aircraft was determined to have hit the ground nose wheel first, 200 feet short of the threshold in approximate alignment with the runway, then to have continued sliding forward as it broke apart in front of the wings. All four engines, the cockpit and the majority of the cargo continued sliding forward, leaving a path of debris 300 feet long on the ground. The remaining fuselage section stopped after a short distance and slid back on the slope toward the original point of impact, where it was almost totally consumed by fire.

Although much of the aircraft had been destroyed by impact and flames, analysis of the available evidence showed it had been in a normal landing configuration prior to contact with the ground. The landing gear had been down and locked, the wing flaps extended past a 030° position, and the landing lights were in the on position. A witness near the runway at the time of the crash, confirmed the airplane had all its landing, anti-collision, and navigation lights illuminated during the final approach.

Many of the control lever positions in the cockpit at the time of impact could not be determined, but the communication systems were found intact and examined. The number 1 VHF radio had been set to the primary ground controlled approach frequency and the number 2 VHF radio was apparently not being used at the time, since it had not been set on any Shemya frequency. It was therefore deemed unlikely that any communication problems existed during the approach, since it would be expected that the crew would have then dialed in the VHF guard frequency, which was the backup frequency for ground controlled approach. Communication systems at the ground facility were also checked and found to be operating normally.

All the propeller assemblies, engines and accessories were recovered and analyzed. Each system was found to be operating routinely and at the correct power settings at the time of impact. There was also no evidence of any fuel or oil contamination, or a malfunction of the aircraft's mechanical components.

The day before the accident, the ground controlled approach equipment at Shemya was given a routine maintenance and operational check by GCA personnel. No deficiencies were noted and during the ensuing twelve-hour period before the accident, six other aircraft executed normal GCA approaches into the airfield without any problems. In addition, the ground controlled approach facility had been flight-checked only six days before by Federal Aviation Administration personnel and was found to be functioning correctly, although it was determined that the radar system was in a deteriorating condition that could possibly cause operational difficulties in the near future.

After the accident, the Federal Aviation Administration conducted two additional flight checks, both of which found the system operating within tolerance. The Federal Aviation Administration pilot who conducted the checks also gave the same GCA controller who was on duty during the accident a "very good" rating for his portion of the evaluation.

The GCA controller on duty during the accident had been working at the Shemya facility since 1957 on a three-month on, three-month off schedule. During his daily work schedule he was the only controller on duty at the facility. His experience included eight years as civilian ground controlled approach controller, and prior to that, four years as a ground controlled approach operator for the Air Force. He had also been rated as a senior controller by the Federal Aviation Administration before being employed at Shemya. In the thirty-day period prior to the accident he had handled over eighty separate ground controlled approaches at the airfield, including both military and civilian aircraft.

During the investigation of the crash site, it was revealed that two days before the accident, airfield personnel had deliberately cut an electrical cable supplying power to several of the approach lighting systems. The cable was temporarily severed and pulled from underneath a utility road being used by construction vehicles so it would not be damaged by heavy vehicle loads. Unfortunately, the cable was completely forgotten, and no notice to airmen was issued to explain the resulting deficiency in the approach lighting system. However, none of the aircraft that landed at the airfield over the two-day period preceding the accident mentioned any problems with the ground lighting systems either.

When the electrical cable was cut, power to all six pairs of red approach lights was terminated, as well as two of the four green threshold lights and the first four pairs of runway lights. Even though the runway lighting system was set on high intensity during the accident aircraft's instrument approach, the reduced number of lights and change in the sequencing probably caused the pilots to become confused. If the instrument approach had been conducted at night with good visibility, the inoperable lights might hardly have been noticed. But if the approach had been flown under an extremely dark night in minimum weather conditions, as was the case in this incident, the ground lights would have been crucial to identifying the proper runway environment and executing a safe approach.

Since the crew was unaware of any problems with the airport lighting system, due to the fact that none were reported, it would certainly seem possible that they might have misinterpreted the lighting indications they were receiving during the approach, which were different from those they expected. Once the aircraft descended through the low overcast, the pilots had only a few seconds to decide either to continue to the runway, or to apply power and execute a missed approach. As visual contact was established and they were in a position to execute a safe landing, they would have continued the approach unless advised otherwise by the GCA controller.

Normal procedure during a ground controlled approach descent would be for the pilot to inform the controller when proceeding visually off the glide slope. As long as the pilot continued flying instruments on the radar approach, it was the GCA controller's responsibility to continue sending the aircraft's position relative to the glide slope. Neither procedure was followed concerning the accident aircraft's situation, at least according to the ground controlled approach controller on duty at the time.

An examination of flight training records following the accident, found all six crew members to be properly qualified for DC-6 flight operations. The only exception was Captain Bowman, who had not yet fully met the qualification requirements for flights into Shemya. As such, his weather minimums for the ground controlled approach approach were increased to a 400-foot ceiling and three-quarter miles of visibility. He had, however, flown the same aircraft into Shemya with the same first officer and flight engineer on two ground controlled approaches the week before, under similar weather conditions. Both the first officer and on-duty flight engineer were qualified, as were the other captain, the other flight engineer and navigator on board at the time of the accident.

Both captains on the flight had over 13,000 total flight hours, with Bowman being the most experienced in night and instrument flying conditions. The first officer had over 2,000 flight hours, and the two flight engineers had well over 1,000. It was the navigator's first regular flight with Alaska Airlines, but he had previously worked for Northwest Orient Airlines, where he had accumulated over 13,000 flight hours as a navigator.

Following completion of the investigation, the accident board determined that the aircrew had properly complied with all policies and regulations concerning the planning and operation of the aircraft. The aircraft had been loaded and serviced correctly at all destinations, and there was no indication that the cargo had moved or come loose inside the fuselage before impact.

There were no indications of any structural or mechanical malfunctions on the aircraft. The airframe had accumulated 10,600 total hours and was specifically manufactured as a DC-6A cargo variant for Alaska Airlines. Since the last major inspection the airplane had flown one hundred and forty-six hours. At no time during the flight did the crew communicate any difficulty with the aircraft or its systems.

Weather conditions at the time of the accident were the same as those reported to the crew, which were also the minimum required for executing the ground controlled approach. The aircraft was operating during the hours of complete darkness, after moonset and before morning twilight.

Icing was not believed to have been a contributing factor in the accident, since conditions did not support the formation of structural icing. Turbulence was not mentioned in the Civil Aeronautics

Board report, but it should not be ruled out as a possible influence. The controller had warned the flight of potential rough air within a mile of the runway and winds in the Shemya area are notorious for being unpredictable.

In the opinion of the accident board, the pilot was aware of the actual weather conditions during the ground controlled approach and did have visual contact with the runway environment prior to impact. Since the aircraft descended below the minimum approach altitude, it was believed that at least some of the lights associated with the runway were visible. In addition, there was no way the crew could have known about the inoperable lights causing the irregular lighting configuration that probably contributed to the crew's false perception of the actual runway location.

The investigation also revealed that the privately owned ground controlled approach system being used at Shemya was considered unsuitable for use in Federal Aviation Administration operated facilities. Ground controlled approach systems under the jurisdiction of the Federal Aviation Administration utilized a safety zone limit of half a degree below the center of the glide slope, while the system in operation at Shemya used a 1.5° safety zone limit. If the controller at Shemya had been operating an approved ground controlled approach system with a 0.5° safety zone at the time of the accident, the aircraft would have been required to execute a missed approach when it was forty feet below the glide slope, a mile from the runway.

The probable cause of the accident, determined by the Civil Aeronautics Board, was stated as the absence of approach and runway lights, as well as the failure of the GCA controller to provide proper glide slope information during the last stage of the approach.

One result of the board's accident investigation was a recommendation that action be initiated to ensure that all instrument approach facilities, including privately owned facilities and the personnel associated with their operation, meet the same federal requirements.

Of the six crew members on board Alaska Airlines flight CKA779, only Captain Bowman had been a long-term Alaska resident. He was born in the village of Ruby and spent most of his adult life flying in Alaska before moving to Washington State in 1958.

Three days after the accident, the six bodies were returned to their families for burial.

Almost twenty years later, an Air Force RC-135 also crashed on a ground controlled approach to runway 10 at Shemya. The aircraft was flying at night and hit the approach lights near the threshold, fatally injuring six of the twenty-four occupants.

Turbulence over Pedro Bay

DECEMBER 2, 1968

It was a crisp winter morning as the twin-engine Fairchild F-27 left Anchorage for Dillingham, with intermediate stops scheduled at Iliamna, Big Mountain and King Salmon. Operated by Wien Consolidated Airlines, flight 55 departed under a layered ceiling that covered Cook Inlet, but soon climbed above the highest cloud layer at 9,000 feet into clear skies. Flying southwest at 16,000 feet, the aircraft crossed the high coastal peaks northeast of Iliamna a short time later, then began a slow descent for its first approach into Iliamna's small airport. The village was already visible in the distance as the airplane cleared the mountains, recognizable against the surrounding frozen tundra about mid-way along the seventy-mile stretch of Lake Iliamna's north shore. All the previous cloud formations had been left behind and blue sky prevailed over the southwest peninsula, except for one single, localized area of ice fog hanging over the lake.

As the aircraft continued its normal descent through 11,500 feet, a violent burst of turbulence suddenly pushed the airplane downward at over 4,000 feet a minute, sharply increasing its airspeed from 220 to 340 knots. A crack opened in the metal support structure of the right wing, widening with each passing second until it ruptured an internal fuel tank and began spewing aviation fuel into the cold air outside the aircraft. The escaping fuel mixed with the hot exhaust of the nearby engine, instantly igniting into a fiery trail behind the wing.

Witnesses on the ground saw fire and black smoke coming from the airplane as the crew tried unsuccessfully to regain control.

Powerful jolts of turbulence continued battering the aircraft for several more seconds until pieces of both wings and the rudder were torn away. Suddenly the flight path changed as most of the right wing separated completely from the fuselage, sending the airplane into an uncontrollable, downward spiral. It impacted the frozen ground approximately twenty-three miles east of Iliamna, near the smaller village of Pedro Bay. All thirty-six passengers and three crew members were killed on impact. The aircraft was completely destroyed.

Most of the fuselage, with one wing still attached, was found in a twisted pile of metal beside an inland pond on a small finger of land southwest of Pedro Bay. The wreckage was located only a few hundred yards from the northeast corner of Lake Iliamna. Other pieces that had separated in-flight were later identified along a one-and-a-half-mile corridor behind the point of impact. The recovered sections included the rudder assembly, vertical stabilizer, left engine, and smaller pieces from the left wing and fuselage. Major portions of the right wing and smaller components of the left wing were never recovered. With the exception of its engine, most of the left wing had stayed attached to the aircraft during the uncontrolled spiral. Somehow the right engine had remained bolted to a small section of wing still attached with the fuselage as the outer wing was torn away.

Immediately following the accident, a bush pilot in the vicinity informed the Federal Aviation Administration controller at Iliamna of the crash. At that time the controller was unaware of the situation and was still attempting contact with the flight. Local villagers who witnessed the accident also reported details of the tragedy by short-wave radio.

When word of the crash reached the military Search and Rescue Headquarters in Anchorage, an Air Force H-21 helicopter was dispatched from King Salmon and reached the scene early that afternoon. Because of the extremely high winds still prevalent in the area, the helicopter could not shut down for fear of damaging the rotor blades. It only remained at the scene for fifteen minutes, long enough to verify that there were no survivors.

The winds on the ground at the accident site were significantly worse than the winds at Iliamna, only twenty-three miles to the west. A special weather observation taken at Iliamna shortly after the accident, showed clear skies with nine miles of visibility and winds at only fifteen knots from the west on the ground, as well as ground fog being visible over the lake and a line of high clouds running east to the southwest in the distance. At the same time, villagers in Pedro Bay estimated the winds were gusting to sixty knots on the ground, while the mountains east of them were observed with even stronger winds, evidenced by long trails of blowing snow on the leeward side of the peaks.

The pilot of a single-engine Cessna, which left Iliamna around 1000 to identify the exact crash location, reported encountering increasing turbulence the closer he approached Pedro Bay. The pilot experienced severe to extreme conditions and stated that the winds were observed burbling over the mountains from the northwest, forcing him to turn back.

Approximately two hours later, a DC-3 cargo airplane, flying the same air route from Anchorage to Iliamna, encountered strong updrafts and severe turbulence during its descent from 8,500 feet around Pedro Bay, forcing the pilot to abort the approach. The turbulence was reportedly severe enough that almost full aileron and three-quarter rudder application were required to remain on course. An Air Force airplane that flew into the area around 1240 confirmed the same violent in-flight conditions.

The severe weather continued throughout the day. Wind gusts of fifty knots and temperatures well below zero were still prevalent the next day. An investigation team and recovery teams could not even reach the crash site until December 4. Because of the delay there was concern that wild animals might be attracted to the human remains at the crash site and disturb the bodies, but some of the local villagers stayed with the wreckage until the proper officials could arrive. Many of the villagers had probably never witnessed such destruction before and must have been stricken by the gruesome scene scattered on the tundra. They surely spent a solemn night watching over the dead.

On December 3, a lone National Transportation Safety Board official managed to reach the accident site in a small airplane and conduct a preliminary investigation. His report on what was observed of the wreckage was submitted to Anchorage that evening by shortwave radio. The following day a team of sixteen investigators from several agencies arrived to begin a detailed analysis of the

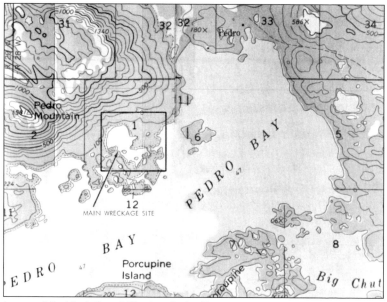

Image of Accident Report Chart at Pedro Bay. *Excerpted from National Transportation Safety Board Accident Report, file no. 1-0038. (For illustration only—not to be used for navigation purposes.)*

crash, while State Troopers also arrived to begin retrieving the bodies. Below zero temperatures and strong winds continued hindering the recovery process, but fourteen victims and both flight recorders were found the first day they arrived. A temporary morgue had already been made available in Anchorage where an FBI disaster team would assist in the identification of remains. All the bodies were located and removed from the crash site by December 5.

On December 12, an Army CH-47 helicopter from the Arctic Test Center at Ft. Greely moved the wreckage from the crash site to the Iliamna airport for analysis by the National Transportation Safety Board. It took five trips to remove the sections and components scattered across the tundra, including the largest pieces of the fuselage. The mission was only completed after the flight crew and three specially trained soldiers responsible for rigging the loads had waited two days for the extreme weather conditions to improve.

The accident investigation team began a more in-depth examination of the wreckage after it was moved to the airport, continuing to recover missing components from the field until the 18th. Other teams were involved in the investigative process at different locations, analyzing maintenance documents, examining crew training records and studying data retrieved from the two flight recorders. Because of the extreme conditions encountered by other aircraft in the vicinity of the accident the same day, as well as statements by witnesses on the ground, a thorough examination of the weather patterns in the area at the time was also conducted. Several important findings were eventually uncovered.

One of the most significant details found in the investigation revealed an error in the compliance of a Fairchild Airworthiness Directive by Wien Consolidated's maintenance personnel. The Airworthiness Directive had established inspection criteria for all Fairchild F-27 wing structures, to determine if deformities exited which could potentially cause stress fractures in the metal supports. Subsequent radiographs of the accident aircraft's wings had taken place during several periodic inspections, as was specified in the Airworthiness Directive, but the details of the radiographs were incorrectly interpreted by the quality control inspector. Analysis of those radiographs by the National Transportation Safety Board after the accident revealed several visible structural cracks in both wings well before the aircraft crashed on December 2. Metallurgical testing of structural pieces recovered from the wreckage later confirmed that fatigue cracks were present in both wings before the crash and that they continued expanding prior to the accident.

Even with pre-existing cracks in the wing areas, it was determined that extreme outside forces would still have been required to cause a structural failure. During the day of the accident, the weather forecast for the area did not reflect any significant weather hazards, but testimony from other pilots and witnesses on the ground contradicted that assumption. An area forecast, obtained by the crew before departure from Anchorage, called for mostly clear skies in the Bristol Bay area, including the village of Iliamna, with occasional light to moderate turbulence below 4,000 feet. The area forecast valid for western Cook Inlet, including the mountains east of Iliamna near Pedro Bay, called only for light turbulence and possible moderate icing in clouds from 6,000 to 12,000 feet. In actuality, conditions were much more severe.

A hired consultant specializing in weather pattern analysis concluded that the accident area was actually experiencing powerful arctic winds being generated by a low pressure trough to the east and a high pressure ridge west of the mountains. The resulting northwest winds of seventy to eighty knots between 2,000 and 4,000 feet would have caused extremely harsh conditions in a mass of turbulent air being funneled out of the valleys near Pedro Bay. Violent wind shears and extreme gust loads exceeding the limitations for transport type aircraft, would have been prevalent for most of the day.

After the accident, the airplane manufacturer conducted tests to determine what vertical load factors would have been necessary for the F-27's wing to fail. It was estimated that a structurally intact wing without cracks would break under a negative force of 5.7g, and a wing with similar fatigue cracks would fail at negative 4.5g. Both levels of negative g forces would easily have been experienced in severe and extreme turbulence.

Subsequent examination of the flight data recorder and cockpit voice recorder revealed the aircraft had indeed been subjected to extremely strong forces before impact. Fluctuations in the binary trace of the flight recorder showed the aircraft experienced approximately a negative 8g change during the first violent downdraft during the descent. That initial shock probably caused the previous crack in the right wing to extend further, breaking through the outer skin and rupturing the fuel tank. Escaping fuel and vapors were then ignited by the hot engine exhaust. The cockpit voice recorder revealed a loud noise at approximately the same time, followed by a warning horn and clacking sound in the background. Eleven seconds later the pilot stated: "Think we're in trouble."

After another three seconds the binary trace recorded an even harder downdraft, this time estimated between negative 20g and negative 30g. A final loud noise was then heard over the cockpit voice recorder, probably the right wing separating from the aircraft. Both recorders stopped functioning at that time due to the loss of electrical power.

The accident board determined that the crew members had been completely unaware of the violent conditions they would encounter until it was too late. There was no way they could have known the weather on approach into Iliamna was significantly more hazardous than forecast. If anything, they were probably anticipating another routine day.

The crew encountered no difficulties during the brief flight from

Anchorage, or during the first five and a half minutes of the descent. Only after the first vertical wind shear occurred could they have realized the severity of the situation. Before they could even react, smoke and fire were probably already trailing behind the right engine. Whether they could have regained control and even landed at that point, is questionable. Their fate was unfortunately sealed when the next wind shear tore the right wing completely away from the fuselage.

Certainly the cracks already present in the wings contributed to the accident, but tests showed that even without these existing cracks, the extreme amount of stress inflicted on the wings would probably have caused the same result. Whether the crew could have recovered from the first severe downdraft and aborted the approach before the initial split in the right wing caused the ensuing fireball, and then exited the danger before encountering even worse winds, is debatable. Certainly other aircraft that flew into the area that morning under similar circumstances were able to do so. In the case of the F-27, however, no one will ever know for sure what might have happened.

The National Transportation Safety Board aircraft accident report, released in July 1970, determined the probable cause to be in-flight structural failure from severe and extreme turbulence. Airworthiness Directives issued for the Fairchild F-27 at the time of the accident were also found to have been improperly complied with, resulting in a failure to identify structural deformities in the wing areas. That failure allowed a further weakening of the wings as the fatigue cracks worsened.

It was believed that the aircraft encountered severe load factors above the carrying capability of the wing, causing a separation at the weakest points in the wing structure. Prior to separation, there was no evidence of a loss of aircraft or engine control.

Additional findings concluded that the aircraft's weight and balance were within allowable limits and the crew did not intentionally exceed any limitations during the flight. The crew was properly qualified and trained for F-27 operations, with both pilots possessing over 22,000 combined flight hours. The aircraft had over 17,000 accumulative flight hours, and only seventy-three hours since its last inspection.

A subsequent recommendation from the National

Transportation Safety Board to the Federal Aviation Administration, suggested that all Fairchild F-27s with more than 5,000 hours be inspected for possible fatigue cracks in the wing structures. The recommendation was subsequently carried out on all general aviation and air carrier aircraft under Federal Aviation Administration jurisdiction meeting that criteria. Out of sixty-seven Fairchild F-27s that were subsequently inspected under those guidelines, eight were found with one or more fatigue cracks present in at least one of the wings. Five of sixty-seven aircraft with more than 5,000 hours belonged to Wien Consolidated Airlines. Two of those five were also found with existing fatigue cracks.

The Wien Consolidated Airlines F-27 that crashed on December 2 was one of three Fairchilds originally placed into operation in 1958 in Alaska. Each of the aircraft was given a name reflecting a significant aviation figure in Alaskan history. The name *Harold Gillam* was given to the aircraft later destroyed at Pedro Bay. Like the famous pioneer, the Fairchild F-27 had a distinguished flying career that ended abruptly in tragedy.

Low and Off Course

SEPTEMBER 8, 1973

As the DC-8 descended through the thick overcast on its approach into Cold Bay, droplets of water were dispersing off the sides of its windshield. Light drizzle had been peppering the aircraft since it first entered the clouds well east of the airport. Winds were blowing hard from the northwest and growing increasingly more turbulent as the airplane descended closer to the ground.

The flight leveled at 3,500 feet, approximately thirty-seven miles east of the airport, while still in the clouds, navigating off the VORTAC (combination VHF omni-directional range and tactical air navigation aid), low-frequency radio range and distance measuring equipment signals at Cold Bay. Six minutes later the cargo DC-8 impacted the east slope of a 4,900-foot mountain, fifteen miles east of the airfield, killing everyone on board and completely destroying the aircraft.

World Airways flight 802 had departed from Travis Air Force Base in California earlier that morning, on a cargo contract with the Military Airlift Command (MAC). Refueling stops at Cold Bay, Alaska and Yokota Air Force Base in Japan were scheduled before its eventual termination at Clarke Air Force Base in the Philippines. The crew consisted of only two pilots and a flight engineer. Three other World Airways employees were on board as non-paying passengers.

The three crew members reported for work at the company's Oakland Airport dispatch office at 2200 the night before departure. After being briefed on the flight, they drove to Travis Air Force Base outside of Oakland, where the aircraft was being loaded and serviced for the overseas flight. Upon arrival, the pilots received a detailed weather briefing from Air Force forecasters for the enroute and destination weather at Cold Bay, then filed an instrument flight rules (IFR) flight plan through military base operations.

The cargo consisted of several heavy pallets of airplane tires that had been secured in the cargo area by military personnel and inspected by the flight engineer before takeoff. The pilots also conducted a pre-flight check of the fuselage, landing gear, engines and control surfaces before entering the aircraft.

Once the cockpit checks were completed, the four large jet engines were started and all systems checked in preparation for departure. An enroute clearance to Cold Bay was received shortly before the airplane began taxiing for departure. The flight lifted off the runway at 0111, turning northwest over the open ocean in a steady climb to 31,000 feet (flight level 310).

Flight 802 continued normally toward Cold Bay for the next four hours, arriving at its last enroute navigation fix south of Kodiak Island at 0525. Radio contact could not be established at that time with the Air Traffic Control Center in Anchorage, so their position report was passed instead through the flight service station at Cold Bay. The flight reported its position as 125 miles east of the airport and estimated an arrival time of 0542 at their initial approach fix into Cold Bay.

The flight service station operator at Cold Bay acknowledged the message then relayed the latest weather observation at the airfield, taken at 0455. A measured overcast ceiling of 500 feet was reported, with seven miles of visibility in light drizzle and winds from 300° at twenty-four knots, gusting to thirty-one knots. A minute later the operator radioed the pilot that air traffic control had cleared the flight for an instrument approach into the airfield, but no specific approach procedure was mentioned.

Flight 802's first officer acknowledged both the weather observation and approach clearance and at 0529 he notified the flight service station operator that they were beginning a descent out of flight level 301 for the approach. It was the last transmission received from the flight.

During the descent while inbound to Cold Bay, there was no discussion between the pilots concerning which particular instrument approach would be flown or how the inbound course would be intercepted, but it was later ascertained from analysis of the cockpit voice recorder that the captain intended to execute the localizer back course distance measuring equipment (DME) approach to runway 32. It also seemed a logical conclusion, since the existing weather conditions only allowed for the localizer back course approach with its higher authorized minimums. In addition, the pilots did discuss a minimum descent altitude of 440 feet at Cold Bay, which was only applicable to the localizer back course approach.

Cold Bay's low-frequency radio range and localizer navigational aids were tuned and identified by the pilots in preparation for the instrument approach during their descent inbound to the VORTAC. An initial altitude of 3,500 feet was also discussed, even though the minimum sector altitude on their approach plate was shown as 6,800 feet. Both pilots misinterpreted the information and confused the minimum approach altitude shown on the first DME fix of the localizer back course, with the minimum sector altitude for the quadrant east of the airport.

Minimum sector altitudes on instrument approach plates establish a minimum of 1,000 feet of clearance above all obstacles within twenty-five miles of the facility. Even though the minimum sector altitudes for Cold Bay were not depicted on the applicable approach plate as well as they could have been, several major obstacles above 3,000 feet east of the airfield were clearly shown. If the pilots had properly reviewed the available information and briefed each other on the correct approach procedures to be flown, their subsequent interpretive errors might not have been so readily accepted.

Only two transitions were authorized for the Cold Bay localizer back course on runway 32. One allowed an aircraft to intercept the localizer back course at the forty-mile DME fix, then to descend and maintain 3,500 feet until reaching the 19.5 DME, before continuing with the step-down approach. The other transition allowed an aircraft to proceed outbound on the localizer back course at 7,000 feet, until reaching the 19.5 DME fix, then execute the published procedure turn and descend to 3,500 feet on the inbound course. The captain used neither transition. Both transitions clearly specified that an aircraft could not descend to an altitude of 3,500 feet until it was established inbound on the instrument course.

Crew coordination was also insufficient over which specific

approach procedure they planned to fly. In the cockpit recordings analyzed after the accident, the captain never clearly stated what transition he would follow to execute the approach. When the first officer inquired if the captain intended to make a procedure turn during the approach, the reply was negative, seeming to indicate an intention of flying the straight-in approach by intercepting the localizer back course. If that was the case, however, they must have known their intercept point would be well within the prescribed forty-mile DME range, which was not an approved procedure.

At 0536, while still in a descent approximately thirty-seven miles east of the VORTAC, the DME signal in the cockpit became erratic and a brief discussion ensued as the aircraft reached 3,500 feet. The first officer stated that the DME signal was "not good" at that time.

The captain then stated several times that an operational DME equipment was required to execute the approach, as specified on the instrument approach plate, yet he continued tracking toward the VORTAC without an accurate DME signal. Only when the first officer began inquiring about mountains in the area a few seconds later did the captain become concerned enough to initiate a climb to a higher altitude, but he only increased power for a few seconds before allowing the aircraft to descend again to 3,500 feet.

A few minutes later the DME apparently registered a stronger signal, showing the aircraft twenty-four miles from the VORTAC. When the first officer confirmed that the signal had returned, the captain turned left onto a heading of 215°, probably to intercept the inbound localizer course, still maintaining 3,500 feet. After flying in a southwesterly direction for only thirty seconds, he began varying the heading between 215° and 275°, possibly because the signal reception in the cockpit was being partially blocked by the higher terrain along their flight path.

About the time the captain turned to the southwest, the first officer announced the radar altimeter was beginning to register the aircraft's height above the ground. A few seconds later he stated they were twenty miles out from Cold Bay, then suddenly declared they were off course, realizing their actual position was different from where they thought they were. As the radar altimeter continued to register a decreasing height above the ground, the captain finally realized the imminent danger and applied power. The first officer

190

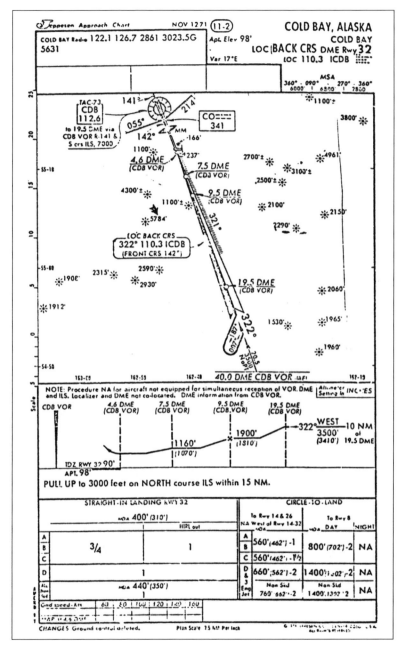

Image of Accident Report Standard Instrument Approach Procedure at Cold Bay.
Excerpted from National Transportation Safety Board Aircraft Accident Report, File No. NTSB-AAR-74-6. (For illustration only—not to be used for navigation purposes.)

191

stated they were only 400 feet above the terrain as the captain attempted to climb, but it was too late. At 0542 the aircraft hit the rapidly rising terrain at an altitude of 3,500 feet, on a bearing of 087° from the Cold Bay VORTAC. The force of impact sheared the wings from the fuselage as it broke open, scattering wreckage over a 1,300-foot area on the snow-covered slope. Fire erupted from the fractured fuel tanks in the wings and quickly spread into the center fuselage, consuming most of the aircraft. Only the tail section and a small area of the forward cabin were left recognizable. Smaller fires outside the main area of wreckage damaged the four jet engines and smaller structural components, which separated from the aircraft at impact. All six occupants died instantly.

When flight 802 failed to report over the initial approach fix at Cold Bay, the flight service station operator attempted contact for several minutes before issuing an alert. A few search aircraft were in the air within a few hours, but the low ceilings and high winds prevented many of the smaller local aircraft from taking off.

Weather conditions at Cold Bay during that time were typical of the area for most of the year. It was said that clear days were rare, calm days even rarer, and when the fog was not accompanied by rain it was usually snowing. The high mountainous terrain that existed over much of the surrounding area compounded the problem. Even though the airport was situated at an elevation of ninety-eight feet in a marshy area beside the ocean, there were four mountains above 4,800 feet within thirty miles, and numerous other mountains that extended above 2,000 feet.

A Coast Guard helicopter from Kodiak and two HC-130 aircraft from Elmendorf searched throughout the first day in spite of the weather, but were unsuccessful in their efforts to locate any signs of the missing DC-8. A Coast Guard cutter dispatched to the area searched the offshore waters while a military ground rescue team stood by in Anchorage.

Initially the search efforts focused over a wide area along the peninsula, since the airplane's last known position was 125 miles east of the airport. Local fishing vessels and weather station personnel near Cold Bay later reported hearing a low flying jet about the time flight 802 was expected to arrive, which indicated it was probably down in an area closer to the airport.

By the morning of the 9th, low clouds had lifted enough for a Coast Guard helicopter to search a few of the mountains east of the airport. Flying just below the cloud deck, the crew spotted the wreckage of the DC-8 on the snow-covered slope of 4,900-foot high Mount Dutton. They were able to land near the site and confirm no one had survived, but high winds and low clouds moving back into the area prevented any quick recovery of the bodies.

Several attempts to reach the crash site by air and ground over the next several days were unsuccessful. An Army mountaineering team was dropped below the wreckage by helicopter, but the persistent rain, high winds and hazardous terrain proved too much of an obstacle, forcing them to return before they could reach the accident scene. Ceilings as low as 300 feet were prevalent on many of the days, with winds reaching gusts of fifty knots on the mountain. Over a week passed before rescue personnel and an investigation team were finally able to reach the wreckage.

Most of the major components of the aircraft were destroyed, but many of the cockpit instruments remained relatively intact. The cockpit voice recorder and flight data recorder, which were extremely important in determining the probable cause of the accident, were also recovered, disclosing crucial information.

Nothing unusual in the aircraft's performance could be determined from the accident board's analysis of the wreckage and flight data recorder. The recorded flight data showed the aircraft had functioned normally during all aspects of flight up to the moment of impact. However, the cockpit voice recorder, which recorded the actual conversations of the crew, did reveal several significant details.

Analysis of the cockpit conversations established that what the crew did discuss was equally as important as what they did not discuss. The most important finding was a lack of crew coordination between the pilots, resulting in their confusion over the correct approach procedures to be flown. It was a critical mistake that cost them their lives. Not only were they flying at an altitude well below the authorized minimum sector altitude, but the approach was continued even after mandatory distance measuring equipment reception became erratic in the cockpit.

The information for the localizer back course DME approach to runway 32, displayed on the applicable instrument approach plate, clearly stated the equipment requirements for executing the approach. The captain even mentioned to the first officer that the mandatory DME requirement was not being met after they lost the signal, but he failed to execute another course of action.

In addition, the captain apparently intended to intercept the localizer back course between the initial approach fix and the first DME fix, which was not an approved transition. On the cockpit voice recording, he clearly stated that he did not intend to execute a procedure turn, which would only have been done after flying the direct transition to the VORTAC. The captain then confirmed the statement by turning southwest away from the station. This was done once the first officer stated they were twenty-four miles out, probably in an attempt to expedite the approach, even though it was an unauthorized procedure.

Another mistake by the captain was in relying on inaccurate signal information from the Cold Bay VORTAC at their altitude of 3,500 feet. The instrument approach plate being used did not mention the usable range of the VORTAC at any specific altitude, but the information had been published in the Alaska Supplement, a U.S. Government Flight Information Publication. The VORTAC was shown as being unreliable beyond a forty-mile range when operating below an altitude of 8,000 feet from the east and below an altitude of 5,500 feet from the southeast. At 3,500 feet, the VORTAC signal would have been inaccurate, but was not apparently disrupted enough in this case to trigger the warning flag on the corresponding cockpit navigation display.

The erroneous VORTAC indications being received in the cockpit probably caused the captain to assume the aircraft was southeast of the station instead of its actual position more to the east. Analysis of the first officer's navigation receiver, which controlled the directional needle indications to the VORTAC on both cockpit remote magnetic imaging (RMI) instruments, supported that conclusion. It was determined that there was an approximate error of 24° between the indications being displayed in the cockpit and the actual bearing to the station.

A month after the accident, another incident with a DC-8 at Cold Bay almost resulted in a similar disaster. The second DC-8 was also proceeding inbound from the east with the intention of executing the localizer back course DME approach to runway 32. It was the first time any of the crew had attempted that particular approach at Cold Bay. While inbound to the VORTAC and descending through an altitude of 4,000 feet twenty-five miles from the station, the DME indications in the cockpit became erratic. As the airplane continued the descent and leveled at an altitude of 3,500 feet, it broke out of the overcast among higher mountains. The crew was startled at the sight of mountains on both sides of their flight path, expecting instead to be over open water. At about the same time the distance measuring equipment signal came back in, indicating a range of twenty-two miles.

The captain wisely discontinued the instrument approach and proceeded with a visual approach instead. Obviously concerned by the near disaster, the crew discussed what had happened immediately after landing. They concluded that each of them had incorrectly assumed the minimum sector altitude east of Cold Bay was 3,500 feet, due to an inaccurate mental image they derived from information on the approach plate.

The circumstances were almost identical to flight 802's, and had it not been for a higher ceiling present over the Cold Bay area at the time of the other DC-8's approach, the result might have been equally tragic. Each crew's understanding of the information on the approach plate was almost identical, but equally misinterpreted.

After the crash of flight 802, all the navigation facilities at Cold Bay were flight and ground checked for possible malfunctions. They were determined to be operating normally during the time of the accident. All signal tolerances were within acceptable limits and no discrepancies were found in any phase of operation.

The accident board concluded no malfunction had occurred with any of the power plants or flight systems aboard the airplane prior to impact. The aircraft was found to be properly certified and maintained in accordance with applicable regulations.

Weather conditions at the time of the accident were also determined to be consistent with the forecast and observations received by the crew and were not likely to have adversely effected the operation of the aircraft.

A review of crew flight records found the pilots and flight engineer to be experienced and qualified for DC-8 operations. Captain Weininger had flown just under a total of 23,000 hours, almost

2,000 of those in DC-8s, while First Officer Evans had nearly 5,000 total hours, 450 in DC-8s. Flight Engineer Brocklesby had amassed over 9,800 total hours, 540 in DC-8 aircraft.

The captain had flown into Cold Bay on twenty occasions in the previous nine years, but there was no evidence he had ever flown the localizer back course to runway 32. It was determined that he was aware of the mountainous terrain east of the airport, yet he did not equate the obstructions as a hazard to their flight altitude of only 3,500 feet.

All the crew members had had adequate rest before the flight and each had been on duty for almost eight hours at the time of the accident. Approximately four and a half hours of their duty period was spent in the air on the flight from Travis Air Force Base.

In the National Transportation Safety Board's final analysis, the flight's altitude of 3,500 feet in an area of high terrain resulted in an unreliable VORTAC signal. A subsequent cockpit display of erroneous heading information caused the captain to believe the aircraft was actually southeast instead of east of the VORTAC and approaching the localizer back course when it hit the mountain.

No explanation could be determined as to why the captain ignored the minimum sector altitudes for the approach, other than he mistakenly believed the minimum altitude for the localizer back course also applied to other areas on the approach plate. In addition, the board determined he was most likely not aware of any published restrictions on the reception of the VORTAC signal.

The probable cause of the accident was stated as the captain's deviation from approved instrument approach procedures, resulting in a descent to an altitude of unreliable navigation signals below the obstructing terrain. His disregard of the published instrument approach procedures, whether intentional or not, resulted in accumulative errors that ultimately ended in disaster.

Because of the obvious confusion of other aircrews with the information shown on the applicable instrument approach plate at Cold Bay, the National Transportation Safety Board forwarded a safety recommendation to the Federal Aviation Administration after the investigation. Several modifications were proposed which more noticeably displayed the pertinent approach information and navigational aid restrictions at Cold Bay. Most were enacted a short time later.

Over the years the Cold Bay area has claimed many aircraft. During World War II, the notorious Aleutian weather caused numerous accidents in the vicinity of Cold Bay. Crashes were not uncommon while taking off or landing at the military airfield. Other aircraft flew into mountains obscured by fog, ditched in the nearby offshore waters when the weather obscured the airfield, or disappeared completely, never to be seen or heard from again.

With the decline in aviation activity after the war, accidents declined, but still occurred when a careless or unsuspecting aircrew was caught in bad weather. In 1951 a Navy PB4Y-2 Privateer crashed into a mountain twenty miles northwest of Cold Bay, killing all twelve servicemen onboard. Another military accident occurred in 1970, when a C-124 Globemaster crashed into Pavlof Volcano while on an instrument approach into Cold Bay, thirty miles northeast of the airfield. All seven occupants were killed on impact.

As has been shown in the previous pages, civilian aircraft were not exempt from fatal accidents at Cold Bay either. The World Airways DC-8 was the second commercial airliner to crash while on approach into the airfield. The first occurred in 1956 and is discussed in a previous chapter.

An Accumulation of Errors

SEPTEMBER 6, 1977

It had been a long day for Captain Crandall and First Officer Bible, even before they departed from Iliamna in the early afternoon of September 6. Both had reported for duty at 0400 and had already flown for over five hours by the time they left the small village airport on the west side of Cook Inlet. In another hour and a half they would be back in Anchorage for a well-deserved rest.

The pilots were flying a De Havilland DHC-6 Twin Otter, a sturdy and reliable aircraft well suited for smaller commercial operations in Alaska. It was one of several aircraft belonging to Alaska Aeronautical Industries and was designated as flight 302 for the scheduled, nonstop passenger service between Iliamna and Anchorage. On board were eleven passengers, most of whom were out of state vacationers returning from hunting and fishing trips in the Iliamna area.

Earlier in the morning, before departing from Anchorage, the crew had received complete weather briefings of the area from the Kenai and Anchorage flight service stations. An additional enroute weather briefing was obtained on the ground at Iliamna for their return flight across Cook Inlet, forecasting predominantly overcast skies at their flight altitude, with winds from 240° at thirty-five knots. Light to moderate turbulence was also expected in the vicinity of rough terrain. Just prior to departure, while waiting in the cockpit, the pilot also asked for and received the current weather observation at Anchorage.

Anchorage Center cleared flight 302 to proceed under instrument flight rules (IFR) via Red Airway 99 to Kakon Intersection, then along Green Airway 8 to Anchorage at a cruising altitude of 7,000 feet. The route would follow the low-frequency airway system, requiring automatic direction finder navigation capability on board the aircraft. No radar service was available in the Iliamna area and the majority of the route would be flown through clouds.

Flight 302 left the Iliamna runway at 1419 then climbed to intercept the Red 99 airway running southeast from the Iliamna nondirectional beacon (NDB) to Kakon Intersection. Kakon was located seventeen miles from Iliamna and was the point where the Red 99 and Green 8 airways intercepted. From there they would track the Green 8 airway across Cook Inlet to Kachemak NDB, then north to Wildwood NDB and on into Anchorage.

Approximately six minutes after departure the flight contacted Anchorage Center, reporting level at 7,000 feet and estimating passing over Kakon at 1434. The crew did not transmit their arrival time over Kakon, but did request a route change into Anchorage a few minutes later when they were established on Green 8.

The alternate route they requested was a published transition extending from where the 192° bearing of the Wildwood NDB intercepted the Green 8 airway, located approximately mid distance across Cook Inlet. From there the flight would fly northeast along the reciprocal heading of the 192° bearing, direct to Wildwood, thus cutting several minutes from their enroute time to Anchorage. Anchorage Center approved the request at 1440, with instructions for the flight to remain at their assigned altitude of 7,000 feet.

One minute later, flight 302 advised the controller it was estimating passing over Clams Intersection at 1515. Clams Intersection was located approximately one-third of the distance between the alternate route's intersection with Green 8 and Wildwood NDB.

No further transmissions were monitored from the flight, but at 1452 some background frequency noise was heard by Anchorage Center, which strongly resembled background interference that occurred during previous communications with flight 302. Subsequent attempts to locate the flight on radar were unsuccessful, and after repeated efforts at radio contact by several air traffic control facilities also proved ineffective, an alert was issued to initiate search procedures.

An electronic and visual search of the area between Iliamna and Anchorage began soon after, but failed to locate any signs of flight

302. None of the military and civilian aircraft involved in the search found any evidence of the missing airplane until the morning of the 7th, when an Air Force HC-130 out of Elmendorf Air Force Base in Anchorage, picked up an intermittent emergency locator transmitter signal in the vicinity of Mount Iliamna. A military helicopter located the wreckage shortly after at the 7,000-foot level of a glacier on the southwest side of the mountain. Because of the hazardous terrain and extreme weather conditions around the mountain, the helicopter was unable to land, but it was able to overfly the site several times. The severity of the impact was obvious, with no signs of survivors.

The crew reported that the aircraft appeared to be completely destroyed, leaving scattered wreckage across a 100-yard area of the rugged ice field. Flight 302's point of impact on the mountain was fifty-eight miles from the Iliamna airport and almost thirty miles north of the IFR route it was supposed to have been on. The airplane apparently hit the glacier on a heading of 012°, which was the same course required to fly the alternate route between Green 8 and Wildwood.

Rescue personnel could not reach the crash site until the morning of the 8th, when an Air Force HH-3 helicopter landed above the wreckage and dropped off a four-man search team. Dangerous glacial conditions on the mountain forced the team to take a longer route through the deep crevasses and ice ridges that surrounded the area. Even though the direct distance from the helicopter to the crash site was only 100 yards, the team traveled nearly two miles on an indirect course before reaching the wreckage.

The four-man military rescue team employed all of their mountain climbing skills as they spent three hours traversing the ice field. When they finally reached the accident site, more than an inch of fresh snow had hidden most of the wreckage under a blanket of white powder, limiting their ability to find and identify anything significant. One of the wings was found near a large crevasse, but the majority of the wreckage was scattered and hidden along the broken surface of the glacier or had fallen inside the deep fissures of ice. It was obvious to the search team that no one could have survived the impact and none of the victims were located during the limited time the team had available on the mountain.

Warmer temperatures were prevalent that afternoon, making the threat of avalanche extremely likely, and the longer the team spent on the glacier only increased the danger. A small avalanche had already been triggered when overhanging snow had broken away from a ledge on their initial descent. They decided that the risk was too dangerous. After a brief stay at the site, the rescue team reluctantly returned to the helicopter.

That evening, fresh snow continued to fall on the mountain, making further attempts even more doubtful. The Alaska State Coroner's Office and Department of Public Safety decided the following day to leave the victims of the tragedy where they were. Since no bodies were found during the initial search, it was likely the victims had been lost with most of the wreckage in the crevasses of the glacier. Future efforts to retrieve the cockpit instruments were put on hold until a mountain climbing expert and officials from the National Transportation Safety Board could overfly the site and make a determination.

A nine-man accident investigation team first arrived in Anchorage on the 8th and began collecting preliminary information from airport personnel, air traffic control facilities and previous passengers. Without any direct evidence available from the aircraft, their task of determining a probable cause was made particularly difficult and it was decided to begin another search of the accident site.

In spite of the danger, another four-man team was dropped onto the mountain by helicopter on the 12th. By then, three feet of snow had fallen since the crash, completely covering even the largest pieces of wreckage. After spending four hours combing the glacier and digging for evidence, the team could not locate anything worthwhile. Neither the cockpit flight instruments, which were essential to the accident investigation, nor any of the victims were found. The aircraft did not carry a flight data recorder or cockpit voice recorder.

Because of the inherent dangers involved with additional search attempts and the extreme difficulty in even locating important pieces of wreckage, the National Transportation Safety Board reluctantly decided that the investigation would have to be concluded with other data. It was agreed that no further teams should be jeopardized on the mountain.

During the ensuing investigation, several important findings were uncovered in the maintenance and training operations at

Alaska Aeronautical Industries. Not only was there a problem with some maintenance procedures, but the company's flight operations and pilot training program also had significant deficiencies. In addition, the Federal Aviation Administration was found to be less than adequate in its handling of periodic inspections and the overall monitoring of the company's aviation program. All the faults were found to have contributed in one way or another to the accident.

A disregard of regulations by the pilots of flight 302 and a failure to follow proper navigation procedures were also listed as probable causes of the accident. There was not one problem or error that stood out among the others as a direct cause of the accident, but rather a combination of several mechanical, operational and human errors, which came together and magnified until they resulting in a terrible tragedy.

In the investigation team's analysis of maintenance procedures at Alaska Aeronautical Industries, it was revealed that many serviceable and unserviceable spare parts were being mixed together in the same bins, without tags or labels identifying their status. Statements from company pilots and maintenance personnel showed there was also a general atmosphere of confusion in understanding maintenance logbook entries and the airworthiness of the aircraft. Although the aircraft logbooks were kept in the aircraft, deficiency write-ups were not carried forward to the next day. Instead, they were transferred onto other maintenance records at the hangar. Pilots who pre-flighted aircraft at the hangar for the first flight of the day had access to those maintenance records, but later crews who pre-flighted the aircraft at the airport terminal a mile away had no access to the maintenance records and could rely on only what was in the logbooks.

One potential problem with the accident aircraft was a series of faults that had plagued both pilot directional gyros over a thirty-day period preceding the crash. Several pilots had recorded seven different problems with both cockpit gyros, some that mentioned directional errors of as much as 030° were occurring over a fifteen-minute time span. Maintenance personnel later annotated each write-up as being either corrected or delayed because replacement parts were unavailable. In one of the entries a malfunction had been signed off as corrected when in fact no actual work was completed.

A problem with the system might have reoccurred on the day of the accident while the aircraft was inbound to Iliamna. The captain told the flight service station operator they were receiving erratic indications on their automatic direction finder and inquired whether the station had direction finder capability. The operator replied they did not, but a minute later the pilot stated that he now had sight of the runway and would proceed visually. Their IFR clearance was canceled at that time. The crew reported no other problems with navigation equipment after landing or during the flight back to Anchorage.

An examination of crew training records at the company showed a pattern of disregarded requirements specified in the company's own training manual. Pilots were often assigned as first officers and captains on flights even before completing mandatory training programs. Of those that did receive the required training, most only completed the absolute minimum hours necessary. Both pilots on flight 302 were in the latter category.

Prior to departure on the day of the accident, the originally scheduled aircraft had a maintenance problem that forced it to be replaced. The replacement aircraft, however, did not have the two fully operational automatic direction finder receivers as required for instrument flights on low-frequency airways in part 135 of the flight regulations. It did have one functioning automatic direction finder receiver and two operational high frequency VHF omni-directional range receivers with distance measuring equipment capability, but they did not meet the requirements for the flight. The airway route in and out of Iliamna only made use of low-frequency, non-directional beacons. The second aircraft should never have been assigned to the flight and the captain should certainly not have accepted the aircraft as a substitute.

From the available information gathered by the accident investigation team, it also appeared as if the crew of flight 302 was completely unaware that they were off course. Since the aircraft had been flying in the clouds during the flight, the crew could not have seen the approaching terrain until it was too late.

Since flight 302 was almost thirty miles off the IFR route when it crashed on Mount Iliamna, the nondirectional beacons forming the airways were checked for possible malfunctions. A post-accident flight check found them all operating normally and within approved tolerances.

The Iliamna, Big Mountain, Kachemak and Wildwood nondirectional beacons were class H navigational aids, which guaranteed signal reception in a fifty-mile radius at all altitudes. Although Wildwood's signal was only guaranteed for fifty miles, it was originally designed for a 100-mile radius and was being used for that purpose on the alternate route between the Green 8 airway and Wildwood nondirectional beacon. The distance was approximately seventy miles.

A Victor (VHF omni-directional range) airway was collocated along the 192° bearing from Wildwood and would normally have been available for use on the route in conjunction with the nondirectional beacon. Unfortunately, the VHF omni-directional range was out of service on the day of the accident. There were no published restrictions limiting aircraft from using the alternate route when the VHF omni-directional range was inoperable.

In a two-day period following the accident, three different aircraft reported automatic direction finder navigational errors along Green 8, when attempting to intercept the 192° bearing from Wildwood nondirectional beacon. In each case a false signal on their automatic direction finder systems showed a location twenty-five to thirty miles further west than their actual position, which was verified by a VHF omni-directional range/distance measuring equipment receiver on board each of the aircraft. Each pilot reported receiving a strong audio signal and steady needle indication from the Wildwood nondirectional beacon while the error occurred. In light of that new evidence, the Federal Aviation Administration discontinued use of the 192° bearing as an alternate route from the Green 8 airway to Wildwood. The investigation also began to focus on the Wildwood nondirectional beacon as one of several potential causes of flight 302's accident.

The accident board subsequently evaluated four probable theories that could have caused a navigational error.

1) One or both directional gyros on the aircraft could have
   precessed in flight, causing an inaccurate heading indication.
2) The crew could have erroneously set the wrong heading on
   the directional gyros by referencing an erratic magnetic
   compass in flight.

3) An inaccurate indication could have been received from the Wildwood nondirectional beacon when the automatic direction finder was cross-tuned to identify how close they were to the 192° bearing.

4) Wildwood nondirectional beacon could have mistakenly been tuned instead of Kachemak nondirectional beacon after passing Kakon Intersection, for the purpose of tracking the Green 8 airway.

The first theory was the more probable since both directional gyros on board the aircraft had previously documented problems. The second theory was also likely if the magnetic compass was fluctuating wildly from turbulence or changes in the airplane's attitude when the pilots adjusted the heading. Either theory would have caused inaccurate heading information to be displayed on the directional gyro.

Since the automatic direction finder receiver on the aircraft was a fixed-card system, any error in directional heading would be reflected as a corresponding error in the automatic direction finder needle indication. Assuming the directional gyros were in error of only 010° to 015° from the actual heading at the time the crew requested the route change at 1439, then once they cross-tuned to the Wildwood frequency the automatic direction finder indication would have shown them already at the 192° bearing intersection. In actuality, their real position would have been over thirty miles farther east, near the Kakon Intersection. If the crew did not notice the navigational error and then began tracking 012°, the reciprocal heading of the 192° bearing, the aircraft would have flown on a direct line toward Mount Iliamna.

For that to have happened, however, would have required the crew to be navigating solely off the automatic direction finder system, without using their VHF omni-directional range/distance measuring equipment receivers or time-distance calculations as a crosscheck. If they had, it should have alerted them to any errors on the automatic direction finder.

The third theory was also probable, considering the indication errors from Wildwood nondirectional beacon that other aircraft observed after the accident. By calculating the winds aloft at 7,000 feet during that time, it was determined the flight would have been approximately fourteen miles east of Kakon at 1439, when the crew requested the alternate route. If the Wildwood nondirectional beacon showed the aircraft already at the 192° bearing intersection after being cross-tuned to that frequency, the pilots would have then turned on a 012° course direct for Mount Iliamna. The time en route to the impact point would have been approximately fourteen minutes, which was the approximate time air traffic control monitored background frequency sounds similar to flight 302's previous radio transmissions.

The first three theories seem even more plausible considering information that had been published in the Alaska Supplement before the accident. It advised pilots to expect disturbances while flying on low-frequency airways in mountainous terrain, causing possible needle deviations and false signals on their automatic direction finder system. In addition, the supplement warned of compass deviations of 5° to 10° near magnetic storms at latitudes above 060° north. The flight route from Iliamna to Anchorage was north of 060° latitude.

If the fourth theory was correct and Wildwood nondirectional beacon was tuned at Kakon Intersection instead of Kachemak nondirectional beacon, it would have also placed the aircraft on a course almost direct to Mount Iliamna. It seemed unlikely, however, since a change in heading of over 090° would have been required and should have been obvious to the crew. In addition, the heading at the time of impact would have been closer to 050° instead of the 012° heading that actually occurred.

Although three of the four theories seemed possible, none could explain why the crew did not use other onboard navigational systems as a backup to the automatic direction finder. Two VHF omni-directional range receivers with distance measuring equipment capability were installed and operational on the aircraft. Either could have given an accurate distance from the VHF omni-directional range station at Homer, if tuned to that frequency, and could thus have given a more precise position of where they were on the airway.

The crew could also have used time and distance calculations to estimate the flight's arrival at points along the route. They could then have determined a more accurate location of where and when the aircraft would be on the airway. If they had used either method, it would have been obvious that they were not actually at the intersection of the 192° bearing and Green 8, as indicated on the automatic direction finder, thus averting the resulting disaster.

No reason could be found as to why the pilot accepted the aircraft when it did not have two operational automatic direction finder systems onboard. It was possible the company had placed undue pressure on him to complete the flight and prevent further delays. Current and former employees reported similar instances of company pressure to the investigation board. In one case a pilot had been dismissed because he refused to fly an aircraft into adverse weather conditions.

The National Transportation Safety Board determined the probable cause of the accident to be the crew's failure to use proper navigational procedures for the IFR route being flown. It also concluded that the automatic direction finder receiver was operating correctly, since the crew did not report any additional problems with the system after landing at Iliamna.

The board believed the crew had tuned in properly to the nondirectional beacon stations along the airways after departure from Iliamna, but because of erroneous automatic direction finder indications, they mistakenly assumed they were tracking inbound to the Wildwood nondirectional beacon when they impacted the mountain. Signal reception from the Wildwood nondirectional beacon was determined to be unreliable within fourteen miles of Kakon Intersection and the crew used no other navigation systems to backup the automatic direction finder indication.

Several important inadequacies were found in the company's maintenance, training and operational procedures, as well as the Federal Aviation Administration's monitoring of those areas. The board issued five safety recommendations to ensure similar aviation problems did not occur with other commercial operators.

Captain Crandall had been employed by Alaska Aeronautical Industries since February 1977. He was a rated flight instructor with over 4,300 flight hours. First Officer Gary Bible was employed with the company in June 1977 and held a total of 1,380 total hours.

The accident aircraft, a De Havilland DHC-6-200, was manufactured in 1969 and had 15,369 total hours on the airframe. The last maintenance inspection had occurred sixty-nine hours previously.

In retrospect, it can be said the accident was the unfortunate result of several errors and it would be easy to single out the captain as the responsible person. After all, any pilot-in-command is ultimately responsible not only for the aircraft, but also the safety of his passengers and crew. Fingerpointing is always the easiest answer, especially in hindsight, but can often hide other serious mistakes. In this incident, the investigation team successfully uncovered several significant problems in the operations at both Alaska Aeronautical Industries and the low-frequency airway system. It is unfortunate that thirteen people had to lose their lives before those faults were revealed.

Fire on the Mountain and a Tale of Lost Gold

MARCH 12, 1948

Bright streaks of luminous green light danced across the evening sky as the Northwest Airlines DC-4 climbed away from Anchorage. Captains Petry and Van Cleef had seen similar light displays from the aurora borealis on many previous flights, but each sight was as breathtaking as the first. Both men had been flying in Alaska since 1942 when they were first employed by Northwest Airlines. The Anchorage to Edmonton route they were flying this night was well traveled by each of them. If not for the brilliant, sparkling streaks playing across the horizon and dancing atop the snow-covered peaks, it would have been just another normal flight. At least as normal as any flight in Alaska could be.

The date was March 12, 1948. All four of the airplane's 2,000 HP Pratt and Whitney engines were operating smoothly and the navigation and communication systems seemed to be in perfect order. In addition to the twenty-four merchant seamen onboard, bound for New York, the chartered flight carried six crew members, all experienced in DC-4 aircraft. Two airline captains, Petry and Van Cleef, a first officer, navigator, mechanic and purser made up the crew. Some of the passengers seemed excited about returning to the United States, but most of them were relaxed and enjoying the flight.

They encountered no problems during their initial flight from Shanghai, China. Arrival and departure at Anchorage airport were equally routine. Flight 4422 departed on its continuing journey from Anchorage at 2012 later that evening. The intended flight route was Anchorage to Edmonton, via the Green 8 and Amber 2 airways, then Minneapolis and finally New York the next day.

The pilots were flying by instruments, navigating off radio signals being transmitted from various ground stations along the course, which allowed for accurate tracking of the intended instrument airway. Instrument flight was especially beneficial at night or during marginal weather conditions when ground references were often indiscernible for visual navigation. By 1948 flying by instruments had become standard operating procedure for most commercial airlines.

A few minutes after departure from the airfield in Anchorage, the flight intercepted the outbound leg of the Anchorage Radio Range. At 2028, sixteen minutes after takeoff, the flight reported over the Wasilla Intersection, thirty-five miles north of Anchorage, then turned east along the Green 8 airway. The DC-4 reached its cruising altitude of 11,000 feet three minutes later.

After flying another fifty miles at a ground speed of 212 knots, flight 4422 reported over the Sheep Mountain non-directional radio beacon (NDB), seventy-four miles southwest of Gulkana. At that point the airway altered course slightly, from 050° to a 046° heading.

With the Talkeetna Mountains now fading behind the aircraft, the terrain changed into a wide expanse of lakes and low areas, stretching between three major mountain ranges that surrounded a confluence of smaller valleys. The coastal Chugach Mountains ran on an almost parallel path before tapering away to the southeast in the distance, while the Alaska Range stretched in a far line across the horizon, well north of their location. Directly ahead, yet still almost 100 miles away, the rugged Wrangell Mountains were visible, extending from Canada to a point less than twenty miles from the aircraft's next checkpoint near Gulkana Airport.

The Chitina River valley lay on the south side of the Wrangell Mountains and the larger Copper River valley opened in an arc to the northeast. Mount Drum and Mount Sanford, the two westernmost peaks of the Wrangell Mountains, towered under the clear night sky, with the northern lights playing tricks across the white walls of rock and ice.

Because many of the peaks of the Wrangell Mountains extended above 13,000 feet and the majority were above 10,000 feet, the Green 8 airway altered course north from Gulkana, on a heading that diverted aircraft safely around the mountains. Pilots would occasionally fly off the airway deliberately, maintaining a direct course between the Gulkana and Snag Radio Ranges, but only when the mountains were clearly visible, and presumably only after air traffic control had authorized the change.

By diverting off the airway in certain situations, pilots could fly closer to the high peaks and shorten their enroute flight time, in addition to providing some spectacular scenery for the passengers. Mount Sanford, the higher of the two western peaks, was located on an almost direct heading between Gulkana and Snag, rising to an ominous height of 16,237 feet.

At 2103 that evening, the flight reported over the Gulkana Station, estimating their arrival over the Northway Radio Range at 2136. This would indicate that the pilots intended to remain on the Green 8 airway and would not divert on a direct heading to Snag, as Northway would not then have been the next reporting point. The crew also did not ask for or receive a change in the route clearance, which was mandatory before proceeding on a different course. However, it was not unheard of for commercial pilots to divert occasionally from their filed flight plans without notifying air traffic control.

Shortly after passing Gulkana at 2103, flight 4422 established initial contact with Northway Radio, which cleared them as filed into the next control area. The pilot acknowledged receiving the clearance a few seconds later. Since both the Northway Radio Range signal and voice communications were on the same frequency, it would seem to indicate that the navigational aid signal was being received normally by the aircraft at that time.

Witnesses on the ground reported seeing the aircraft pass three to four miles south of the Gulkana Radio Range, on a easterly heading around 2100. No other transmissions were received for approximately fifteen minutes, until the flight repeated its previous Gulkana position report to Northway Radio. One minute later a fire was observed high on the western slope of Mount Sanford. When the Gulkana and Northway stations received reports of the fire, they attempted unsuccessfully to contact the flight several times. All radio facilities along the flight's intended route were immediately notified of a probable crash involving the Northwest Airlines flight. Subsequent attempts at contact by the other stations were also unsuccessful.

When the navigation facilities along the route at Sheep

Mountain, Gulkana and Northway received news of the possible accident they immediately conducted ground checks of their systems. All were found operating normally. There were no evident mechanical malfunctions that could explain why the Northwest Airlines diverted off course and impacted the mountain.

A couple of hours after the fire was first observed on Mount Sanford, a private pilot from Gulkana decided to investigate. Flying a small airplane, he climbed to 10,000 feet while circling around the mountain, but saw no visible signs of fire or wreckage. He did report that the Gulkana Radio Range signal appeared to be operating correctly and his compass indications in the aircraft were unaffected by atmospheric interference. Flight conditions were stated as clear skies with fifty miles of visibility, but with diminishing visibility in the vicinity of the mountain from the effect of the northern lights. The lights were apparently unusually bright and hanging like a curtain, completely obscuring Mount Sanford from view for several minutes at a time.

A military search aircraft from the 10th Rescue Group in Anchorage was delayed by mechanical problems, but was able to launch a few hours after the initial report of an accident was received. Once it arrived at the mountain, the Air Force crew confirmed there were no signs of fire.

The reduced illumination at night, even with the aurora borealis, could not provide enough visibility to adequately scan the snow-covered slopes for signs of wreckage. The crew returned to base, radioing air traffic control their findings, or lack thereof, and also reported normal radio reception and compass indications during the flight.

The search intensified the next day when a DC-3 carrying officials from Northwest Airlines, the Civil Aeronautics Administration and Civil Aeronautics Board, duplicated flight 4422's route from Anchorage. More airplanes from the 10th Rescue Squadron in Anchorage and Fairbanks joined the search as well. There was little doubt by then that the airliner had impacted Mount Sanford. Locating the wreckage and any possible survivors became a priority.

Civil Aeronautics Administration officials conducted mandatory flight checks of all the navigation facilities along the airway while en route to the presumed crash site. If one of the navigational aid stations had been transmitting an inaccurate signal, it would at

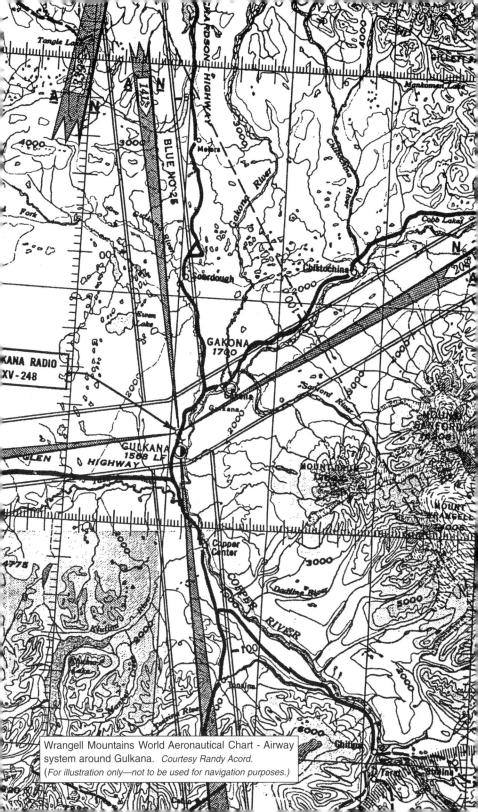

Wrangell Mountains World Aeronautical Chart - Airway system around Gulkana. *Courtesy Randy Acord.*
(*For illustration only—not to be used for navigation purposes.*)

least explain how the accident could have occurred and could then have been repaired before causing another potential incident. No discrepancies or errors were found in the navigation signals, however. Reception and course indications were accurate at all the radio range stations and non-directional beacons along the airway route.

As each navigational facility was ruled out as a possible cause of the accident, concerns about the circumstances of flight 4422's crash were a matter of in-depth discussion on board the DC-3. Some type of mechanical failure, atmospheric interference or pilot error was a possibility, but the last seemed the least likely. Senior pilots Petry and Van Cleef had almost 13,000 combined flight hours between them, many of which were flown in Alaska since being employed by Northwest Airlines. Both had flown the very same Anchorage to Edmonton route many times over their careers. First Officer Stickel was also very experienced with over 4,700 flight hours, many of his hours in Alaska and on the same route. Even the navigator had over 2,500 total flight hours, although he had been certified as a navigator for only six months.

After the DC-3 with the government officials on board arrived over Mount Sanford, it flew several search patterns before finally sighting the wreckage. They confirmed the airliner had indeed struck the western slope of the mountain where the fire had been observed the night before. A large blackened area of snow at the 11,000-foot level confirmed the point of impact, but the wreckage had tumbled and slid down an almost vertical wall of ice, leaving behind a discernible trail of destruction. The remaining hulk and pieces of debris came to rest in a small glacial basin at the 8,500-foot level. It was readily apparent that no one could have survived the violent collision.

A mass of thick, blue ice hung precariously from the cliffs around the wreckage, making the site almost inaccessible from the ground or air. Other areas of the mountain were extremely rugged, especially at the higher elevations where hundreds of feet of accumulated snow and ice completely covered the surface year round. Only a few patches of exposed rock were even visible along the upper slopes, and they were just as foreboding as the rest of the mountain.

Officials and observers who flew over the crash site in the next few days were unanimous in their opinion that any attempt to reach the wreckage would be extremely dangerous. It was decided that risking further lives in an attempt to recover the bodies would serve no real purpose. A team from the Air Force's elite rescue unit in Anchorage, which had been standing by in Gulkana for permission to attempt a recovery of the bodies, was reluctantly sent home. The victims would have to remain entombed where they had fallen.

Falling snow and ice from the upper slopes had already begun to cover the wreckage by the time it was discovered a day after the accident. Each new storm added a little more depth, eventually hiding the destruction under a thick layer of white camouflage. In a few months the location was completely invisible from the air, hidden beneath a solid shroud of heavy snow. The secrets of why flight 4422 crashed into Mount Sanford would remain buried with the passengers and crew.

Several days after the tragedy, three chaplains circled in an airplane above the ice-encrusted mountain and conducted a brief but touching memorial service for the victims. Somehow the ceremony must have brought at least a small measure of closure to the families, but it could never fill the gap of unanswered questions that would linger for generations.

The official Accident Investigation Report from the Civil Aeronautics Board was released on July 28, 1948. The board determined the probable cause as the pilot's failure to see Mount Sanford, which was probably obscured by either clouds or the aurora borealis or both, while attempting to fly a course well off the airway. It was their contention that the flight diverted south of the airway for the purpose of flying a straight-line course between Gulkana and Snag, with an intention of visually circumnavigating around Mount Sanford.

That conclusion, however, raises some additional questions. Although the ultimate cause was the crew's failure to see the mountain, it is difficult to believe their initial intention was to fly off the airway. One interesting bit of information not mentioned in the accident report, was the fact that the airway from Wasilla Intersection to Gulkana Radio had a 004° heading change after passing over the Sheep Mountain non-directional beacon. If an aircraft flying the airway failed to make the 004° course correction at Sheep Mountain and continued on a 050° outbound track from the radio beacon, it would eventually pass approximately four miles south of the

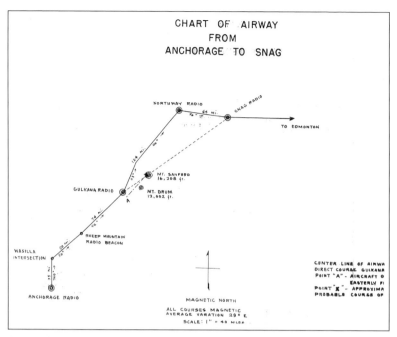

Image of Accident Report flight route and airway structure.
Excerpted from Civil Aeronautics Board Accident Investigation Report, File No. 1-0025.
(For illustration only—not to be used for navigation purposes.)

Gulkana station. That is the same location where witnesses observed the airplane about the time of its 2103 position report.

There is also a possibility that in-flight winds blew the aircraft south of course. If the crew had adjusted for the 040° course correction at Sheep Mountain, but failed to correct for the winds aloft at 11,000 feet, which were forecast from 275° at twenty-two knots in the Gulkana area, the subsequent error would also have placed the aircraft several miles south of Gulkana.

If the aircraft turned left to the new 023° course after station passage at Gulkana and from a point four miles south, the subsequent heading would have taken it within close proximity of Mount Sanford's summit. For that to happen, however, the crew would have had to completely disregard the automatic direction finder needle indications to and from the Gulkana Radio Range, and to have only navigated off a compass heading.

Another fact not discussed in the accident report is the question

216

of why the pilot would give an estimated arrival time over the Northway station if they had no intention of flying there. The airway route crossed directly over the Northway Station, while the straight-line course from Gulkana to Snag passed well east of Northway. If it had been the pilot's intention to fly the straight-line course, the estimated arrival time over Snag Station, not Northway, would have been reported.

It is possible the pilot decided to change the initial route because of predominately clear weather conditions, assuming Mount Sanford could be seen from the aircraft and safely circumnavigated. But why was air traffic control not informed of the change, unless the crew was violating regulations deliberately? All commercial pilots knew it was mandatory to advise the controlling station of any intended changes in the flight route.

Assuming for a moment the pilots did decide on the direct route between Gulkana and Snag without advising Northway Radio, why would they continue on a direct course toward Mount Sanford for another fifteen minutes without it being visible? It seems illogical when other factors are considered. After all, the crew was aware of the mountain's proximity to the direct line course.

The Civil Aeronautics Board's accident report also mentions the fact that flight 4422 repeated the position report over Gulkana Station approximately one minute before impact on Mount Sanford. The first report was sent at 2103, the second sent to Northway fifteen minutes later. Why the delay? Is it possible the crew was confused at some point about their exact location and tried to verify their position before sending the same report again?

Mount Drum, which is approximately twenty miles southwest of Mount Sanford, would have been almost directly off the nose of the aircraft if the flight had continued on a 050° track from Sheep Mountain. Mount Sanford would have been off the nose if the flight was tracking the airway correctly on the 046° radial. If the crew was unaware of being several miles south of the Gulkana station, and decided to proceed visually by referencing the mountain, Mount Drum could easily have been mistaken for Mount Sanford. Any confusion between the two mountains would have critically altered their perceived flight path to either Northway or Snag.

On the other hand, if they were flying only by instruments, they would probably have realized their navigational error after station passage at Gulkana, while turning north to follow the 023° radial to Northway. It seems equally possible that in an attempt at either intercepting the airway, relying on a false visual identification of Mount Drum, or both, they then flew into Mount Sanford. There is little doubt that Mount Sanford was obscured at different times by the brilliant light display of the aurora borealis. The private pilot who departed from Gulkana after the accident confirmed it. It is also possible that a thin layer of high clouds could have formed around the mountain, as stated in the accident report, but this is rather unlikely since the weather forecast and in-flight observations from the private pilot and Air Force crew did not mention it.

The actual weather forecast for flight 4422, prepared at 1820 that evening, called for excellent visibility and an unlimited ceiling between Anchorage and Snag. Winds over Gulkana at 11,000 feet were forecast out of the west at 275° at twenty-two knots, and at Northway at 285° at twenty-eight knots. Without correcting for winds aloft, the aircraft would have been pushed east toward the mountain after passing Gulkana.

Although the crew of Northwest Airlines flight 4422 was very experienced, the one weak link seemed to be the navigator. He had only been certified in navigation for less than six months, and it is doubtful if he had much experience in Alaska or over that particular route, since it was not mentioned in the personnel data of the official Accident Report. Whether or not the navigator contributed to the accident is unknown, but it is ultimately the pilot's responsibility for ensuring the safety of the aircraft, the passengers and the crew.

Another consideration is a lack of adequate crew rest. The long overseas flight from China the previous day could have caused increased fatigue among the crew, even though there is no information to support that particular conclusion. Flight 4422 originally left Shanghai, China at 2010 Pacific Standard Time on March 11. However, the accident report states that an entirely new crew was added in Anchorage before departure.

Perhaps the crew simply flew past Gulkana without paying attention to their en route time or to an indication of station passage over the Gulkana Radio Range, and continued on the same course until impact with the mountain. No one will ever know for sure.

The crew of flight 4422 reported no mechanical or communication difficulties. Only light turbulence existed in the area of the crash and the weather conditions were not conducive to the formation of aircraft icing. The moon had set approximately an hour before the accident, decreasing somewhat the ambient light available that night.

As in most fatal accidents when the wreckage cannot be analyzed, the circumstances causing the mishap can never be positively determined and will remain a matter of speculation. The accident was probably a result of several accumulative errors.

No one knows for sure when the rumors of gold aboard flight 4422 first began. Rumors of secret treasure and mysterious cargo always seem to follow unexplained disasters. A lack of certainty somehow fosters imaginative and intriguing tales of untold wealth, replacing fact with fantasy. Alaska alone has many stories, most of them fiction, of missing ships and airplanes carrying great riches. There are stories of an Air Force cargo airplane that crashed with a fortune in government payroll aboard, a corporate airplane that disappeared with hundreds of thousands of dollars in cash for pipeline workers on the North Slope, and a steamship that sunk in southeast Alaska with millions of dollars in silver bullion. A search for truth is often replaced by more entertaining thoughts of unexplained riches.

None of the evidence in the accident report showed any link to a cargo of gold, which was supposedly carried by the twenty-four seamen as payment for the sale of an oil tanker they delivered to the Nationalist Chinese government. And no insurance claims were filed after the accident, as would be expected had a valuable cargo been on board.

One individual interviewed by a newspaper reporter about the cargo after the accident had been a radio officer and ship's secretary on a similar tanker delivered to the Chinese during the same time. He stated that the ships were not actually sold to the Chinese but were leased on a two-year contract. In addition, the crew's wages would only have been paid by the shipping company on their return to New York, and not by the Chinese government. Someone else who helped load the airplane in Shanghai stated that he did not witness any cargo of gold or cash being carried by the ship's crew. Even with evidence to the contrary, it did not take long before incredible tales of gold on the Northwest flight enticed curious expeditions to investigate. By 1974 there had been at least fifteen attempts to find and salvage the presumed treasure, some by professional mountain climbers. All failed to reach the inaccessible wreckage. One expedition supposedly came within a few hundred feet before being forced back by the threat of an avalanche.

Not until July 1999 was an attempt to reach the crash site successful. In 1997, two pilots who had spent years researching the accident and flying over the area finally located pieces of the debris from the air. The wreckage had been slowly carried by the movement of the glacier over the decades, until it was finally revealed in a more accessible location, lower on the mountain. Having obtained a special permit from the National Park Service, the two adventurers hiked up to the glacier and retrieved several artifacts, later confirmed as being from flight 4422.

Alaska State Troopers and a National Transportation Safety Board investigator also visited the site in the days following the discovery. Some pieces of visible human remains were retrieved for identification. One engine and two propeller assemblies were also found along the narrow, mile-long debris trail. No evidence of any gold or cash was found. The pilots who found the crash site kept secret the exact location to deter any future adventurers. Perhaps now the dead will be left in peace.

Without Warning

JANUARY 20, 1949

January 20, 1949 was a clear night. Flying several thousand feet above the ground in such conditions must have seemed tedious to the two pilots of the Alaska Airlines DC-3. Visibility was unlimited and they could just as easily have navigated low level over the terrain where the spectacular scenery could be better appreciated. Perhaps that is why a requirement that all night flights be conducted using instrument flight rules (IFR) flight plans did not seem relevant when they departed from Homer Airport on the second leg of their flight to Anchorage.

They departed at 1950, heading northeast initially along Kachemak Bay before turning inland over the Kenai Peninsula. The area was covered with a blanket of snow, but plenty of trees and darker vegetation dotted the landscape, clearly contrasting against the horizon for easy navigation. As the elevation began rising further inland, the pilots varied their altitude to maintain a constant separation with the ground, keeping the DC-3 on a general heading toward Anchorage.

At approximately 2005, fifteen minutes into the flight, the aircraft hit the south slope of Ptarmigan Head, 300 feet below the 3,100-foot summit. Both engines were torn loose by the force of impact and the wings separated from the fuselage as it was thrown sideways into an inverted position. Debris was strewn over a 250-foot area as the main cabin broke apart and slid down the snow-covered ground. The nose and cockpit were heavily damaged in the crash before breaking away completely at the forward bulkhead and coming to a stop further up the hill.

Two of the three passengers plus the co-pilot were killed instantly. The pilot-in-command and surviving passenger were transported to Providence Hospital in Anchorage for medical treatment after being rescued the next afternoon. Several days later the passenger also succumbed to his extensive injuries. Serious trauma prevented the pilot-in-command, now the only survivor, from remembering many details of the flight.

Alaska Airlines flight 08 departed originally from Naknek, a village on the northeast end of Bristol Bay, earlier in the evening on a return flight to Anchorage. An instrument flight rules clearance was issued by air traffic control, with intermediate stops scheduled along the route at Homer and Kenai. A weather briefing for the Cook Inlet area was received before departure, calling for clear skies and unlimited visibility.

Federal requirements dictated that as a condition of the airline's certification in Alaska, an IFR flight plan would be used when flights were conducted at night. The accident report did not mention if the requirement had been clearly stated and emphasized by Alaska Airlines as a mandatory policy among its pilots.

After taking off from Naknek at 1805, the flight intercepted the low-level airway across Cook Inlet and proceeded on course without incident. Approximately twenty-five miles southwest of Homer, the captain advised the controller they would be continuing visual flight rules (VFR) to Kenai and Anchorage instead of IFR, after stopping to transfer passengers and cargo. That information was relayed by air traffic control to the Alaska Airlines dispatch office in Anchorage at 1925. Ten minutes later the flight touched down safely at Homer and taxied in front of the airport office.

While on the ground an additional passenger and some baggage were loaded on board. The flight now had three passengers along with the original pilot, co-pilot and flight attendant. The remainder of the cabin area was filled with over a ton of cargo from Naknek. Once the extra baggage was secured and the passengers re-seated, the crew made a quick turnaround, advising the tower operator they would be proceeding by VFR to the next destination at Kenai. After taxiing into position and accelerating down the runway, Alaska Airlines flight 08 climbed away from the small city, only fifteen minutes after arriving.

A few minutes after the DC-3 departed, the tower operator also relayed the flight's intention to proceed under visual flight rules to the

Alaska Airlines dispatcher in Anchorage. No one at the dispatch office questioned the information or attempted to contact the flight and advise the crew of the violation, even though it was the second report they had received. Either the dispatch office was unaware of the carrier's requirement for IFR flight at night (which would seem unlikely), or simply chose to ignore it. Since the pilot also openly admitted his intentions over the radio, it would seem probable that VFR flights at night were not an uncommon occurrence.

Seven minutes into the flight, Kenai Radio advised the crew there were no passengers or cargo waiting at their next stop in Kenai. In response, the DC-3 captain stated the flight would bypass that location, and instead fly direct to Anchorage. The crew then made a minor heading correction to the right of the previous course, continuing their visual navigation over the Peninsula in the direction of Tustumena Lake. A new estimated time of arrival at Anchorage of 2050 was passed to air traffic control at that time.

When no further communication could be established with the flight after its ETA at Anchorage had passed, search and rescue facilities were notified. Several aircraft in the Kenai area departed from and flew the same route as the DC-3, but nothing could be identified on the ground in the dark. The crews were forced to wait until 0200 the following morning, when ambient light conditions increased during a late moonrise.

A ski-equipped search plane spotted the wreckage at 0220, near the 2,800-foot level of Ptarmigan Head in the Caribou Hills, twenty-seven miles northeast of Homer. The small airplane was able to land on the barren summit above the crash site, allowing an easier hike down the slope.

At first it was assumed all the occupants had died during the impact, since the airliner had sustained such extensive damage. Major sections were found in pieces and partially crushed, leaving the two wings and tail assembly as the three largest pieces among the wreckage. The first people to arrive on scene were so certain of the occupants' fate that they sent a radio message to say no one had survived the crash.

High winds howling across the snow-covered slope at the time prevented any rescue sounds from carrying more than a few feet. It was only when searchers began moving around in the wreckage later that day that the survivors heard the voices and shouted for help.

Captain Land, the pilot-in-command of the DC-3, was found trapped in the smashed cockpit among a pile of twisted metal and tangled electrical wires. He was suffering from a punctured lung, broken ankle, frostbite and several facial lacerations. A passenger named Poumirau was located in a forward section of the demolished cabin, still hanging upside-down in his seat. He had serious internal injuries and frostbite.

Initially, because the heavily damaged pieces of fuselage were so twisted and crushed, there could be no immediate rescue of the survivors. A crash team from the 10th Rescue Squadron at Elmendorf Air Force Base in Anchorage had to be flown in with special cutting equipment to free them. During the hours before the crash team arrived, the survivors were kept as warm as possible and given medical aid, but the extreme cold temperatures kept freezing the blood plasma and morphine capsules that had been flown in by another rescue party. The Air Force crash team reached the wreckage to free the survivors that afternoon, almost twenty hours after the accident happened.

After being carried on stretchers through the chest deep snow around the accident site, both survivors were flown from the scene by a ski-equipped bush-plane. They arrived in Anchorage in critical condition, but Captain Land was later downgraded to fair. A statement he made while at the hospital indicated there was no warning of an impending collision and he could not recall any problems with the aircraft. Other important details of the flight, from the time they left Homer until being rescued the next afternoon, were permanently blocked from his memory.

Another pilot, from a different aircraft, was also injured at the site on the 21st, when his airplane was caught in a downdraft while circling over the accident scene. It crashed in the same area as the DC-3, hitting hard and flipping several times down the slope. In this incident, however, the pilot walked away with only a few cuts and abrasions. A doctor from one of the rescue teams already on scene helped administer minor first aid before the pilot was transported back to Homer.

On January 22, three of the four bodies were recovered from the wreckage. The remaining body, that of the flight attendant, was not found until the 23rd.

An investigation by the Civil Aeronautics Board showed no evidence of either mechanical or structural failure prior to the accident, and no discrepancies were found in the maintenance records. The aircraft was determined to be airworthy and properly certified for both passenger and cargo service.

Analysis of the wreckage revealed the aircraft had hit in a wings level attitude, while slightly nose high, on a heading of 355°. The landing gear and flaps were fully retracted and the trim tab control had been set correctly. A current barometric pressure setting for Homer had been properly dialed in the altimeters at the time of the accident. Other cockpit instruments could not be properly interpreted, due to a zeroing of the needle indications when the electrical wiring was torn loose during impact.

Examination of the propeller and engine assemblies indicated they were operating at a high power setting, indicating normal flight. Because of excessive damage to the cockpit area, the control lever positions could not be accurately determined.

The aircraft was manufactured in 1944 and had accrued slightly over 8,000 hours on the airframe. Both engines had flown approximately 400 hours since their last overhaul.

Post-crash testing of the radio components found them to have been operating normally. The automatic and manual compass systems were determined to be operating correctly and tuned to the Anchorage Radio Range at the time of impact. Subsequent flight checks of the navigation facilities at Homer, Kenai and Anchorage the day after the accident found them to be functioning normally. There were no indications of any malfunction in the navigational equipment on board the aircraft or on the ground.

Analysis of the weather patterns at the time of the accident verified the conditions were clear and unlimited with northerly winds at twenty to thirty knots around the impact point. Because of the likelihood of blowing snow off the top of Ptarmigan Head, and limited vegetation on the upper slopes, it was surmised the crew might have had insufficient references to see and avoid the approaching terrain. A lack of contrast between the higher hills and lower elevations, influenced by a decrease in visibility from blowing snow on the summit, could have given the crew a false perception of their height above the ground.

Although the crew's failure to see the higher terrain is a consideration, it does not explain why they were not using a map, leaving themselves unaware of their actual location in proximity to Ptarmigan Head. After all, the mountain was the highest point of land on a direct course between Homer and Anchorage. It also does not explain why the crew would continue flying a straight-line course at the same altitude when the visible horizon became obscured by higher terrain and blowing snow; both of which should have been obvious indications of an obstruction along their intended flight path.

Another possibility is that the aircraft experienced a sudden downdraft on the leeward side of the mountain as it flew over at a low altitude, forcing the airplane into the slope before corrective action could be applied. It is also probable that the pilots were complacently flying a few hundred feet above the terrain, while following a signal from the Anchorage Radio Range, and never bothered verifying what obstructions, if any, were in front of the aircraft.

VFR flights at night were prohibited for very good reasons, most particularly because of a reduced amount of ambient light for identifying visual references and the safety of the passengers. The crew foolishly chose to violate that restriction, ultimately taking the lives of five of the six occupants on board.

Captain Land had 7,500 flight hours at the time of the accident, most of those in DC-3s. He had been rated as a good pilot during previous flight checks with the airline, and was signed off for captain duties a month earlier.

The co-pilot had 2,500 flight hours, of which the majority were in multi-engine aircraft. During his four previous flight checks over the same route, however, Alaska Airlines had rated him as a below-average pilot.

The accident board identified several factors as contributing to the crash. Predominate was the captain's intentional disregard of company requirements for IFR flight at night. In addition, the board cited the crew's failure during the fifteen minutes before impact to climb to a sufficient altitude to clear the obstruction. The company dispatcher in Anchorage was also faulted for not reminding the crew that their intentions of flying visual flight rules at night were not authorized.

The Civil Aeronautics Board determined the probable cause of the accident as the pilot's attempt at flying off the airway at an insufficient altitude above the terrain.

A Tomb of Ice

JUNE 14, 1960

Pacific Northern Airlines flight 201, a Lockheed Constellation out of Seattle, climbed steadily after departure from Cordova and intercepted the Amber One airway over Hinchinbrook Island. Bound for Anchorage with nine passengers and a crew of five, it proceeded on course for several minutes before abruptly turning 035° right of course on a heading northwest away from the instrument airway. Approximately seventeen minutes later the aircraft struck an almost vertical wall at the 9,000-foot level of Mount Gilbert, twenty-eight nautical miles north of its intended route. There were no survivors.

The accident was a terrible tragedy. Questions as to why the aircraft was off course arose immediately, with several different theories put forward by other pilots and the investigation board. Some considered it just another aircraft accident in the aviation community, one of many that occurred every year in Alaska, but airline officials and the federal government looked at it from a different perspective.

If similar accidents were to be prevented in the future, an accurate determination of the cause had to be found. Commercial aircraft did not arbitrarily change flight directions on their own nor did the pilots flying them change course without good reason. It had to be established whether the crash of flight 201 was caused by mechanical or human error, or weather phenomena, so procedures could be put in place to ensure there were no repeat incidents.

Flight 201 originally departed from Seattle late in the evening on the 13th, arriving at its first scheduled stop in Cordova at 0346 local time. A company flight dispatcher in Seattle provided a routine briefing to the pilots before departure, including the status of navigation aids along the route, expected weather conditions and pertinent airfield information. The crew did not ask for or receive an official weather briefing from the U.S. Weather Bureau.

Sixty-one passengers and five crew members were on board the Constellation when it left Seattle. No problems were encountered during the five hour and twenty minute flight along the coast and during the landing at Cordova. The aircraft only stayed at the terminal long enough to off-load the passengers, baggage and cargo, and be refueled before getting underway again. Less than thirty minutes after landing, it taxied into position for departure.

The sleek Constellation had recently been added to Pacific Northern's Alaska route to handle increased passenger traffic during the summer months. Most of the fifty-two occupants who disembarked when it arrived in Cordova were cannery workers and fisherman who had been hired for the upcoming fishing season.

Anchorage Air Route Traffic Control issued an instrument clearance shortly before takeoff from Cordova, clearing flight 201 as requested to the Anchorage low-frequency radio range at 10,000 feet, via Egg Island and the Amber One airway.

Visibility at Cordova was reported as fifteen miles, with winds from the northeast at fifteen knots and a ceiling of 2,800 feet. An updated weather briefing was not available from the company dispatch office in Cordova and the pilots did not obtain a weather forecast from the U.S. Weather Bureau for the remaining route. However, the pilot did receive the Anchorage Airport weather from the Cordova Flight Service Station after takeoff.

Immediately after departure the flight advised the Anchorage Air Route Traffic Control they were off Cordova at 0417, climbing to the assigned altitude and estimating a 0425 arrival over Hinchinbrook. At that time the controller amended their clearance to an new altitude of 9,000 feet, which the pilot acknowledged. The airplane continued a steady climb to intercept the instrument airway at the Hinchinbrook Radio Range, subsequently reporting over the station at 0427, level at 9,000 feet and estimating their passing the next checkpoint at Whittier at 0447.

For several minutes following the position report, flight 201 correctly tracked the Amber One airway, then suddenly turned 035° to the northwest. The crew did not request any change of route, and since Anchorage Air Route Traffic Control did not have radar coverage of the area, the controller was unaware of the deviation.

The last radio contact with the flight was at 0432, when the Anchorage Air Route Traffic Control transmitted traffic information and a current weather update at Anchorage. The information was acknowledged by the flight, which at the time was already several miles north of the instrument course.

An Air Force defense radar site on Middleton Island, sixty-three miles south of Hinchinbrook in the Gulf of Alaska, was tracking the flight on radar, however. The operator was already aware of the Pacific Northern aircraft's intended route and destination, from the instrument flight plan that had been passed to him by Anchorage Air Route Traffic Control. It was normal policy for military radar sites and civilian air traffic control centers to inform each other of aircraft in their respective areas.

A joint agreement between the Federal Aviation Administration and Alaska Air Command had already been established to assist civilian aircraft with radar advisories and flight monitoring. The main purpose was to ensure commercial aircraft avoided conditions that could jeopardize their safety, such as restricted areas, extreme weather conditions and hazardous terrain. Whenever an airplane was observed flying off course or approaching dangerous terrain, the radar site was required to immediately notify either the pilot of the flight or the Anchorage Air Route Traffic Control. In this case it was not done.

After the defense radar site at Middleton Island received Flight 201's instrument flight plan, the operator waited for the expected radar signature and identified the airplane on his screen as it departed from Cordova. He continued tracking its progress during subsequent radar plots over different time intervals.

The aircraft was observed following the correct flight route until 0435, when its position changed to approximately twenty miles off the intended airway. At that time it was plotted over Bligh Island on a heading of 295°. The next radar scan at 0440 showed a position further off course, approximately three miles west of Columbia Glacier, but on a different heading that approximately paralleled the coastal mountains on the north side of Prince William Sound and the Amber One airway, twenty-eight nautical miles south.

When the Air Force radar operator advised his supervising officer of the situation, it was decided that flight 201's pilot was only deviating over the glacier for the viewing benefit of the passengers. There was no attempt by Air Force personnel to contact the crew or to alert Anchorage Air Route Traffic Control of the aircraft's position off the airway. Before the next radar plot was taken at 0445, the blip had disappeared from the screen.

Numerous attempts were made by Anchorage Air Route Traffic Control to contact Flight 201 after it failed to report arriving over Whittier. Two other commercial flights on the same airway also attempted contact with the missing airplane, but there was no response. Anchorage Air Route Traffic Control initiated standard emergency procedures for an overdue aircraft at 0503, and when further inquiries also failed, search and rescue units were notified.

Coast Guard and Air Force assets began a search of the area as soon as they could get airborne. By late morning over twenty aircraft were involved in the effort, including assets from the Alaska Air National Guard, Civil Air Patrol, Pacific Northern Airlines and Cordova Airlines. A general alert notice was also issued to all fishing vessels in Prince William Sound, and two Coast Guard cutters were dispatched from Kodiak to assist with a sea search of the coastal waters.

A wide area along the missing airplane's suspected flight route between Hinchinbrook and Whittier was systematically searched before further efforts began concentrating around the Chugach Mountains on the northwest side of Prince William Sound. Even then the search area encompassed several hundred square miles of the most extreme terrain in Alaska.

Huge, seemingly endless glaciers and towering, ice-encrusted peaks litter the landscape along the coastal range. The highest mountain rises over 13,000 feet and several more reach well above 10,000 feet. Countless snow-covered slopes, vertical canyons and smaller, but equally formidable mountains, stretch inland in every direction. Finding a missing airplane in such a vast territory, even one as large as the missing Lockheed Constellation, was almost an exercise in futility.

At 1830, an Air Force C-123 transport spotted an unusual color pattern near the summit of Mount Gilbert on the western side of Prince William Sound. As the pilot circled for a closer inspection, a

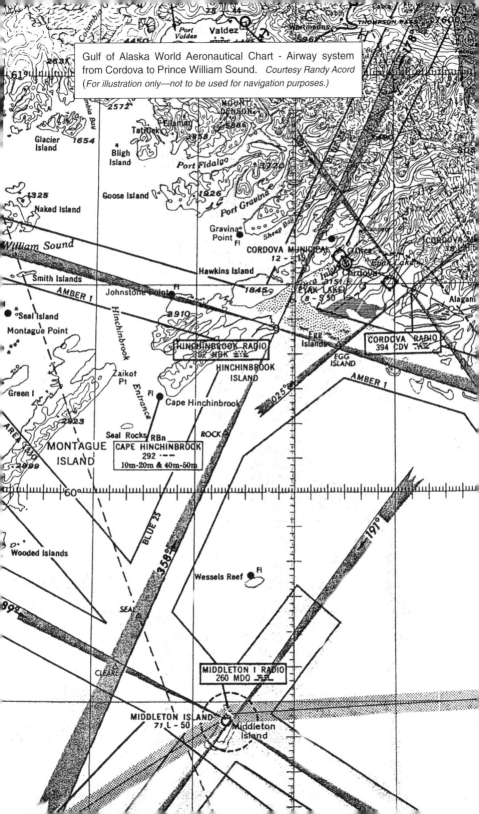

Gulf of Alaska World Aeronautical Chart - Airway system from Cordova to Prince William Sound. *Courtesy Randy Acord* (*For illustration only—not to be used for navigation purposes.*)

bright yellow life raft was revealed partially buried atop the snow in the scattered wreckage of an aircraft.

What were first thought to be only rocks and snow from a distance were in fact pieces of the missing airplane that had been carried down the slope by a recent avalanche. The crew stared in horror at the destruction below them, realizing they could easily have overlooked the area had it not been for the conspicuous yellow raft drawing their attention. Another avalanche or snowstorm could easily have covered the wreckage in the next few days, hiding any evidence of the airplane's location. Only their chance sighting prevented the Constellation from being added to the long list of Alaska's missing aircraft.

Mount Gilbert is located some forty-five nautical miles east of Anchorage and twenty-seven miles north of Whittier on the western edge of the Chugach Mountains, at an elevation of 9,638 feet. The Lockheed Constellation hit the eastern slope near the summit of the mountain, disintegrating on impact. What remained fell several hundred feet into deeper snow, with a resulting avalanche dispersing and burying most of the wreckage under a blanket of white powder. Only a small patch of blackened ice on the near vertical slope marked where the aircraft had first struck the mountain. No large pieces remained.

An Air Force medevac and two Army helicopters carrying a six-man rescue team were the first to land at the crash site that evening. It was their job to positively identify the aircraft and to search for any possible survivors. After arriving and overflying the site, it became immediately obvious from the amount of destruction that their second task would only be a search for the dead.

The helicopters were forced to land in the only safe area they could find, several hundred feet below the slide, which forced the search team to hike through deep snow and across a glacial ravine before reaching the wreckage. A piece of the fuselage was eventually found, identifying the debris as being from the missing Pacific Northern Constellation, but only one partially intact body was located. The search team also recovered several bags of mail and payroll checks that had been thrown clear of the other wreckage during the impact.

The ensuing accident investigation involved several government officials from the Civil Aeronautics Board, Federal Aviation

Administration, FBI and even the U.S. Postal Department. Overflights of the crash site were conducted by the agencies, but because of the inherent danger of further avalanches and the extreme difficulty involved in recovering the buried wreckage, it was decided a ground investigation would not be feasible. A ten-man team from the Alaska Rescue Group offered to return and search for more bodies, but Pacific Northern officials decided the hazards involved precluded any further attempts. The potential loss of even more life was not worth the risk. A tomb of snow would be the remaining victims' final resting place.

In the days following the accident, the government investigation continued gathering information that could help explain the circumstances of the crash. Inspections of the aircraft maintenance records and crew qualification records kept on file at the company did not uncover any irregularities.

It was revealed that no problems with the flight occurred between Seattle and Cordova, indicating the onboard communication and navigation equipment were working correctly. Both flight and ground checks of the navigation aids between Cordova and Anchorage also found them within tolerance and operating normally. Analysis of the weather patterns on the day of the accident showed no severe or extreme conditions near the flight route and all in-flight conditions that were encountered would have been as briefed. Other commercial aircraft, flying only minutes behind flight 201, also verified this.

When the initial investigation failed to uncover any clues to the accident, bench and flight tests were conducted on similar navigation equipment carried by flight 201. Different circuit and component failures were induced to see if an error could be caused on the corresponding flight instruments. Surprisingly, the test revealed a malfunction of the aircraft's fluxgate compass that could cause a subsequent error of as much as 80° on the remote magnetic imaging display, which was the primary instrument in the cockpit for indicating direction and course. In some situations the RMIs even remained on a fixed heading after a 090° course change.

An RMI was installed in front of each pilot on the instrument panel, allowing for separate tracking of the desired course. Both RMIs received their heading information from the fluxgate compass. Other heading information was available to the pilots in the

233

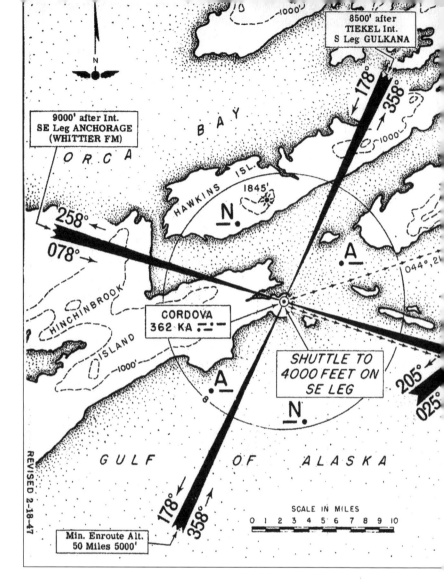

cockpit, however, including a magnetic compass and directional gyros. In order for the fluxgate compass to have caused the accident, the crew would have had to remain completely focused on the remote magnetic imaging system, without cross-checking their other instruments during the twenty minutes before impact.

The Amber One airway was a low-frequency radio range course between Hinchinbrook and Anchorage, which was established by radio signals being transmitted from ground stations along the route. Each side of the course line, approximately 015° in width, had an

234

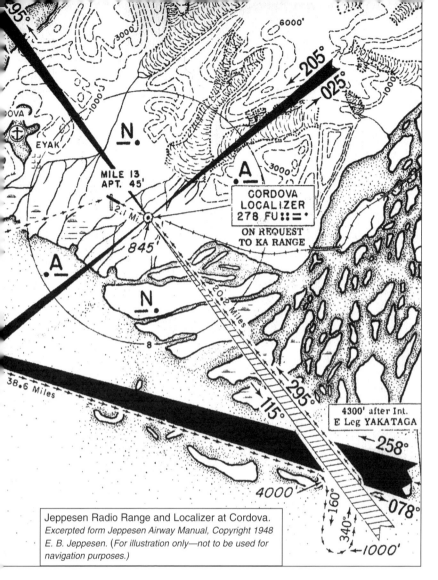

Jeppesen Radio Range and Localizer at Cordova.
Excerpted form Jeppesen Airway Manual, Copyright 1948 E. B. Jeppesen. (For illustration only—not to be used for navigation purposes.)

area of signal reception that gave off a distinct audio tone. Depending on where an aircraft was in relation to the course, the pilot would hear different audio tones at different volumes, providing the receiver was set on the correct frequency.

An automatic direction finder was also used on the aircraft for tracking the low-frequency airway, which displayed a heading indication on the RMI for the correct course to the station. Although it was not as accurate as newer VHF omni-directional range navigation systems coming into use, a large discrepancy would have had to exist between the automatic direction finder indication and actual heading when the aircraft turned off the airway, and should have alerted the crew.

If the crew had used the audio signal and automatic direction finder to continually verify their position, as was mandated by company policy, any erroneous display on the RMI should have become obvious by a loss of audio signal and increased deflection of the automatic direction finder needle. A deflection of approximately 035° would have existed once the aircraft turned north away from the airway.

It is also difficult to believe that the crew would not have noticed a sharp change in the aircraft's flight attitude as it turned off the airway, either from cockpit indications, such as the attitude indicator, turn and slip and other compass systems, or from possible visual references with the ground.

The pilot, Captain Chamberlain, should have noticed even a slight deviation from the normal enroute course. He had over 14,000 hours in the air, had been flying the same route for fifteen years and was equally familiar with the instrument procedures required for navigating the instrument airway. Other company pilots who had flown with him on the route stated that he always flew the Amber One airway along the "A" side of the course so he could monitor the audio signal and always utilized the automatic direction finder as a cross-check. For some reason known only to him, those course tracking procedures were not followed during his final flight.

Another possible theory is that the captain decided to divert off the airway and fly over the Columbia Glacier on the edge of the Chugach Mountains for the enjoyment of the passengers. It was not uncommon at that time for airline pilots to alter their flight path near scenic areas, and in fact continues today. For the captain to do so under instrument flight rules without a clearance from air traffic control, however, would have been an obvious violation of federal regulations. It is questionable why he would attempt a scenic flight along the coastal mountains anyway, when weather conditions along the coast at the time were predominately overcast below their flight level.

Weather conditions between Cordova and Anchorage included scattered to overcast cloud layers from 600 feet up to 15,000 feet, with only light precipitation and winds twenty to thirty knots at their flight altitude. Then again, as the crew did not receive an official U.S. Weather Bureau forecast, they might have been unaware of the expected cloud formations over Prince William Sound and wrongly assumed better sky conditions would exist around the glacier and mountains to the north of their flight path.

Crew incapacitation also seems unlikely since the last radio contact with the flight was at 0432, when the aircraft was already several nautical miles north of the airway and heading 035° to the right of the actual instrument course. Air defense radar was able to track the flight clearly as it proceeded on a northwest heading, then turned left on a parallel course to the airway before impacting the mountain.

The altitude of flight 201 also remained constant from the time it passed the Hinchinbrook Radio Range. Ironically, the last course change the aircraft made was southwest away from the higher coastal mountains. Mount Gilbert was the only obstruction above 9,000 feet between it and Anchorage.

The official Aircraft Accident Report determined the probable cause to be the crew's failure to employ all available navigation systems, with a contributing factor being the failure of Air Defense Radar to advise the flight or Anchorage Air Route Traffic Control of the potential hazard.

On June 19, five days after the accident, clergymen and airline officials flew over the crash site to conduct a memorial service for the passengers and crew. It was a solemn event only briefly mentioned in the local newspapers. Neither wreaths nor markers were dropped on the victims' final resting place. The mountain itself, encased with granite pillars and natural sculptures of ice, served as a much more fitting tribute.

A similar accident occurred in 1952, when an Air Force transport plane hit the south side of Mount Gannett at 8,900 feet while en route to Anchorage under instrument conditions. Mount Gannett lies only five miles south of Mount Gilbert in the same mountain range. All fifty-two military personnel onboard were killed on impact.

The Air Force believed this accident was caused by inadequate radio navigation from severe precipitation static occurring in the area at the time, as well as stronger than predicted winds pushing the aircraft north of the airway.

Unforeseen Circumstances

NOVEMBER 27, 1970

Most accidents are not as dramatic as a crash into a mountain or vanishing without a trace while on a long cross-country flight. Often accidents occur while on or near an airport during the takeoff or landing phase. A pilot's momentary distraction, or a minor mechanical failure during those critical moments, can easily place the aircraft outside its already slim margin of safety. When hundreds of people are added to the equation, the chance of fatalities increases dramatically.

On November 27, 1970, a DC-8 belonging to Capitol International Airways, and a military charter flight, was on a refueling stop at Anchorage International Airport. It carried 219 military passengers and ten crew members on a route to South Vietnam from McChord Air Force Base in Washington State. A second refueling stop was scheduled later in the route at Yokota, Japan, before continuing on to its final destination.

It had been a long day for the flight crew. The duty period had already exceeded seven hours when they touched down in Anchorage at 1532, with an equal amount of time still ahead. The long schedule was not unusual for them and they were accustomed to it, having flown the same route several times before. They were all experienced, senior crew members, selected for the charter flights because of those very reasons. Between the two pilots, flight engineer and navigator, they had over 52,000 combined flight hours, with more than 12,000 total hours accumulated in DC-8s.

The three-hour-and-forty-five-minute flight from McChord Air Force Base to Anchorage was routine except for an inoperable

238

engine pressure gauge on the number 1 engine. Freezing drizzle had been falling at the airfield for forty minutes by the time they arrived, coating the runway with a thin layer of clear ice that made for poor braking action. Reverse engine thrust and heavy braking pressure were necessary to stop the airplane before it could taxi to the terminal. After being directed into transient parking, company ground personnel chocked the wheels, all four engines were shut down and passengers deplaned before refueling began. A mechanic also conducted a walk-around inspection of the aircraft after it was shut down, checking visually for defects or potential problems. He specifically checked the landing gear assemblies for proper condition and serviceability. Nothing unusual was noted.

A maintenance technician also checked the engine pressure gauge that had malfunctioned in-flight and verified it as inoperable. It was not replaced at that time, however, since continued flight under those circumstances was still authorized by the company. Power settings for the number 1 engine could still be adjusted by correlating the readings from the other engine pressure gauges. It was a minor task that could easily be handled during the conduct of normal cockpit duties.

Fuel was added within a few pounds of the maximum gross weight of the aircraft while it sat on the ramp. Once the servicing was completed the engines were restarted, passengers reboarded and an instrument flight rules (IFR) clearance was requested for the next flight segment. The pilots had already filed a new flight plan and checked the enroute weather conditions while the aircraft was being serviced. Because of the persistent freezing drizzle falling at the airport, the aircraft was also de-iced before being allowed to taxi away from the terminal. It left the ramp at 1654 with clearance instructions to proceed to runway 06R, and hold for departure.

Current weather conditions at that airfield were reported as a 300-foot ceiling in freezing drizzle and fog, winds southeast at six knots and visibility five miles. Night had already descended over the area. Official sunset occurred at 1459, approximately a half-hour before the flight arrived at the airport. Temperatures were in the low 20s, a striking contrast to what they could expect on arrival in South Vietnam.

After taxiing into position for takeoff, the pilots waited for a minute and a half on the runway for their departure clearance to be issued by air traffic control. The captain briefed the crew on takeoff procedures at that time, stating that the first officer would handle the takeoff roll, while he assisted with the brakes, engine power settings and calling out of the airspeed. Once they received their IFR clearance, the final takeoff checks were completed.

At 1703 the captain adjusted the engine power to 80 percent, then released the brakes. The first officer took over, advancing the throttles to takeoff power while simultaneously aligning the nose with the runway centerline as they moved forward, being careful not to overcompensate and slide on the ice. As the aircraft increased in speed past 130 knots, the acceleration hesitated for a split second then continued normally until reaching approximately 145 knots. The speed and acceleration of the aircraft seemed to hesitate again for a brief moment before increasing to a rotational speed (the point at which an aircraft begins to pitch up into a takeoff attitude) of 153 knots, 1,500 feet from the end of the runway.

With the runway length decreasing rapidly, both pilots stayed on the controls, rotating the nose off the ground. The required takeoff safety speed was 163 knots, but the aircraft would not accelerate further past the rotational speed to attain the necessary lift. The pilots kept the nose up, trying to force the heavy aircraft into the air, but it stayed fixed on the ground until abruptly rolling off the end of the paved runway and onto the dirt surface extending beyond the threshold. Shutting off power to the engines was the only option at that point, which they did, but they could only watch in horror as the momentum carried the aircraft into increasingly rougher terrain.

The pilots held the nose wheel off the ground as long as they could, so it would not absorb the forward weight of the aircraft and collapse from pounding against the uneven surface. They succeeded initially, but 545 feet past the end of the runway the tail began dragging into the snow and dirt. A moment later the airplane plowed through a wooden fence, causing a fire near the left side engines. Continuing forward, it impacted an instrument landing system support structure a 1,000 feet from the runway, tearing loose components from the undercarriage and wings. Galley equipment, overhead racks and ceiling panels began breaking away from their mounts, injuring passengers and blocking emergency exits.

As the aircraft began slowing down and losing some of its momentum, the nose dropped, contacting the ground. Forward speed was still excessive, however, and it continued traveling unchecked for another 1,600 feet, before hitting a twelve-foot-wide drainage ditch running perpendicular to the runway, causing extreme structural damage.

The aft cabin was split open by the impact and all interior lights immediately stopped functioning. More pieces of the fuselage and wings were ripped away as the landing gear also collapsed, forcing the aircraft on its belly over the rough surface. Aviation fuel began spraying from the right wing and another fire erupted closer to the fuselage, spreading into the cabin area. Several flight attendant seats near the emergency exits folded in on themselves, injuring the very crew members responsible for assisting passengers during an evacuation.

The DC-8 finally came to a complete stop 3,400 feet from the end of the runway, after having split into three large sections. Most of the center fuselage remained intact, but the tail section had broken away thirty feet behind the main wreckage and the cockpit had separated from the fuselage near the forward bulkhead. Spilled fuel began entering the rear cabin area, adding to the already dangerous situation as the fire spread in from the wings.

With most of the flight attendants injured or incapacitated, several passengers took control of the situation and quickly began evacuating the others. Many in the forward cabin area were able to escape through the emergency doors, except for the forward galley exit, which was blocked by loose debris. All but one of the overwing exits was still usable. Once outside the aircraft, the passengers hurried away from the fire, which was rapidly turning into an inferno. Fuel was still spilling over the ground from the ruptured tanks as they moved away. A maintenance crew working on the east end of the runway at the time of the crash, arrived shortly after the airplane stopped and assisted many of the passengers in getting clear.

Other the passengers remained trapped toward the rear of the cabin area behind the wing exits. They perished in the flames and in the toxic smoke from the fire. A few managed to jump through a small break in the fuselage or squeeze through a partially blocked aft galley exit. Some near the wings also escaped by using the overwing and forward exits, but many had no chance of survival. Two rear-escape doors and another aft entry door could not be opened at all, blocking any escape during the brief seconds that were available. In the few minutes immediately following the crash, the fuselage was completely engulfed in flames.

The captain and first officer managed to escape through the forward windows, after finding the cockpit entry door blocked. The captain then helped several passengers exit from the fuselage before returning to assist the first officer in evacuating the injured flight engineer and navigator.

Within a few minutes of the accident the first airport fire-rescue vehicle arrived on the scene and began to spray chemical-retardant onto the raging fire, with little effect. Additional firefighting trucks from the airfield arrived shortly afterward, followed by emergency vehicles from several city, borough and local military units.

Explosions began in and around the aircraft shortly after the crash, hampering many of the firefighting and rescue attempts. Flames reportedly reached a height of 150 feet and continued for over an hour, completely consuming major portions of the center fuselage and wing areas. The cockpit and tail section were the only large pieces left intact after the fire was extinguished.

In all, forty-seven of the 229 occupants perished from the fire or resulting explosions, including one passenger who died two days later from severe burns. All the crew members managed to escape, with the exception of one flight attendant seated in the rear of the cabin. Over 100 survivors received some type of injury, many with severe burns from the ignited fuel. Eleven of the more seriously injured victims were transported to the military Burn Treatment Center in San Antonio, Texas.

Although the accident was later determined to be survivable, many more might have died had it not been for the fact that most of the passengers were disciplined military servicemen. Their training helped ensure an orderly exit of the aircraft without undue panic during the emergency, saving countless lives.

A recent disaster exercise conducted under similar circumstances at the airfield also contributed to the reduced number of fatalities. The previous training had properly prepared the different state, federal and military agencies for an actual disaster when it did occur. Well-rehearsed procedures and organized medical support that were coordinated during an earlier crash simulation helped to save numerous lives on that day.

An investigation into the incident began almost immediately.

The runway condition was checked only fifteen minutes after the accident, and showed a thin coating of clear ice covering the surface. Skid marks, pieces of rubber and fibers from the aircraft's tires were also found along the runway length. It appeared as if the tires had begun to deteriorate a short distance after the takeoff roll first began, disintegrating completely from subsequent blowouts and shredding of the outer casings.

Seven of the eight tires from the main landing gear, which had separated during the last moments of the crash, were later recovered. All seven tires exhibited some degree of blowout damage. Each had subsequently begun to deteriorate, and none appeared to have rotated during the takeoff acceleration. Each wheel brake assembly was also recovered, but none showed any signs of overheating or malfunction. The parking brake mechanism was found and checked as well, revealing no evidence of scarring or failure.

Both the flight data recorder and cockpit voice recorder were salvaged from the wreckage, but the cockpit voice recorder had been subjected to extreme heat and was unusable. The flight data recorder showed the aircraft had remained stationary on the runway for ninety-four seconds, then turned a few degrees to align with the runway centerline as it accelerated. A maximum speed of 152 knots was reached seventy-two seconds after initial application of takeoff power. As the aircraft ran off the runway and power was terminated, the speed barely decreased at first, but seconds later slowed dramatically as the aircraft hit the obstacles and began breaking apart.

A post-crash analysis of the cockpit showed the wing flaps had been properly set for takeoff. The pitot-tube switch was in the on-position, and both probes and airspeed indicators had functioned correctly. All the instrument indications were found to be normal. Other than the obvious deterioration of the main landing gear tires during takeoff, the accident board could identify nothing else as contributing to the accident.

A witness at the airport stated he heard two or three loud booming sounds from the aircraft during its long takeoff roll, and thought they were caused by tire blowouts. Most of the survivors also heard the loud reports, which they too associated with blowing tires. The sounds were not heard by the cockpit crew, probably due to their location forward of the main landing gear and the rapid acceleration of the aircraft.

The captain and first officer both stated that although the aircraft hesitated momentarily during acceleration, there appeared to be more than adequate runway available at the time for a successful takeoff. Even as the aircraft nose was rotated 009° off the ground near the end of the runway, they still thought they would make it safely into the air. At that point there was not much else they could do anyway, even if they knew there was a problem. Established procedures stated that once a critical engine failure speed of 138 knots was reached in the DC-8, the takeoff sequence should be continued until becoming airborne. In this case, both pilots still thought the aircraft would keep accelerating and reach takeoff speed before running out of useable runway.

Because of the substantial evidence pointing at multiple failures of the landing gear tires, the accident board investigated several factors possibly causing the malfunction. The chance that the parking brake might have been unintentionally left on before takeoff, or had not completely released, was investigated but could not be supported. A statement from the captain confirmed that even though the aircraft was parked and chocked on the ramp for refueling, he had released the braking mechanism specifically so it would not stick during the long wait, and did not reset the parking brake again. The rest of the cockpit crew substantiated his statement.

Improperly installed brake systems or wheel assemblies were other probabilities, but post-crash inspections of the recovered components revealed no unusual wear patterns or scoring of the surface areas. After the aircraft first arrived at the terminal in Anchorage, a mechanic had inspected each tire and wheel assembly and found no evidence of malfunction. Tire inflation pressures and tread conditions were also observed at the time as being normal.

A third possibility was a malfunction of the brake system after the aircraft began taxiing or while holding in position on the runway. It seemed the most likely scenario since other major airlines experienced some incidents of slow or incomplete brake release on a few of their DC-8 aircraft.

By analyzing the track patterns of the accident aircraft as it taxied to the runway, it was determined that the tires rotated correctly before the airplane stopped on the runway, while awaiting the takeoff clearance. From that point the marks and tire remnants along the runway indicated that the tires did not rotate at any time after takeoff power was applied, and subsequently began a catastrophic deterioration as the aircraft increased in speed. Because of the sliding effect that occurred on the ice-covered surface, the friction caused by the non-rotating tires was comparable to a normal acceleration and undetectable by the crew. As the momentum continued, however, the frictional drag being applied on the tires and wheels increased accordingly, limiting the airspeed necessary to attain takeoff.

After an in-depth analysis of available evidence, the accident investigation board determined the tires had overheated during the long, two-mile taxi to the departure runway, because of the heavy gross weight of the aircraft. While it remained in position for takeoff, the heat and weight on the tires caused them to melt through the ice. As takeoff power was applied, braking action of an unknown source was somehow applied to all eight main wheels, causing the tires to skid forward over the surface instead of rotating. The tires' inability to rotate resulted in degradation and subsequent blowouts.

The accident board also concluded that the impact forces encountered during the crash sequence were not severe enough to cause fatal injury. All the deaths were attributed to post-crash fires and explosions.

The board submitted several recommendations to alleviate similar occurrences in future incidents. They included a recommendation that the Federal Aviation Administration determine and implement updated takeoff procedures for appraising time and distance references during acceleration, which were currently used to establish critical engine failure speeds. In addition, upgraded fuel-system fire safety devices were recommended on all commercial carrier aircraft, for the prevention and control of in-flight and post-crash fires. Design improvements were also urged for airline interiors, to correct unsafe crew seats and restraining devices, as well as the dangerous use of flammable cabin materials.

The procedure for using 100 knots as the critical engine failure speed, which was in effect at the time of the accident, was later discontinued by the Federal Aviation Administration as being ineffective. The recommendations for improved fuel system safety devices were also implemented. New design improvements for passenger safety have also been advanced with each new generation of aircraft. How much safety is ultimately enough, and at what point it becomes cost prohibitive, depends on who is making the final argument.

A Matter of Intoxication

JANUARY 13, 1977

The normal duties of an aircrew member encompass many additional responsibilities over and above their everyday routine. Whether as a captain, first officer, flight engineer, navigator, or flight attendant, the crew member is responsible not only for performing his or her individual tasks, but also for operating as a cohesive member alongside the rest of the flight crew. Communication is a principal part of that process. Without adequate communication, essential crew coordination breaks down, severely jeopardizing the safety of the aircraft, the passengers and the other crew members.

The pilot-in-command is ultimately responsible for the conduct and accomplishment of the flight, and the final authority for the safe operation of the aircraft. An individual is placed in that position of authority because of superior experience and judgment. Sometimes that authority can negatively influence the amount of communication between the rest of the crew and the pilot-in-command, but it should never be allowed to progress to the point of becoming a safety issue.

For any crew member to be reluctant to address a potentially unsafe situation is inexcusable, regardless of the circumstances. If one of the crew should become mentally or physically impaired it would be an obvious safety issue. Regardless of what any individual's position of authority, reputation, or influence might be, their condition should never be allowed to endanger the aircraft. Other crew members must step forward and bring the situation to someone's attention, especially when it concerns the pilot-in-command.

Several decades ago alcohol abuse might have been more socially acceptable, but an intoxicated person was still not permitted to operate a vehicle, much less a commercial airliner. How then could a noticeably impaired pilot be allowed to assume his duties without any of the crew or company officials saying or doing anything about it? It seems unlikely, yet that is exactly what happened in the following accident. Five people lost their lives because of a captain's obvious intoxication and his crew's choice to ignore it.

Japan Airlines flight 8054 was a chartered DC-8 transporting livestock from Moses Lake, Washington to Tokyo, Japan. An en route stop at Anchorage was planned for refueling and a change of crews. The entire cargo consisted of fifty-six cattle, enclosed in specially designed holding pens mounted to the cabin floor. A sales agent from the Colorado-based export company that had contracted the flight and the company's director of operations were also on board with the three crew members.

There were no problems with the aircraft or cargo during the flight to Anchorage. It arrived at 0503 and promptly taxied to the service ramp for refueling. The crew shut down the engines, completed their post-flight checks, then disembarked to brief the oncoming crew. A maintenance team from Japan Airlines and some contract mechanics began servicing and inspecting the aircraft in preparation for the next flight.

During the walk-around inspection of the aircraft, two contract mechanics noticed ice accumulation on the inlet guide vanes and outer surfaces of the engines, and reported their findings to the Japan Airlines representative. They requested that the next crew be advised to use the anti-icing system before departure, so the ice could be properly cleared. No icing was observed on any wing surfaces or other structural components, and no other problems were identified.

At approximately 0445, the oncoming crew left their hotel in Anchorage for the Japan Airlines dispatch office at the airport. A local taxi driver who was transporting the captain, first officer and flight engineer, became so alarmed at the apparent intoxication of the captain that he immediately informed his company dispatcher of the situation once he had dropped off his passengers at the airport. He stated that the appearance and actions of the captain were reflective of a very strong influence of alcohol. The taxi driver explained

247

the captain's movements as being uncoordinated, his speech slurred and incoherent, and his face flushed with a glazed look in his eyes.

The taxi company's dispatcher did not inform Japan Airlines directly about the intoxicated captain, but instead called the operations office of the local maintenance company, which was under contract with the airline.

When the dispatcher told the operations agent that an apparently drunk pilot had been driven to the airport for an outgoing flight, the agent stated that if it were true, Japan Airlines would certainly notice the condition of the pilot and act accordingly. A half-hour later the agent did notify his own line manager of the phone call, but they agreed that if the captain was indeed intoxicated, personnel at Japan Airlines would stop the flight.

When the oncoming crew entered the Japan Airlines office, the outgoing pilots and flight engineer briefed them on the status of the aircraft and Japan Airlines operations personnel supplied new weather and flight planning information. The dispatch procedure was accomplished fairly quickly, with apparently no one in the office noticing anything unusual in the captain's behavior. Even more remarkable was the fact that the first officer and flight engineer, who had been with the captain since earlier that morning, seemed unconcerned about his condition, or at least not enough to bring it to anyone's attention.

At 0515 the crew was taken out to the aircraft by a company vehicle. They boarded with the two officials from the export company and began preparing the cockpit for departure. The driver of the vehicle, who also happened to be a friend of the captain, later stated he appeared in good condition.

After the cockpit checks and pre-start checks had been accomplished, air traffic control issued a weather update and instrument flight rules clearance. Conditions at the airport were reported as sky partially obscured, and visibility one-quarter-mile with fog. All four jet engines were then started in sequence, with each verified by the corresponding instruments in the cockpit as operating correctly.

Once the after-start checks had been completed, the first officer asked the tower controller for taxi instructions. A moment later the flight was cleared to runway 24L. As they moved toward the runway the taxi checks and before takeoff checks were completed. The captain also briefed the crew on abort procedures, but he had to be reminded of the previously reported icing in the inlet guide vanes of the engine. Only then was the engine anti-icing system engaged. The aircraft de-ice system, which was different from the anti-icing system and designed to keep the airfoil surfaces free of ice accumulation, was not turned on.

There was some confusion in the cockpit when the captain taxied onto runway 24R instead of 24L. At one point the captain even disagreed with the tower controller when advised they were on the wrong runway. A moment later the situation was cleared up and the tower provided further taxi instructions. They taxied into position on 24L and called ready for takeoff at 0633.

The confusion in the cockpit was not only a result of the captain's condition. From cockpit voice recordings recovered after the accident, both the first officer and flight engineer seemed uncertain about some instructions being received from the captain and over the radio, but were reluctant to ask questions. This was probably due in part to the cultural difference and language barrier, since the captain was American and the two crew members were Japanese. There was also a wide difference between the experience level of the captain and that of the two junior officers, leading to a possible over-confidence by the crew in the captain's abilities.

At 0634 the aircraft began its takeoff roll and accelerated normally down the runway. During takeoff the aircraft pitched up above a steeper than normal climb angle, causing a corresponding reduction in airspeed and subsequent loss of lift. Buffeting was heard in the cockpit almost immediately after takeoff, which was indicative of an approaching stall, but nothing was done to correct the excessive pitch angle. The first officer called gear up, and a second later the flight engineer announced they were too steep.

Instead of correcting for the impending emergency, the captain increased the pitch angle even further and began drifting left. There was an exclamation of alarm from the first officer and sounds of the stick shaker could be heard in the cockpit. The flight engineer then shouted in alarm as the stall audio warning system was activated. A second later the airplane hit the ground, broke apart and burst into flames. None of the five occupants survived.

One witness who was replacing a light on the taxiway near the end of the runway, saw the flight climb about 100 feet then drift left and fall back rapidly toward the ground. Later examination of the crash site revealed that the airplane initially impacted a small hill 1,000 feet beyond the runway and almost 200 feet left of the centerline. The aircraft remained airborne from that point while continuing over an access road, then hit the ground again 800 feet past the first point of contact. All four engines broke away from their mounts as the wings and fuselage separated into several sections.

Small fires started in several areas along the aircraft's debris trail immediately after the initial impact. A larger fire soon engulfed the main wreckage, heavily damaging the cargo section and wings. The cockpit and tail sections, which had separated from the fuselage during the collision, were the only portions left relatively untouched by the ensuing fire. Impact forces caused severe damage to the cockpit area, where all five occupants were located, crushing or separating most of the seats and internal structures. Death from multiple injuries was almost instantaneous.

As the fuselage hit the ground and broke apart, the eight cattle pens were torn loose from their fittings, scattering dead animals and twisted pieces of metal throughout the wreckage. It was a gruesome sight, and one observer who arrived shortly after the accident described the scene as comparable to a battlefield.

Airport fire and rescue vehicles reached the site approximately five minutes after the accident, but by then the small amount of flame retardant they carried had little affect on the raging fire. Other emergency vehicles responded from several local fire stations a short time later and eventually succeeded in dousing the flames. Heavy fog over the area remained throughout most of the morning, hampering many of the response and recovery efforts. The airport was closed to further traffic until much later in the day.

National Transportation Safety Board investigators from Anchorage were on scene shortly after the accident and an additional twelve-man team arrived from Washington D.C. the following day. A thorough examination of the evidence and recovery of the black boxes began almost immediately.

It was determined that the impact occurred on a heading of 230°, scattering wreckage over a 1,600-foot area southwest of the runway. There was no indication of fire or explosion before the crash, and no signs of structural failure or flight control malfunction prior to impact. All four engines were examined, showing normal operation comparable with takeoff power being applied.

Each engine's anti-icing valve was determined to be in the open position. The aircraft weight and balance was determined to have been within allowable limits. There was also no evidence of the cargo having shifted in-flight. The small pens holding the cattle were small and designed to restrict forward and lateral movement, although there was no established Federal Aviation Administration criteria for doing so. Another accident involving a cargo of live animals eventually resulted in the Federal Aviation Administration requiring that specific design and installation standards be implemented for all livestock restraining systems.

An examination of aircraft maintenance records and interviews with the previous crew revealed no pre-existing problems or maintenance concerns about the aircraft. No communication difficulties were reported and analysis of the radios after the accident found them functioning correctly. The radio transmissions that had to be repeated by tower personnel to the captain during the airplane's taxi to the runway were probably reflective of the mental state of the captain at the time.

The Pitot-static system on the aircraft, which measures ram and static air pressure for an accurate determination of airspeed, was found free of any obstructions during post-crash analysis, indicating normal airspeed indications should have been present in the cockpit. However, if the system had been obstructed with ice at the time of the accident, heat from the resulting fire would have destroyed any evidence. The stall warning system was also recovered, showing no signs of malfunction.

Runway lighting conditions were not believed to be a factor. Even though the accident occurred during the hours of darkness with reduced visibility, the high-intensity runway lights, runway centerline lights and approach lights were on and functioning correctly.

Weather conditions at the time of the accident were as previously stated. The freezing level was at the surface and temperature and humidity were conducive to icing. It was determined that when fuel was added after the ground inspection, the warmer temperature of the added fuel could possibly have caused rime ice to form on the outer surface of the wing as water vapor in the fog came into contact with the metal skin. Since the de-ice system was not activated before takeoff, any accumulation of wing ice would still have been present at the time of takeoff.

After analysis of the flight data recorder and a comparison with other DC-8 takeoff criteria in similar circumstances, the accident board determined rime icing was probably present on the airfoils at takeoff, which contributed to the aircraft stall. The ice would have reduced the angle of attack necessary to cause a stall, and would explain why the stall warning system did not activate earlier in the accident sequence.

Even without the stall warning system, the accident board believed the captain still had ample notice of an impending stall by the increased buffeting occurring in the aircraft. If not for the excessive pitch attitude applied during takeoff, it was doubtful if the stall would have occurred at all. After the buffeting began and the flight engineer stated the climb was too steep, the captain aggravated the situation by increasing the pitch attitude even further.

Examination of the crew's flight records showed all had received proper certification and training. The captain was well qualified and experienced, with over 23,000 flight hours. Both the first officer and flight engineer were also experienced, although not at the high-hour level of the captain. Captain Marsh's DC-8 flight experience exceeded 4,000 hours, while First Officer Akitani and Flight Engineer Yokokawa had 1,200 and 2,500 hours respectively.

Autopsies conducted on the bodies revealed no drugs or alcohol in the first officer or flight engineer, but the captain had a blood alcohol level that was over twice the legal limit. The amount was high enough to cause significant mental confusion and physical impairment. Thirteen people who had been in contact with the captain during the twelve hours before the flight gave conflicting testimony. Friends of the captain said he had not been drinking in their presence and he displayed no indications of having done so. Six other individuals, however, stated he had been drinking or showed definite signs of being under the influence of alcohol.

In the accident board's final analysis, it was determined the aircraft had initially lifted off the runway in a 015° pitch attitude, 005° higher than normal. Airspeed was 164 knots during rotation, but began decreasing almost immediately. As the airplane's airspeed began slowing, a buffeting effect occurred from the subsequent reduction in lift, which continued to intensify. The angle was further increased to 018° of pitch, at which time the aircraft reached a height of 160 feet. It then stalled and abruptly fell at 3,000 feet a minute until hitting the ground.

The performance of the aircraft was found to be a direct result of the captain's improper control inputs, which were compounded by airframe icing. His physical and mental capabilities were determined to have been diminished by the effects of alcohol, to the point he was incapable of performing his duties.

The following facts were specifically mentioned: Marsh got lost while taxiing to the specified runway, rotated off the runway at a faster than normal airspeed, applied an excessive pitch angle after takeoff, failed to recognize the indications of an approaching stall and did not apply appropriate corrective action.

The crew's failure to stop the captain from flying and to notify company officials of his condition was a contributing factor.

An Accident Waiting to Happen

NOVEMBER 23, 1987

The Beech 1900C twin-engine fixed-wing was a sleek-looking aircraft, ideal for small capacity passenger flights. Ryan Air Service, a rapidly expanding commuter airline in Alaska, owned three of the Beech 1900s in addition to twenty-six other aircraft. The company primarily used the airplanes for cargo and passenger service into mid-sized communities with improved runways and service capabilities.

In 1987 Ryan Air Service was the largest air-taxi operation in Alaska, maintaining eight different crew bases and four maintenance bases employing over 250 people. It provided service to eighty-five villages and cities across the state, including Dawson, Yukon. At the time, Ryan Air Service was also negotiating for a commercial contract on the proposed Alaska-Siberia air route.

On the day of the accident, Captain Deliman and First Officer Stoltzfus arrived for work in Anchorage at 0600 in preparation for their flight assignments. They were assigned the newest Beech 1900C in the fleet, purchased only one year earlier.

By 0730 they were in the air flying a round-trip flight to Iliamna, followed by another round-trip flight early in the afternoon to St. Marys. Their last flight of the day was to be a regularly scheduled run from Kodiak to Anchorage, with brief intermediate stops planned at Homer and Kenai.

Deliman had been upgraded to captain from a flight officer position only six months previously, but he had over 7,000 total hours in the air and over 4,000 hours in Beech 1900s. Other pilots in the company considered him to be a competent, well-trained pilot, very thorough in the operation of the aircraft.

First Officer Stoltzfus was a designated flight instructor and check pilot in single and small twin-engine aircraft for Ryan Air Service, as well as the company's director of training. He had been flying the larger Beech 1900s for one year and was working toward his captain rating. His total experience included over 10,500 flight hours, with 300 of those hours in Beech 1900s as a first officer.

Upon landing in Kodiak at 1709, the pilots taxied the aircraft in front of the operations building and shut down the engines. They both exited the cockpit to assist with off-loading of the passengers and cargo. A company agent who came out and met them was instructed to add no additional fuel for the return flight, since there was already more than an adequate amount remaining in the tanks. The available weight could be used for cargo instead.

A full complement of new passengers and baggage was waiting to be loaded. Most of the nineteen individuals were sportsmen returning home from recent hunting trips in the Kodiak area. The cargo consisted of personal luggage, hunting gear, numerous packages of wild game and seafood, and two hunting dogs in kennels.

The first officer made a rough calculation of the useable weight on the aircraft and told the service agent it could hold 1,500 pounds of cargo, which he requested be brought out for loading. At the time it seemed like an unusual request to the agent, but she did not mention her concern and complied with the first officer's instructions, even though other Beech 1900 pilots never hauled more than 1,200 pounds of cargo.

Both pilots helped the passengers into the aircraft and assisted the baggage loader with positioning the cargo in the small nose compartment, forward cabin compartment and two large aft cargo compartments. The company manifest showed them taking a total of 1,437 pounds of cargo on board. When they had finished, the baggage loader noticed the tailstand on the airplane was pushed down within an inch of the ground, considerably lower than he had seen on any previous flights.

After using every available space in the cargo compartments, the pilots secured the doors and prepared for takeoff. Flight 103 was issued an instrument flight rules (IFR) clearance to Homer by air traffic control at 1737, and they lifted off at 1742 under a clear winter sky. Their estimated time en route was thirty-three minutes. One of the passengers would later state he thought the aircraft would never get aloft. He said that at one point during the takeoff, the airplane lifted off the runway for a short distance, then fell back onto the runway and continued accelerating until finally becoming airborne again.

A few minutes after departure the flight reached a cruising altitude of 12,000 feet on the V-438 airway. Neither pilot reported any problems or concerns with the aircraft. At 1810 Anchorage Center cleared the flight to descend and maintain 6,000 feet, with an expected holding delay for other traffic. Current Homer weather was reported as a 3,500-foot ceiling, visibility twelve miles, winds 340° at nine knots, and a local altimeter setting of 29.31 inches.

After reaching the localizer at Homer and entering a holding pattern until 1819, air traffic control cleared the flight for the localizer/distance measuring equipment instrument approach to runway 3. Five minutes later the first officer reported they were on a two-mile final for the runway. Nothing more was heard from the flight. Witnesses near the airport observed the airplane rocking back and forth a few hundred feet short of the runway, then apparently stall and drop suddenly toward the ground. It hit hard just outside the airfield perimeter fence, then slid forward on its belly a short distance before crashing through the eight-foot-high chain-link fence and coming to a complete stop.

The landing gear was down and locked on approach, but collapsed on impact with the ground. Both sides of the empennage buckled from the severe force of impact, while the fuselage sustained wrinkles all along the outer surface between the nose and rear cargo compartment. Each wing was heavily damaged and part of the left cabin area was crushed.

All the passenger seats in the cabin separated at their attachment points as the frames twisted and bent during the crash, leaving thirteen passengers dead. The two cockpit seats remained attached to the floor, but were left torn or bent from the force of impact. Captain Deliman died during the crash, and the first officer and three other passengers died within the next twenty-four hours. The three remaining passengers sustained severe injuries, but survived, as did the two dogs that had been loaded in the rear cargo compartment.

City fire department vehicles arrived on scene within fifteen minutes of the accident and immediately doused the aircraft with foam retardant to reduce the chance of a post-crash fire. Rescuers then found most of the occupants strewn about the cabin, still in their broken seats with the seatbelts attached, but they were delayed in their efforts to extract the survivors.

Only the left front cabin door was accessible from outside because of loose cargo and structural damage blocking the other entry points, which severely limited the recovery effort and caused an extensive delay. Each individual had to be carefully moved and repositioned onto a stretcher board then passed through the narrow door opening before the next person could be taken care of.

Rescue workers also had a problem locating the master switch in the cockpit that shut off all the electrical power. None of the rescuers were familiar with the aircraft and the switch was not clearly marked. They could not locate it for forty-five minutes, and an attempt to remove the injured first officer before the power was shut off resulted in electrical arcing from the instrument panel wiring. Fearing a possible electrical fire, they were forced to leave him in place until the battery was finally located in the right wing and disconnected. All the survivors were eventually removed to the nearest medical facility for treatment.

The ensuing National Transportation Safety Board investigation uncovered several problems with the aircraft and Ryan Air Service that had contributed directly to the accident. They determined that the pilots involved in the accident had not accurately computed the weight and balance or center of gravity limits for the flight, resulting in an excessive aft center of gravity and eventual loss of control during the approach. Federal regulations specifically placed responsibility for computing the weight and balance on the crew. According to the company's own operations manual, which was approved by the Federal Aviation Administration, center of gravity computations were to be recorded by the crew prior to each leg of flight and kept on file for thirty days at the home base.

By the accident board's most conservative estimate of the cargo weight, which allowed for an increase in weight due to wet conditions at the accident site when the cargo was recovered, it was determined that the actual load carried on board the aircraft was 2,231 pounds. The maximum cargo capacity for the three baggage compartments was only 1,910 pounds, including 150 in the nose, 250 in the forward baggage compartment and 1,510 in the aft cargo area. Flight 103's actual takeoff condition was therefore 321 pounds over the allowable weight. Company policy also limited the 1900's maximum cargo and baggage weight, when departing from Kodiak with a full passenger load, to 1,100 pounds.

In the computation of the aircraft's center of gravity by the accident board, again using the most conservative estimate for the placement of the cargo, it was found the aft center of gravity was 8.43 inches past the maximum limit at takeoff and 8.64 inches past the maximum limit upon arrival at Homer. Additional calculations using the least conservative estimate of cargo distribution placed the aft center of gravity 10.86 inches past the maximum limit at takeoff and 11.2 inches over during the landing attempt. A shift in the center of gravity further aft between the takeoff and landing was caused by a change in weight distribution due to fuel consumption.

Flight tests were then conducted on a BE 1900 with similar loading conditions, revealing that the aircraft's controllability began deteriorating as its center of gravity moved further aft. It was determined that when the center of gravity was seven inches past the aft limit, the aircraft would require constant control inputs to maintain level flight, and if it was executing an approach with full flaps applied, a loss of control could result. At eleven inches past the center of gravity limit it was almost impossible to control the aircraft under the same conditions. Any abrupt control inputs, turbulence or power changes were especially critical in that they could easily place the aircraft in a nose high flight attitude that became unrecoverable.

Another problem was uncovered in the weighing of cargo at the company's Kodiak office. Agents had been memorizing the weights of different items instead of writing them down on individual pieces of cargo, and were using informal worksheets for computing aircraft loads. On the day of the accident the loading agent's own calculations for the cargo showed errors of 110 pounds above the 1,500 pounds the first officer had asked to be loaded. In reality, the total weight of the items was well over 2,200 pounds. Ironically, postcrash analysis revealed that if a cargo weight of 1,500 pounds had actually been loaded at Kodiak, which would have moved the center of gravity 3.5 inches beyond the aft limit, the aircraft would still have been controllable.

The average weight of passengers being used for weight and balance calculations was also found to be well below normal. A winter weight of 165 pounds was being used for passengers at the time of the accident, which included small carry-on bags. However, it was still the crew's responsibility to ensure the average passenger weight was accurate for each flight. The average weight of the passengers on flight 103 was determined to be 190 pounds. The Federal Aviation Administration later changed the average passenger weight for flights in Alaska to 180 pounds.

Structural icing was not believed to have been a cause of the accident, even though 0.38 inches of rime ice were found on the leading edge of the wings after the crash. Icing certification tests conducted on the aircraft showed no noticeable changes in the handling characteristics or controllability with up to one and a half inches of ice on the leading edge. The pneumatic de-icing boots installed on the aircraft allowed flights into icing conditions, but the Operator's Manual recommended an accumulation of one to one and a half inches of ice before the system was activated. The 0.38 inches of rime ice found on the leading edge were therefore found to be insignificant.

A weather forecast for the Cook Inlet area at the time of the crash called for occasional moderate rime icing in clouds and precipitation, from the freezing level to 10,000 feet. Thin ice had also been reported on the runway at Homer prior to the accident and a pilot reported encountering moderate rime icing in clouds at 5,000 feet, approximately forty miles north of Homer, ten minutes before flight 103's arrival.

Testing of the passenger seats was conducted after the accident by Beech aircraft. The designs were found to exceed federal requirements, although impact forces during the accident were determined to be significantly above the structural capability of the seats. It was estimated that they were subjected to over 8g of downward force and 12g of longitudinal force during the crash.

Analysis of the accident aircraft showed the trim wheel and corresponding trim cables were against their stops in the full nose-down position. The position of the wing flaps before impact could not be determined, but the cockpit's flap handle was in the up position, and the right flaps were found at a transient position between 007° and 012°. Company policy stated the flaps would be set at 035° during each landing.

Numerous violations by Ryan Air Service were also uncovered

during the accident investigation. They found that the Federal Aviation Administration had recorded twenty-two violations since 1980, and the company had a history of fatal accidents and aircraft damage incidents. A Federal Aviation Administration report still in progress at the time of the accident, detailed even more violations, many categorized by the inspecting officer as "flagrant".

A month after the accident the Federal Aviation Administration initiated a special investigation of Ryan Air Service. It found many of the company aircraft were not maintained in accordance with regulations during the previous six-month period. The extent of the violations was so obvious to the inspectors that they concluded the company's maintenance operators were deliberately disregarding regulations. Further inspections were subsequently discontinued by the Federal Aviation Administration and a consent order was issued for Ryan Air Service to cease operations.

A particularly noteworthy incident had occurred in September 1986, when a Ryan Air Service mechanic had approached the Federal Aviation Administration with allegations that the company was pressuring its crews to fly unsafe and over-gross aircraft. He reportedly represented three of the company pilots. The mechanic stated that the pilots were willing to cooperate, providing they received immunity from any prosecution.

The Federal Aviation Administration denied the request, giving the reason that only the U.S. Attorney's office had the authority to grant such immunity. No further attempt was made to negotiate with the pilots or to obtain supporting documentation, nor was the U.S. Attorney's office contacted on the pilots' behalf. The Federal Aviation Administration district office did inspect the company's weight and balance records soon after, but found only one minor violation. One of the pilots who had made the complaint through the mechanic was first officer Deliman, later to be the captain of flight 103.

The findings of the accident board were released in December 1988. It was determined that both pilots were properly trained and qualified for the flight, but had failed to compute a center of gravity computation for the weight distribution on the aircraft. The excessive weight and placement of the cargo caused an extreme aft center of gravity of between eight and eleven inches past the allowable limit. A loss of aircraft control then resulted from an excessive nose high attitude during the attempted landing.

In an attempt to control the aircraft, it was believed the pilots probably retracted the flaps from the initial full up position, causing an increasing nose high attitude and loss of airspeed during the approach. They then applied additional power to recover the airspeed, which only increased the excessive pitch attitude further, until the airplane finally become uncontrollable.

The board also found that the Federal Aviation Administration's oversight of Ryan Air Service before the accident was ineffective. Previous inspections revealed a pattern of violations that were not fully corrected, and an accident history that justified a thorough examination of the entire operation by the Federal Aviation Administration. At a minimum, the board determined some degree of remedial action should have been taken. Other than a few minor fines imposed on the company by the Federal Aviation Administration, nothing substantial was initiated prior to the accident.

After Ryan Air Service ceased operations in January 1988, new management and operation policies were implemented. The company resumed air service in the summer of 1988, but on a significantly reduced scale.

This accident was the last involving ten or more fatalities on a civil aircraft in Alaska until the year 2001.

Whiteout

APRIL 6, 1944

Encountering a whiteout condition is an experience no pilot will ever forget. It has been compared to staring into a Styrofoam cup or flying inside a ping-pong ball. Whiteout occurs when a solid overcast condition exists simultaneously with a complete ground covering of snow or ice. The combined effect obscures the horizon and all visible terrain features. The loss of those visual references can then cause the pilot to become disoriented and lose control of the aircraft. Over-reaction by the pilot, or not reacting at all, can easily lead to disaster.

Avoiding a whiteout in the first place is, of course, the best procedure. But if the condition is encountered, the pilot should transition to the aircraft instruments and immediately attempt to either exit the whiteout condition or proceed under instrument flight rules. Any continued attempt at visual flight will usually result in vertigo and eventual impact with the ground.

Pan American Airways flight 08, an American Pilgrim 100-B out of Fairbanks, had arrived in Nome earlier in the day on a scheduled round-trip flight. The single-engine, ski-equipped aircraft departed on the return flight to Fairbanks at 1535, with scheduled stops at Moses Point, Nulato, Galena and Tanana. On board were the pilot, two company flight mechanics and three passengers. Cargo containers and mail sacks took up most of the remaining cabin space.

Captain Robert Bullis had been flying the Fairbanks to Nome route since August 1943 when he was first hired by Pan American. He had a total of 3,477 flight hours, was rated as a single- and multi-engine land and sea pilot, and was a qualified flight instructor. His experience in Pilgrim 100 type aircraft was limited, however, with slightly over 100 hours accumulated.

On departure from Nome the flight was cleared to operate under visual flight rules, and Captain Bullis was familiar with the instrument airway system and radio range stations along the route. Because of the relatively flat terrain in the Nome area, which provided limited visual references for navigation in the winter, pilots usually flew along the coast when traveling to the next stop at Moses Point, eighty-six miles to the northeast. By following the contrasting patterns between the landmass and sea ice, pilots could usually maintain visual contact with the surface of the ground without becoming disoriented. The radio stations along the route could also be tuned and fixed to verify the aircraft's position, or for direct instrument navigation between the two points.

Weather at the time of departure from Nome was reported as a 2,000 foot overcast ceiling with haze, light snow, and winds fifteen to twenty-five knots. Visibility would have been five or six miles if enough terrain features had been available for reference, but with no visible horizon or identifiable marks on the ground, forward visibility was almost non-existent further inland from the coast. There were no trees, large rocks or man-made structures to help distinguish the snow-covered surface from the overcast sky.

Shortly after departure, Captain Bullis established radio contact with another Pan American flight that was inbound to Nome along the coastal route from Moses Point. A few miles east of the airfield he turned the airplane inland away from the shoreline, intending to maintain a safe separation from the approaching aircraft until they had passed each other. It was probably his intention to turn back along the coast and resume navigation once the other aircraft was clear of his area. They passed abeam each other's position at approximately 1542.

A witness on the ground saw flight 08 turn north from its original heading along the coast, descending from an approximate altitude of 600 feet. The airplane continued to lose altitude until it disappeared below an area of low, rolling hills. The witness's view was partially distorted by haze and blowing snow over the several mile distance, but he stated that he thought it reappeared one more time at a very low altitude before vanishing completely.

Nothing further was heard from the flight and after it failed to arrive at Moses Point a search was initiated. The wreckage of the missing aircraft was located later that evening, three-quarters of a mile south of the low-frequency airway beam between Nome and Moses Point. It had impacted the eastern slope of a 240-foot hill at an elevation of 125 feet, about nine miles east of Nome and a few miles north of the coastline. The airplane appeared to have hit wing first while in a descending right turn at a high rate of speed, then flipped forward, tearing the engine away from the nose mounts. After skidding down slope into a shallow depression, the aircraft bounced over the edge and came to rest approximately sixty feet from the impact point on its right side. There were no survivors.

Rescuers at the scene reported that the occupants had died instantly upon impact. The pilot was found at his station in the cockpit, and the other five people were still in their seats along one side of the cabin. All the bodies were removed and taken back to Nome the first night.

A representative from the Civil Aeronautics Administration arrived at the crash site the following day, accompanied by three senior pilots from Pan American Airways and several mechanics to assist with the identification and recovery of aircraft components. The wreckage had been left relatively undisturbed once the bodies were removed, although some cargo and mail sacks that were easily accessible had also been carried away and properly secured. The weight and loading of the aircraft were later found to be within allowable limits for the flight.

A post-crash examination of the aircraft found no evidence of mechanical or structural failure prior to impact. The engine had been operating at normal power, and the controlled pitch propeller was set for cruise flight at the time of the crash. It was apparent that the occupants were unaware of any impending impact with the terrain. An analysis of the cabin area revealed the passengers were in the process of eating dinner, and the pilot had made no corrective inputs before hitting the ground.

The Civil Aeronautics Administration official flew the same route a short time later under similar weather conditions, finding there were insufficient references available on the ground for maintaining visual flight. It was established that the aircraft had been operating in predominantly whiteout conditions since shortly after

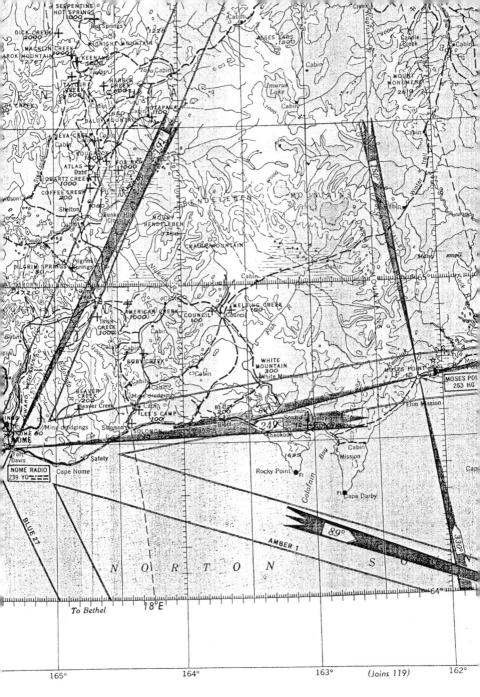

Seward Peninsula World Aeronautical Chart - Airway system around Nome and Moses Point. *Courtesy Randy Acord.*
(*For illustration only—not to be used for navigation purposes.*)

departure until impact at approximately 1548. A clock on the instrument panel had stopped working at precisely that time.

The accident board could not determine why Captain Bullis did not climb to a safer altitude to clear the terrain after turning inland from the coast. He was familiar with the area, the weather hazards and the radio range systems at Nome and Moses Point.

Since the temperature and precipitation at the time of the accident were conducive to icing, the board believed the venturi system on the aircraft could have malfunctioned, thus providing the pilot with false attitude and compass readings on his instruments. The resulting confusion, combined with a continued attempt at low-level flight in whiteout conditions, could have led to the impact. There was no substantiating evidence to support that conclusion, however.

It is also likely that the pilot simply experienced vertigo while turning in different directions over an area with no visual references. The subsequent false sensations of movement and position, due to a lack of visual information, could easily have caused him to simply fly the aircraft into the ground. Hundreds of documented accidents detail the same occurrences in all too many cases. Any pilot's continued attempt at visual flight while still operating under prevalent instrument conditions, especially while maneuvering the aircraft, will usually result in fatal consequences.

The Civil Aeronautics Board released the findings of the accident investigation in November 1944. The probable cause was determined to be the pilot's failure to recognize the aircraft's height above the ground due to heavy snow cover that masked all visual references.

Following the accident, all six occupants were returned to their homes for burial. Two of the three passengers were from Elim, near Moses Point, and the other had resided in Nulato, further east on the Yukon River. Captain Bullis' body was shipped back to his family in Yakima, Washington. Flight mechanics Moller and Seltenreich were buried in Fairbanks on April 12.

Fred Moller was a veteran Pan American mechanic at the time of his death, and one of the most respected individuals in the Alaska aviation community. He was raised in the territory after arriving there as a young boy in 1897 with his father. Most of his adult life had been spent around aircraft and he had earned a reputation as an outstanding mechanic. Some of his many close friends included the famous aviators Ben Eielson, Wiley Post and Joe Crosson.

During Moller's storied aviation career he was reputedly involved in more airplane accidents than any other Alaskan. Only fourteen months previously he had survived another crash in a Pilgrim 100-B near Nulato. He had walked out with the pilot whom he had pulled from the wreckage.

The airplane had crashed in the Nulato Hills in early 1943 after encountering bad weather, pinning the pilot in the cockpit when the engine was shoved backwards against his legs. Moller was uninjured and managed to crawl free of the wreckage, where he was then able to pry the pilot loose from the cockpit with a piece of steel pipe he found in the cabin. Luckily, the pilot sustained no more than a few minor injuries.

They waited at the crash site for two nights in the hope of being spotted by a rescue plane, but with no luck. Even if they were spotted, they feared a rescue was not feasible because of the rough terrain in the area that precluded a safe landing. Instead, they decided to try and walk out toward Nulato. Over the next five days, with only limited survival gear that included neither sleeping bags nor blankets, The two survivors walked eighty miles through terrible winter conditions before finally being rescued.

A year later, in the spring of 1944, Moller informed the airlines that he intend to leave his job on April 1, in order to start a mining business in the Interior. After twelve years with the company he had decided it was time to try a new career. Pan American was shorthanded at the time, however, and convinced Moller to remain a few days longer until another mechanic was available.

Ironically, he died on what was planned to be his last flight for Pan American Airways. Ted Seltenreich, the other experienced mechanic on board the aircraft, was to be his replacement. Moller was giving Seltenreich a check-out as a company flight mechanic at the time. They had been close friends for years since first meeting in Fairbanks in 1930.

The accident was the first to involve a fatality in eleven-and-a-half years of flying in Alaska by Pan American Airways.

Trust Your Instruments

DECEMBER 30, 1951

Flying is a dangerous business. Instrument flight can be especially hazardous, requiring the pilot to depend on instrument indications received inside the cockpit and his correct interpretation of those indications. It demands a much higher skill level than normal visual flight, and is developed through hours of instrument instruction and hands-on training. A pilot must not only have confidence in the indications on the instruments, but at the same time must recognize when they might be in error.

Instrument flight is much more of a challenge than visual flight, even when operating in weather conditions under predictable and repetitive circumstances. It is during unexpected circumstances that a pilot's ultimate ability to react and respond successfully will determine the difference between completing a flight safely, or not at all.

Transocean Air Lines was operating under contract with the U.S. Navy to provide transport service in the North Slope region of Alaska. Daily flights were often flown from the company's main supply hub in Fairbanks to any of several remote locations. Weather conditions were often harsh, even extreme at times, and always unforgiving. Experienced Arctic pilots were in great demand.

Flight 501 was a C-46F owned by the U.S. Air Force and under lease to Transocean Air Lines. At the time of the accident it was on the return leg of a round-trip service flight between Fairbanks and Point Barrow. After arriving at the northern coastal village earlier in the day, the twin-engine cargo airplane lifted off the runway at 1655 on an instrument flight rules (IFR) flight plan back to Fairbanks. An intermediate stop was scheduled at Umiat, located 150 miles southeast on the Colville River. Two pilots, six passengers and approximately 9,500 pounds of cargo and baggage were on board.

At 1754 the flight arrived at Umiat, where it off-loaded some of the cargo and four of the passengers. The crew reported no problems. Approximately two hours were spent on the ground. Both pilots received updated weather information for the remaining flight into Fairbanks and were advised of a recent change concerning the north leg of the Bettles Radio Range by the Civil Aeronautics Administration station operator. The north leg quadrant signal had been changed by a few degrees.

IFR flights between Umiat and Fairbanks were by low-frequency airway navigation, using the radio range signals at Umiat, Bettles, Nenana and Fairbanks. The flight plan specified that flight 501 would follow the Amber 2 airway south from Umiat to Bettles to Nenabank Intersection, then would intercept and follow the Green 7 airway east, direct to the Fairbanks Radio Range. A cruising altitude of 10,000 feet would be flown from Umiat to Bettles, then at 8,000 feet until Nenabank Intersection and 5,000 feet into Fairbanks.

The weather forecast that was received called for strong southwesterly winds from forty to sixty knots at the flight's cruising altitude between Bettles and Nenabank Intersection, and thirty to forty knots from the intersection into Fairbanks. Low ceilings were reported over areas of higher terrain, especially north and east of the destination. Light turbulence and light rime icing were expected along the flight route, along with periods of light snow.

Once the flight departed from Umiat at 1950 it proceeded normally and reported over the Bettles Radio Range a little over an hour later. From there the crew apparently did not compensate for the high wind speeds present on the south side of the Brooks Range. As the aircraft continued heading toward what the crew thought was Nenabank Intersection, the winds pushed them well east of the airway centerline. Their actual course track should have been apparent by the amount of increasing needle deflection on the automatic direction finder, but for some reason the pilots did not interpret the signal correctly.

At 2144 the flight reported twenty-five miles northwest of Nenabank Intersection, when their actual position was only twelve miles west of Fairbanks. The difference between their estimated position and actual position from the Nenana Radio Range was over 80° in error.

Both pilots were obviously confused by the signal indications they were receiving in the cockpit at that time, which was emphasized by the fact that they initiated a circling pattern for over three minutes in an attempt to establish their bearings. The pilots eventually confirmed they were on the west leg of the Fairbanks Radio Range, but falsely assumed they were much farther west on the beam than was actually the case.

After circling for a few minutes the pilots began tracking east again at 2148, mistakenly reporting to the controller that they were over Nenabank Intersection, descending to 5,000 feet and estimating passing over Fairbanks at 2200. Their position at that time was actually fifty miles further east, almost directly over the Fairbanks Radio Range station.

Nenabank Intersection is the point where the west leg of the Fairbanks Radio Range and north leg of the Nenana Radio Range meet. For some reason the pilots simply refused to believe their instruments or wrongly interpreted the indications, but if there was any doubt they could easily have done a cross-check by tuning in KFAR in Fairbanks, a local civilian broadcast station. They could also have asked for a position fix from the military radar operator at Eielson Air Force Base, located thirty miles to the east of Fairbanks, or verified the indications with other onboard navigation receivers.

Air Traffic Control was unaware of the aircraft's exact position, since no civilian radar existed in the area at that time. The controller assumed the pilot was where he said he was, and subsequently provided clearances based on those false position reports.

At 2155 the flight reported reaching 5,000 feet, and two minutes later air traffic control cleared it for the standard instrument approach into Fairbanks, with instructions to cross the Radio Range at 4,000 feet. The flight was actually well east of Fairbanks at that time by some thirty miles.

The flight acknowledged the message, but at 2205 the captain told air traffic control their automatic direction finder was not working and they had missed the cone of silence. He stated that they were turning back on the west leg at that time and would call when over the station. A minute later air traffic control asked the flight to confirm the message. The captain repeated that they were proceeding out on the west leg, which was a heading of 239°, when they were in actual fact still much further east of the station and well north of the beam.

It was probably the captain's intention to fly out on the west leg, but he was still initiating a left-hand turn at the time of the radio call. The instrument approach procedure at Fairbanks only authorized a right hand turn when reversing course on the east leg back to the station. Both pilots were familiar with the requirements, but for some reason decided to turn left toward higher terrain. Whether the turn was initiated from the pilots' estimated position or the actual position of the aircraft did not matter, since in both cases the location was still east of the station, requiring a turn on the south side of the airway for course reversal, not the north.

No further messages were received from the flight. Moments after the flight's last radio call at 2207, the aircraft impacted the 4,421-foot summit of Chena Dome, completely destroying the aircraft. All four occupants were killed instantly.

The airplane smashed into the slope only 100 feet below the crest of the dome while in a slight left turn, approximately thirty-four miles northeast of Fairbanks and fourteen miles north of the east leg of the radio range. Most of the aircraft's forward section disintegrated in the collision and the left wing was torn away by the impact. Forward momentum forced the fuselage further upslope, scattering debris in all directions before it flipped inverted onto the summit. What remained of the fuselage came to rest with only the right wing still attached and the tail assembly lying a short distance behind after it separated from the aircraft.

Within a few minutes of flight 501's last radio transmission, air traffic control attempted numerous contacts with the airplane. When it became apparent no response was forthcoming, several civilian and government agencies were notified of a potential emergency situation. Two Air Force C-47 search and rescue aircraft from the nearby military base were launched soon after, looking for possible signs of impact fires or flares in the area, but nothing was observed.

At the time of the accident, Fairbanks Radio was unaware of flight 501's confusion and assumed the airplane had gone down somewhere west of the radio range. Only when a military radar track of the flight path became available a short time later, was a more accurate area of the possible crash location established. The

Yukon River World Aeronautical Chart - Airway system from Fairbanks to Nenana. *Courtesy Randy Acord.*
(For illustration only—not to be used for navigation purposes.)

delay was not significant, since there were overcast cloud conditions over the city restricting visual flight. Lower conditions in the surrounding hills prevented much of the area from being adequately searched for the next three days.

A widespread search was initiated for the missing cargo plane the next day, with several military and Civil Air Patrol aircraft taking part. Continued low ceilings and persistent snowfall hampered the efforts, especially over higher terrain, while extreme low temperatures prevailed in the lower valleys. By then the focus of the search had been concentrated in the area where the flight was last tracked by radar.

Hope of finding survivors from the Transocean Air Lines C-46 increased when a blinking light was seen by one of the search aircraft the night of the 31st, fifty miles northeast of Fairbanks on the Chena River. A military helicopter dispatched to the area reported an SOS had been trampled in the snow. Unfortunately, the message was not from the missing airplane, but from a trapper who was stranded and near starvation. A local bush pilot soon supplied him with provisions to help him through the winter.

Marginal weather conditions existed over much of the search area until January 3rd, when the clouds finally lifted above the higher hills. Aircraft were able to overfly some of the mountains north and east of Fairbanks for the first time. Twenty-six military and civilian airplanes were dispatched for the only full day of decent flying weather since the C-46 had first disappeared. In addition to Air Force assets from Elmendorf and Ladd Field, the local Army base had ground and air equipment involved from its Cold Weather Testing Unit. The Civil Air Patrol, Civil Aeronautics Administration and Wien Alaska Airlines also had several aircraft assisting.

At 0950 on the morning of January 3, an Air Force Cessna LC-26 flew over Chena Dome and spotted the wreckage of flight 501. An H-19 military helicopter arrived a short time later, but was unable to land because of the heavy accumulations of snow and steep terrain around the accident site. It was able to hover over the crash site and confirmed the full extent of destruction and absence of any survivors.

Military "Weasel" snow-tracked vehicles attempted to reach the wreckage over the next two days, but were continually hampered by mechanical difficulties and snowdrifts up to five feet high. Local dog sled teams also tried reaching the crash site, but were equally unsuccessful.

Finally, on the 5th, an Air Force helicopter landed below the summit, allowing three officers to climb to the accident site. They conducted a preliminary investigation of the accessible wreckage before removing the bodies. Further attempts to land and examine the evidence were delayed until summer by the Civil Aeronautics Board, because of the continued risk of cold injuries and heavy snow cover that hid much of the debris.

From the initial examination of the wreckage by the Air Force officers, it was determined that the aircraft had hit the dome on a heading of 240° while in a slight left turn. Very little useful evidence was found in the cockpit and nose area, which had disintegrated on impact.

One engine and its propeller assembly were located under the snow, indicating that it was operating at full power at the time of impact, but the other engine could not be found. Examination of the broken tail assembly showed the rudder and elevators in a neutral position.

The aileron of the attached right wing was found extended a few degrees. The radios and instruments were located in and around the wreckage, but they all had extensive damage that did not allow an accurate determination of their operation at the time of the accident. A wristwatch from one of the survivors was also found, apparently having stopped at the exact time of impact. The fractured face showed a time of 2207.

A six-man investigation team from the Civil Aeronautics Board began an investigation of the accident after the wreckage was first discovered. Most of their findings were already completed before an extensive examination of the crash site was accomplished in June, when the snow had melted from Chena Dome. No significant evidence was uncovered at the accident site to change the Board's initial conclusions. If anything, additional analysis of the wreckage only further supported the information already obtained from the preliminary investigation.

On June 2, a Civil Aeronautics Board investigator was flown to the accident site by Air Force helicopter. He remained at the scene for two days, examining the available evidence from the wreckage. Both engines and propellers were located, confirming that they were

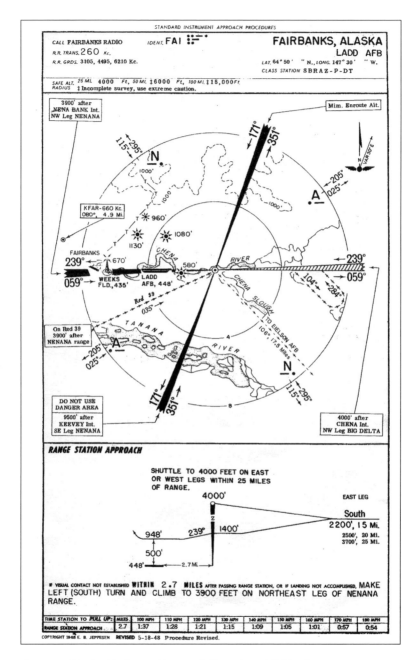

Jeppesen Standard Instrument Approach Procedure at Fairbanks.
Excerpted from Jeppesen Airway Manual, Copyright 1948 E. B. Jeppesen
(For illustration only—not to be used for navigation purposes.)

operating at full power before the impact. Even though the aircraft control systems were heavily damaged, the investigator was able to determine there were no indications of a malfunction prior to the accident.

The automatic direction finder control head from the cockpit was recovered and showed the frequency had been properly set to the Fairbanks Radio Range station. There was no evidence of fire either before or after the impact. The only change uncovered between the Civil Aeronautics Board investigation in June and the previous Civil Aeronautics Board findings, was the conclusion that the aircraft had hit while in straight and level flight, instead of during a slight left turn. The investigator did conclude, however, that the airplane appeared to have contacted the ground left wing first.

During the investigative process, analysis of the weather data showed the conditions to have been basically the same as forecast. It was determined that the maximum wind velocities were sixty knots from the southwest, although the flight probably experienced those higher winds as they flew closer to Fairbanks.

Another Transocean airplane had flown the exact same route ahead of flight 501, landing at Fairbanks fifty minutes before the accident. The captain of that flight stated radio reception was poor after passing Bettles due to precipitation static, making it impossible to receive the Nenana Radio Range and to fix Nenabank Intersection. He also explained that high winds became apparent only when his flight intercepted the west leg of the Fairbanks Radio Range, several miles east of Nenabank Intersection. From that point on he said the reception was reliable and their flight continued into Fairbanks without incident. The military radar plots of flight 501 recorded less than an hour later, showed the aircraft intercepting the west leg of the Radio Range over thirty miles east of Nenabank Intersection.

During the ensuing investigation of flight 501, the Fairbanks and Bettles low-frequency radio ranges were determined to be operating normally for the duration of the flight, as was the loop-type system in place at the Nenana Radio Range. Monitor reports from all three stations revealed no malfunctions or discrepancies. The radio range for Fairbanks was also flight-checked again on December 31, showing it to be functioning correctly. All radio communication between the pilot of flight 501 and the Civil

Aeronautics Administration operator in Fairbanks was found to be normal, and at no time did the pilot express a problem or concern before the flight's arrival over the Fairbanks Radio Range.

The accident board believed that when the automatic direction finder was reported as inoperative by the pilot of flight 501 it was probably operating correctly, but the crew had rejected the needle indications on the instruments because they thought their position was much further west. Even if the automatic direction finder had been malfunctioning, there were still two additional low-frequency receivers on the aircraft that could have been used to cross-reference their position and execute the approach on the radio range. One of the receivers was manual loop and the other was a marker beacon.

Once the flight passed over the Brooks Range from Umiat to Bettles, the crew failed to calculate the wind correction for the increased wind velocities, and began tracking a course away from the airway. Position reports and ground speed computations began increasing in error as the flight progressed further south. By the time the pilots made their 2144 position report, they were fifty-two miles southeast of their estimated position. There was also obvious confusion in the cockpit as estimated and reported arrival times over subsequent reporting points varied dramatically, showing their ground speed calculations jumping from 147 knots to as much as 425 knots between Nenabank and Fairbanks.

How two instrument-qualified transport pilots could become so confused inside the cockpit seems almost incomprehensible. The fixing of Nenabank Intersection and the Fairbanks Radio Range required two completely different interpretations of the appropriate instrument indications. Apparently the crew used none of the other navigation systems, nor did they cross-tune other radio facilities to verify their position. After passing what they falsely assumed to be the Fairbanks Radio Range, the pilots executed an unauthorized left turn to the north in an attempt to reverse course, resulting in impact with Chena Dome.

The Civil Aeronautics Board found the aircraft was properly loaded within center of gravity limits and below the maximum gross weight for the flight. It was determined to be airworthy upon departure from Point Barrow. Total time on the airframe was just under 2,000 hours. A 125-hour phase inspection had been completed on December 14. Weather data analyzed after the accident showed

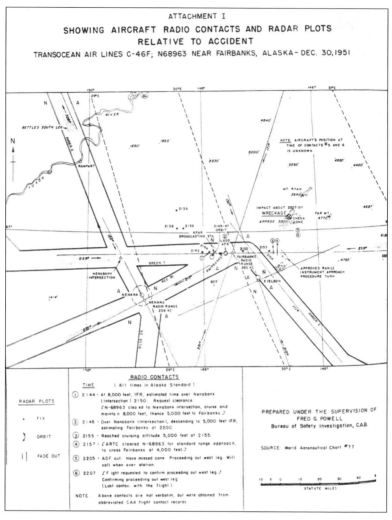

Accident Report image of flight route and airway structure
Excerpted from Civil Aeronautics Board Accident Investigation Report, File No. 1-0116
(*For illustration only—not to be used for navigation purposes.*)

instrument conditions were prevalent for most of the flight and substantially the same as forecast. In addition, the pilots reported no malfunctions of any aircraft systems, except for the failure of the automatic direction finder receiver once the flight passed the Fairbanks station.

The probable cause of the accident was determined to be the

failure of the pilot to follow instrument procedures and employ the enroute radio facilities correctly for navigation, which resulted in the aircraft becoming lost.

Although the crew was also found to be properly trained and certified for the flight, there were some previous weaknesses shown in the captain's instrument ability. Civil Aeronautics Administration records showed Captain Warren initially took the written airline transport pilot examination in October 1945, failing the section on radio navigation three separate times before eventually passing a year later in October 1946. He also subsequently failed the flight portion of the exam on two occasions. Test results at that time revealed a below-average ability in certain phases of instrument flight.

From early 1948 to mid-1950, Warren flew in the Fairbanks area, primarily as a single-engine pilot and flight instructor. He was hired by Transocean Air Lines in July 1950 as a first officer on C-46 aircraft and spent most of his time with the company flying the same Fairbanks routes with experienced captains.

In November 1951 he successfully passed the flight portion of the airline transport pilot examination with above-average ability on cone identification, but below average ability on automatic direction finder tracking and intersection fixing. A subsequent company flight check for his captain rating on the Fairbanks to Point Barrow route was passed on December 11. At the time of the accident he had over 7,000 flight hours, of which 116 were under instrument conditions, and 150 hours in link simulators.

The first officer joined Transocean in September 1951. He possessed over 2,500 flight hours, and had successfully passed the written and flight portions of the airline transport pilot exam in September and November respectively. The instrument portion of his exam reflected an average score.

All pilots hired by Transocean Air Lines for the Alaska Division were first employed as first officers to gain experience. Pilots had to have at least 2,000 previous flight hours, hold valid instrument and multi-engine ratings and pass a flight evaluation before being considered for employment. The majority of pilots had Arctic flying experience as well. Before a first officer could be upgraded to captain in the company's Alaska Division, he had to possess a current airline transport pilot rating with a minimum of 5,000 flight hours and pass a flight evaluation with the division's chief pilot, who was a certified Civil Aeronautics Administration examiner. Captain Warren met all the requirements for instrument flight, as did First Officer Irwin. Even though their instrument experience was not extensive, it certainly reflected the training and qualifications necessary for conducting safe flight operations in adverse instrument conditions. Whatever circumstances transpired in the cockpit that fateful evening, the result serves as a hard lesson of improper instrument navigation.

On January 12, 1952, only two weeks after the crash of the Transocean C-46, an Air Force C-47 out of Eielson Air Force Base disappeared under similar circumstances. The crew of five was on a round-trip instrument training flight over the same airway system from Fairbanks to Umiat. After passing Bettles on the return leg, a fifty-knot wind and the recent but unknown change in the Bettles Radio Range signal direction caused the crew to become disoriented.

Completely lost after six hours of flight and nearly 150 miles off course, the crew bailed out near the village of Ft. Yukon. The wreckage was not discovered until July of the same year. All of the crew had initially survived the bailout, but perished over the next several days from a lack of food and extreme weather conditions.

Some of the search crews were also confused by apparently erroneous signals from the Bettles Radio Range in the days following the C-47's disappearance, until it was determined the southeast leg radio signal had been swung 009° from the previous bearing, placing it in a different magnetic quadrant with a corresponding audible tone opposite from what was normally expected. Apparently the Air Force flight crews had not been properly notified of the scheduled directional change to the Bettles Radio Range, raising the question of whether the Transocean crew was also unaware of the discrepancy.

Visual Flight in Instrument Conditions

August 30, 1975

A low ceiling with moderate winds prevailed over Norton Sound as the twin-engine Fairchild F-27B departed southwest from Nome for St. Lawrence Island, 145 miles away. Flight 99 was a weekly Wien Air Alaska passenger and freight service flight to the Savoonga and Gambell villages on the island, only fifty miles from the Russian mainland.

An instrument flight rules (IFR) flight plan for the route was filed and a forecast obtained for enroute weather before takeoff. The first stop would be Savoonga on the north side of the island, then Gambell on the northwest corner of the island before returning to Nome.

Weather conditions at Savoonga were reported as marginal, with 600-foot ceilings, visibility ten miles in light rain and winds from the southeast at nine knots. Gambell was reporting conditions below the published minimums for the instrument approach, with the ceiling obscured, visibility one mile in rain and fog and winds from the south at nine knots. The crew knew the coastal fog that frequented the island had a tendency to shift indiscriminately, and was in fact reported to be moving east across the airport. They had little reason to doubt the landing conditions would improve by the time they arrived.

Flight 99 lifted off from the Nome airport at 1216, arriving in Savoonga fifty minutes later. After a brief twenty-minute layover to pick up additional passengers, the aircraft departed on its next leg to Gambell. As soon as they lifted off from the runway, the pilot notified the Wien agent at Gambell to activate the nondirectional beacon

(NDB) at the airport, allowing them to track inbound to the station. An estimated enroute time of fifteen minutes was also passed to the agent, along with a request for the current weather observation.

The reply was not what the crew had hoped for as the agent explained the low sky coverage was still present over the airport, with only a half to one mile of visibility in fog. When the captain questioned the accuracy of the observation, the agent changed the report, adding that the visibility was difficult to judge and would occasionally increase up to five miles.

It seems unlikely that the crew actually assumed visibility would be anywhere near five miles, however, and as they approached Gambell the captain even told the first officer the fog would pose a problem during the approach. He further stated his intention of executing the instrument approach. If unsuccessful, he announced he would attempt visual approaches from different directions by flying below the cloud cover, even though a visual approach was in conflict with established company procedures.

Flying over the ocean from the north side of the island, the captain was on the controls as they turned inbound on the NDB-A approach, descending to cross the beacon at the published minimum descent altitude of 500 feet. Once they crossed the beacon at the minimum descent altitude, the correct procedure was to continue visually only if the runway environment was in sight. If it was not in sight, the proper procedure was to execute a missed approach by turning clockwise onto the 335° bearing from the nondirectional beacon, while climbing to 1,600 feet. Instead, the captain elected to continue south over the island at a low altitude after passing the beacon, then made a sharp left turn back toward the airfield in the hope of locating the runway visually by following references along the shoreline.

During the turn toward the northwest after initially flying away from the beacon, the captain dropped the aircraft altitude as low as 100 feet to maintain visual contact with the ground. A few minutes later he recognized a landmark on the shoreline, still southeast of the airport, then made another sharp left turn to line up with where he thought the runway should be.

Following the western shore inbound to the north, the captain saw the airport too late to make a safe landing attempt and continued north over the water, climbing back to 400 feet. After a few miles he made a steep left turn back south toward the airport, this time descending well below 100 feet to maintain visual references. Only a few feet above the threshold, he realized the aircraft was going to overshoot the runway and applied power, turning back north over the water for a third visual attempt at landing.

From cockpit voice recordings analyzed by the National Transportation Safety Board after the accident, both pilots seemed confident they could make the runway on the next attempt. After proceeding out away from the island for less than a minute, the aircraft made a final turn back toward the village.

A heading of 155° would have brought the aircraft over the beacon in alignment with the runway, but the captain held a 140° track instead, probably because he was trying to fly visually from references on the ground. The aircraft actually passed northeast of the village where the nondirectional beacon was located, but continued on a southeast track at an angle away from the airport. It passed over a new housing area before impacting the 600-foot high Sevuokuk Mountain, one mile east of the airport.

Witnesses saw the aircraft fly over the beach and boat racks northeast of the village with the landing gear extended, maintaining a course inland toward the mountain, then disappear in the fog before they heard a crash. Visibility was estimated at one-quarter to one and a half miles.

Some of the passengers who were familiar with the area could see the ground from their windows as they flew inland and realized the airplane was on a collision course with the mountain. They had just enough time to brace themselves before the crash.

Flight 99 impacted a ridge on the northwest slope of Sevuokuk Mountain at an altitude of 424 feet. The landing gear, tail cone and outboard tip of the right wing were sheared off as the aircraft hit. Forward momentum pushed the fuselage over the rough ground, crushing the cockpit area before flipping it onto its back. As the aircraft rolled inverted, the right wing and tail assembly separated completely from the torn fuselage and the outboard half of the left wing broke loose. The cabin structure split into three separate sections, although they all remained relatively close together near the wings.

As violent as the collision was, most of the occupants survived. Had fewer passenger seats failed, far less injuries would also have occurred. Many of the seats collapsed or were torn loose from their mounts during the force of impact, flinging bodies against the cabin supports and each other. Luckily, only seven passengers and three of the crew members died out of the thirty-two people on board. Of the twenty-one surviving passengers, two had minor injuries, while the other nineteen sustained various levels of trauma, including fractures, lacerations and bruises. The lone surviving crew member, a flight attendant, fractured both legs.

A fire erupted near the left engine immediately after impact and spread toward the cabin area. Fortunately it moved slowly enough to allow the escape or rescue of all but one of the injured passengers. An Alaska State Trooper on board at the time, who received only minor injuries during the crash, was responsible for rescuing most of the survivors from the aircraft. He pulled fifteen people out of the wreckage and carried many of them to safety.

Other survivors managed to escape on their own while some were assisted by villagers who arrived within thirty minutes of the accident. The fire was even fought with portable fire extinguishers that local residents had carried to the site, but eventually it subsided and burned out on its own.

All of the survivors were helped or carried off the mountain, many over several miles of rugged terrain, before arriving in Gambell. A village health nurse was the only person in the community trained to administer first aid, and for several hours she did her best treating the various injuries. Additional medical personnel and supplies arrived from Nome later that evening. In spite of their injuries the survivors were obviously grateful to have survived the terrible tragedy. A Coast Guard C-130 aircraft transported them to medical facilities in Anchorage the next morning.

By September 2 seventeen of the survivors were listed in stable or satisfactory condition, three were in serious condition and two had been discharged almost immediately upon arrival. The three dead crew members and seven dead passengers were recovered from the destroyed fuselage after the crash. All seven passengers were Gambell residents who had been returning home. Ironically, the hill on which they lost their lives was the village burial ground.

An official accident investigation began almost immediately. At one point twenty-four different government and state officials were involved at the accident site. Much of the evidence was removed from the wreckage for analysis, including all the flight and navigation instruments inside the cockpit. The cockpit voice recorder and flight data recorder, improperly referred to as "black boxes," were also found and removed for examination. In addition, hundreds of photographs and measurements had to be taken at the scene before a determination could be made. By September 5, the site investigation was completed. It would be another four months before an in-depth examination of all the evidence could be finalized and the National Transportation Safety Board accident report released.

The accident board concluded that there was no evidence of mechanical failure or system malfunction at any time before impact. Weight and balance limitations were within allowable limits and the aircraft was found to be completely airworthy, with no discrepancies uncovered. All four crew members were properly trained and certified in accordance with Federal Aviation Administration standards. Autopsy and toxicology results on the pilots revealed no evidence of drugs or disease.

A thorough analysis of the wreckage revealed the aircraft was in a landing configuration at the time of impact. Wing flaps were set in an approximate 016° position, with the landing gear fully extended. Some survivors and witnesses on the ground said they heard the engines increase in power moments before the crash.

All the fatalities resulted from injuries received on impact. The post-crash fire resulted in most of the forward fuselage and several bodies being severely burned. Numerous seat failures during the crash were determined to be responsible for the majority of survivor injuries.

An examination of the wreckage by the investigation team did not provide any initial clues as to the cause of the accident. Tests conducted on the recovered navigation and communication equipment found them to be functioning properly up to the point of impact. Only when information from the cockpit voice recorder and flight data recorder were retrieved was a sequence of improper actions by the crew revealed as the probable cause. Statements from survivors and witnesses further substantiated the information.

It was shown that the captain did not follow his own company policy for executing the Gambell instrument approach procedure and that he continued to operate the aircraft in an unsafe manner by repeatedly flying in and out of instrument conditions. There was also limited flight planning by the crew and virtually no cockpit coordination during the series of approaches into the airfield. The captain's persistence in flying visually without adequate cloud clearance and visibility requirements was in direct violation of federal regulations.

The instrument approaches at Gambell required that a missed approach be initiated if visual flight could not be maintained at a minimum descent altitude of 500 feet for the NDB-A approach, or 980 feet for the NDB-B approach. Both missed approach procedures required a climb to 1,600 feet while intercepting an outbound track from the beacon. Neither one of the approach procedures was followed correctly.

Wien Air Alaska operated the nondirectional beacon at Gambell with a generator. It did not have a standby power source and was only activated on request by the Wien agent at the airfield. This was done on the day of the accident once flight 99 departed from Savoonga. A flight check of the nondirectional beacon system after the accident found it to be operating normally. The nondirectional beacon is located approximately one mile northwest of the airport on the outskirts of the village, requiring a 155° heading to the runway centerline.

Even though the accident could have been prevented had the crew followed the appropriate instrument approach procedure, other problems were uncovered with the airport operation that contributed to the crash. A notice to airmen was not issued for an inoperable rotating beacon at the airport and several of the runway lights were out of service. Those problems were magnified by the lack of visual approach aids at the airport and no runway markings that could help identify the landing environment. There were also no air traffic control facilities or controlled airspace on St. Lawrence Island.

The accident investigation board further determined that weather conditions at Gambell before and during the flight's arrival, were below minimum requirements for an instrument approach and visual flight. It was the captain's responsibility to ensure those procedures were properly followed. By not doing so he endangered the

Opposite: NDB-A Standard Instrument Approach Procedure at Gambell.
Excepted from NTSB Aircraft Report, report number NTSB-AAR-76-1.
(For illustration only—not to be used for navigation purposes.)

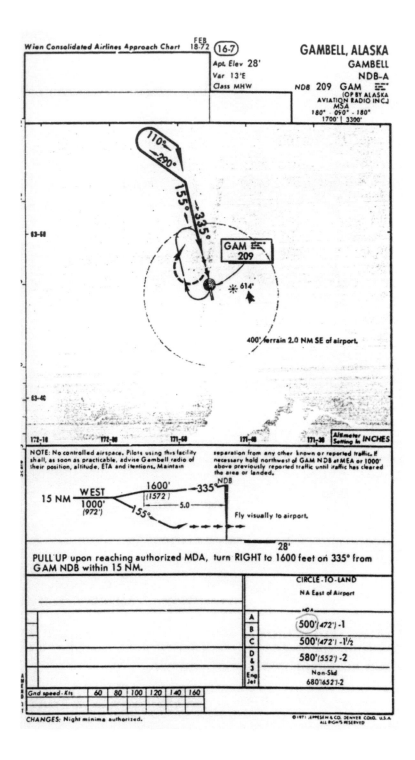

GAMBELL, ALASKA

GAMBELL
NDB-A

Apt. Elev 28'
Var 13°E
Class MHW

NDB 209 GAM ≖
(OP BY ALASKA AVIATION RADIO INC.)
MSA
180° - 050° - 180°
1700' | 3300'

GAM ≖ 209

614'

400' terrain 2.0 NM SE of airport.

172-10   172-00   171-50   171-40   171-30 Altimeter Setting In INCHES

NOTE: No controlled airspace. Pilots using this facility shall, as soon as practicable, advise Gambell radio of their position, altitude, ETA and itentions. Maintain separation from any other known or reported traffic. If necessary hold northwest of GAM NDB at MEA or 1000' above previously reported traffic until traffic has cleared the area or landed.

15 NM — WEST 1000' (972')   1600' (1572') -335° NDB

5.0

155°

Fly visually to airport.

28'

PULL UP upon reaching authorized MDA, turn RIGHT to 1600 feet on 335° from GAM NDB within 15 NM.

					CIRCLE-TO-LAND
					NA East of Airport
					MDA
				A	500' (472') -1
				B	
				C	500' (472') -1½
				D & 3	580' (552') -2
				Eng Jet	Non-Std 680' (652') -2
Gnd speed - Kts	60	80	100	120	140	160	

CHANGES: Night minima authorized.

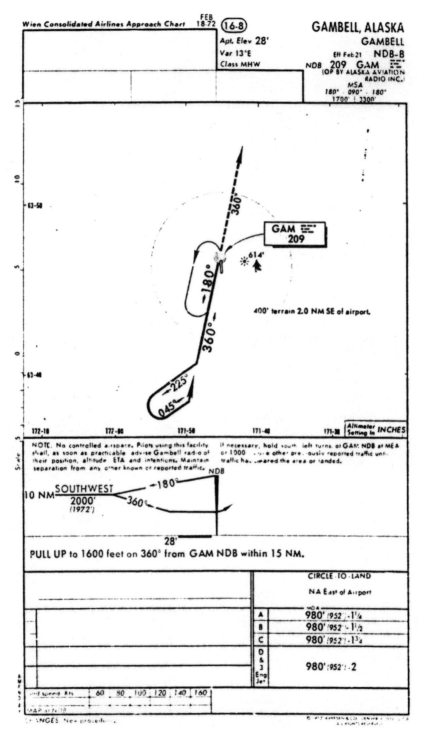

NDB-B Standard Instrument Approach Procedure at Gambell.

Excepted from NTSB Aircraft Report, report number NTSB-AAR-76-1.

(*For illustration only—not to be used for navigation purposes.*)

twenty-eight passengers and three other crew members, resulting in fatal consequences.

Both pilots were familiar with Gambell airport, having flown into the area numerous times over the preceding six months. Together, they had over 9,000 flight hours, half of those in F-27 type aircraft. Each was a skilled instrument pilot.

Most likely, it was their own overconfidence and perceived familiarity with the area that enticed them to violate regulations and push a bad situation to the point of disaster. Ten people perished in the resulting crash. Only the prompt actions of one of the passengers and local residents precluded a greater loss of life.

Russian Mission

JULY 20, 1996

During Alaska's long aviation history the DC-6 has endured as a reliable workhorse for over four decades, serving as one of the safest piston-engine commercial aircraft on record. Many passenger and freight carriers that have operated in the state over the years have used the DC-6 in their inventory. Even today, the aircraft is still being used by several aviation companies. Ideal for large capacity loads that newer and smaller turbo-prop aircraft cannot handle, the DC-6 will no doubt continue to operate into many remote and unimproved airfields throughout Alaska for years to come.

In July 1996 Northern Air Cargo in Anchorage operated thirteen DC-6 aircraft, flying freight and charter service flights into many of the native villages and mining camps scattered across the state. During the company's forty-year history, none of its aircraft had been involved in a fatal accident. This was such an outstanding achievement that an honorary award was presented to Northern Air Cargo by the Federal Aviation Administration in 1995.

Spanning forty years, the prestigious safety record cannot be attributed to luck. Instead, it was most certainly a combination of pilot training, experience, aircraft maintenance, management and policy. Unfortunately, in this case, the record did not endure.

Flight 33 was a Northern Air Cargo DC-6A, being operated as a cargo flight from the western coastal village of Emmonak, near the mouth of the Yukon River. The flight departed from Emmonak at 1410 for a planned stop at Aniak, located 185 miles southeast on the

Kuskokwim River, with a scheduled return to Anchorage later in the afternoon.

The pilot filed a visual flight rules (VFR) flight plan before departure, estimating an enroute time of slightly over an hour to the first destination. On board were the captain, first officer, flight engineer and a pilot from another company, who was catching a ride back to Anchorage.

Good weather conditions prevailed as the DC-6 took off from Emmonak and proceeded southeast along the Yukon River. For the next forty-five minutes the flight was routine. All four Pratt and Whitney engines were running smoothly, registering normal indications on the instruments, until a strong shudder was suddenly felt in the cockpit at 1455. The fire warning light and fire warning horn sounded a moment later, indicating a fire in the number 3 engine.

Both pilots confirmed the malfunction before the firewall selector knob was placed in the appropriate position, shutting off the fuel and oil supply to the number 3 engine. The fire handle for the engine was then pulled, discharging an extinguishing agent into the engine area.

After the chemical had been fully discharged, the first officer asked if the number 3 engine propeller had been feathered, which was required before engaging the fire suppressant system. Feathering changes the angle or pitch of the propeller blades to align with the direction of flight, effectively stopping the rotation of the propeller, and consequently the engine. This had not been done and the captain at that time instructed the first officer to go ahead and do so. The first officer and flight engineer both then tried feathering the propeller, but were only partially successful. Fire was still spotted coming from the engine at 1456, and a few seconds later the flight engineer announced the engine was starting to overspeed.

The emergency procedure for an in-flight engine fire on the DC-6A specified that the engine should always be feathered before pulling the fire extinguisher handle. This was important since the effectiveness of the extinguishing agent would be significantly reduced if the propeller assembly was still rotating. In some cases an engine fire could even be caused by the rotation of the propeller assembly. In addition, if the flow of oil to the propeller governor was stopped before feathering took place, an excessive and uncontrollable RPM could result. Any subsequent attempts at feathering

291

would not only be difficult, but could cause a failure of the feather pump and repeated tripping of the pump circuit breaker, potentially causing an even more serious malfunction.

With the engine still not properly feathered and the fire intensifying in the engine area, the captain took control of the aircraft from the first officer and turned on a direct heading to the nearest airport at Russian Mission, only a few miles south of their flight path. At 1457 he asked for and received the before-landing check, then once again instructed the crew to try and feather the number 3 engine. Almost another minute passed before the flight engineer announced it had finally feathered, but by then the fire was burning unchecked.

As the DC-6 approached the airport on the southeast end of the village adjacent to the Yukon River, the fire appeared to go out for a few seconds but quickly resumed with increased intensity. The fire warning horn sounded for a second time, moments before the flight engineer announced he detected the odor of something burning.

At 1459 the captain stated he planned to cross the airport and enter an abbreviated downwind approach for landing on runway 35. Their flight path was at an angle to the runway as they descended over the western hills, which probably did not allow adequate time to turn toward the airfield before crossing the river, although fuel tanks and people near the north end may have caused the captain to alter his approach and attempt a landing from the other direction. The airport only had one gravel runway, 2,700 feet long, and no control tower or emergency services were available.

Less than a minute after the captain announced his intention to enter a downwind approach, smoke began entering the cockpit. The fire also continued to spread along the wing, trailing flames along the length of the fuselage as the first officer earnestly informed the captain they needed to get on the ground.

The captain continued with the downwind entry after passing over the airfield, turning sharply to intercept a parallel course before finally shallowing out their turn. As the aircraft continued the downwind leg and began its turn to base, the fire alarm sounded again. The flight engineer then announced the instruments were indicating that all four engines were becoming hot. The crew's agitation increased as they began vocally urging the aircraft toward the runway.

Just as they began the turn to final at 1502, the flight engineer uttered an exclamation of alarm as the right wing folded upward and completely separated from the fuselage. The flight recorder stopped functioning at that time, only seconds before the aircraft plunged earthward onto a small island in the Yukon River, less than a mile from the approach end of the runway. Fire quickly spread through the main wreckage, consuming most of the fuselage and left wing. There were no survivors.

Witnesses on the ground saw the aircraft fly across the airfield from the west at about 400 feet, with a fireball surrounding the inboard engine on the right wing and flames extending all the way back along the fuselage to the tail. They watched it turn downwind on the opposite side of the river, as burning pieces began falling away from the wing into the trees, starting a small fire.

The villagers watched the DC-6 continue flying a few hundred feet above the ground while turning base and then final, when the right wing appeared to come off in slow motion. It fluttered behind the trail of smoke for a few seconds then fell to the ground as the aircraft rolled right and nosed over into the trees.

Local residents were able to reach the island within half an hour, but the intense flames prevented anyone from doing much of anything until the fire had subsided. When Alaska State Troopers arrived at the scene three hours after the crash, the wreckage was still smoldering. They secured the area until investigators from the National Transportation Safety Board and Federal Aviation Administration arrived later that evening to begin a preliminary investigation. One of the first things recovered was the cockpit voice recorder, which did not sustain any extensive damage. A flight data recorder was not installed on the aircraft.

By the next day the accident team was able to find all but a few components of the aircraft. Most of the right wing was located approximately 100 feet behind a cut in the trees where the main wreckage had first made contact. It was determined that after the wing had separated outward from the number 3 engine, which was the closest to the fuselage, it fell at a forward angle through the trees with the number 4 engine still attached. During the ensuing impact the engine was torn loose and the wing ended up lying perpendicular to the flight path. A fire then partially damaged the engine, which was found beside the right wing.

The rest of the aircraft hit the trees left wing first, before plowing a swath through the timber for several hundred feet. Portions of the outer wing tip and tail assembly broke free, but were found near the main wreckage. The remaining fuselage was partially destroyed by a post-crash fire, which also damaged the inboard number 1 engine on the left wing. The number 2 engine had been ripped from its mounts by the force of impact and was thrown in front of the cockpit, where it lay unaffected by the fire.

Extensive damage was evident from the initial in-flight fire on the number 3 engine, which consumed the entire power accessory section. There was also heavy damage to the outboard wing spar near the engine, where wing separation had taken place. Burning and melting had occurred from the intense heat and all the inside portions of the wing were coated with soot. A severe amount of stress was evident on the spars, fuel tank and skin, where the wing had folded and separated. The firewall shutoff valve for the engine was found only partially closed, which probably provided a continuous fuel source for the fire.

All the propeller assemblies were located in the wreckage, but only the number 3 propeller was found completely intact. It had been feathered before impact. The total time on the engine was 2,354 hours, of which only 109 hours had accumulated since the last major inspection three months before.

Later analysis of the number 3 engine revealed the crankcase was cracked in front of the cylinders, with the master rod and all connecting rods broken. The components were subjected to metallurgical testing, which revealed the master rod had initially fractured at two points where corrosive pitting had weakened the metal, causing further destruction of the engine and the resulting fire.

An examination of the crew's flight records found all three to be properly qualified and trained. Captain Bruce Bell possessed over 14,000 total hours, half in the same make and model of DC-6 aircraft. He was first certified as a DC-6 captain in October 1995. First Officer Gary Claiborne had logged over 9,000 hours, mainly while serving as a flight engineer before May 1994. Half of his total hours were also in DC-6s. Flight engineer Rex Ketchum had been flying off and on in that capacity since December 1994, splitting his schedule to work as an independent A&P mechanic during the winter months.

No specific explanation could be found as to why an incorrect emergency procedure was performed in response to the fire in the number 3 engine. The training program at Northern Air Cargo was well managed, emphasizing the exact procedures detailed in the DC-6 checklist. Less than four months earlier, the captain had received a satisfactory company proficiency flight evaluation and had also previously attended a Crew Management class that emphasized cockpit communication. The first officer passed a bi-annual flight evaluation in May and had also previously attended the same Crew Management class. The flight engineer successfully accomplished his proficiency evaluation only three weeks before the accident.

The accident board determined the probable cause to be the failure of the engine master connecting rod, which subsequently compromised the integrity of the engine, igniting the escaping oil. Also mentioned as an equal cause was the crew's failure to follow the prescribed emergency procedure, by improperly pulling the fire handle before feathering the engine propeller, thus significantly reducing the capability of the fire suppression system.

It was possible that the aircraft might have been able to land sooner on a straight-in approach to Russian Mission from the north, and therefore allow the crew to escape without injury, but only the captain knew his exact intentions. One of the witnesses on the ground was certain the flight could have landed safely without entering a downwind pattern, but thought the pilot deliberately turned away from a straight-in approach to avoid some fuel tanks and children playing near the approach end of the runway. If so, he and his crew made the ultimate sacrifice.

Bibliography

PUBLISHED WORKS

Books

Alaska Geographic. *Frontier Flight*. Anchorage: Alaska Geographic, 1998.

Billberg, Rudy. *In the Shadow of Eagles*. Anchorage: Alaska Northwest Books, 1993.

Brown, Dale (chief editor). *The Bush Pilots*. Alexandria, Va.: Time-Life Books, 1984.

Bruder, Gerry. *Heroes of the Horizon*. Anchorage: Alaska Northwest Books, 1991.

Clark, Harry Chester Sr. *Alaska's Silent Birdmen*. Phoenix: Harry Chester Clark, 1986.

Cloe, John Haile. *The Aleutian Warriors*. Missoula, MT: Pictorial Histories Publishing, 1990.

_____. *Top Cover for America*. Missoula, MT: Pictorial Histories Publishing, 1984.

Gregory, Glenn R. *Never Too Late to Be a Hero*. Seattle: Peanut Butter Publishing, 1995.

Helmericks, Harmon. *The Last of the Bush Pilots*. New York: Bantam Books, 1990.

Jackson, Donald Dale. *Flying the Mail*. Alexandria, VA: Time-Life Books, 1982.

Janson, Lone E. *Mudhole Smith*. Anchorage: Alaska Northwest Publishing, 1981.

Jefford, Jack. *Winging It!* Anchorage: Alaska Northwest Books, 1981.

Jeppesen. *Jeppesen Airway Manual*. Jeppesen Standard Instrument Approach Procedures, 1948.

Juptner, Joseph P. *U.S. Civil Aircraft*. 9 vols. Falbrook, CA: Aero Publishing, 1962-81.

Levi, Steven C. *Cowboys of the Sky*. New York: Walker and Company, 1996.

Maclean, Robert Merrill. *Flying Cold*. Seattle: Epicenter Press, 1994.
Mills, Stephen E. *Sourdough Sky*. Seattle: Superior Publishing, 1969.
Nevin, David. *The Pathfinders*. Alexandria, Va.: Time-Life Books, 1985.
Nickerson, Sheila. *Disappearance: A Map*. New York: Doubleday, 1996.
Page, Dorothy. *Polar Pilot*. Danville, IL: Interstate Publishers, 1992.
Potter, Jean. *Flying Frontiersmen*. New York: MacMillan, 1956.
_____. *The Flying North*. New York: MacMillan, 1965.
Routsala, Jim. *Pilots of the Panhandle*. Juneau: Seadrome Press, 1997.
Satterfield, Archie. *Alaska Bush Pilots in the Float Country*. Seattle: Superior Publishing, 1969.
_____. *The Alaska Airlines Story*. Anchorage: Alaska Northwest Publishing, 1981.
Smith, Blake. *Warplanes to Alaska*. Surrey, BC: Hancock House Publishing, 1998.
Stevens, Robert W. *Alaskan Aviation History*. 2 vols. Des Moines, Wash.: Polynyas Press, 1990.
Worthylake, Mary M. *Up In The Air*. Woodburn, Oreg.: Mary M. Worthylake, 1977.

Newspapers and Magazines

Alaska Fishing News. Various articles. Ketchikan: various dates.
Alaska Living. Various articles and dates.
Anchorage Daily News. Various articles. Anchorage: various dates.
Anchorage Daily Times. Various articles. Anchorage: various dates.
Anchorage Times. Various articles. Anchorage: various dates.
Daily Alaska Empire. Various articles. Juneau: various dates.
Fairbanks Daily News Miner. Various articles. Fairbanks: various dates.
Flightline. Various articles. Alaska Aviation Heritage Museum, various dates.
Gebo, Robert and Dassow, Ethe. *The Alaska Sportsman*. "The Gillam Plane Was Missing," 1943.
Jessen's Weekly. Various articles. Fairbanks: various dates.
Ketchikan Daily News. Various articles. Ketchikan: various dates.
Nome Nugget. Various articles. Nome: various dates.
Rearden, Jim. *Alaska*. "Clarence Rhode," 1980.
Seattle Post-Intelligencer. Seattle: 1973.

Government Documents and Records

Accident Investigation Report. Civil Aeronautics Board. Various accidents an dates.
Aeronautical Information Manual. Federal Aviation Administration, 1998.

Air Occurrence Report. Department Of Transport, Civil Aviation Division of Canada, 1951.

Air Taxi Safety in Alaska. National Transportation Safety Board, 1974.

Aircraft Accident Briefs. National Transportation Safety Board, various publications and dates.

Aircraft Accident Report. Civil Aeronautics Administration. Various accidents and dates.

Aircraft Accident Report. National Transportation Safety Board. Various accidents and dates.

Alaskan Air Command. "Final Mission Report". Department of the Air Force, 1972.

Aviation Safety Network. Various accident descriptions. Internet web site, 2000.

Cold Weather Flying Sense. U.S. Army General Publications, 1978.

National Oceanic and Atmospheric Administration. *IFR Enroute Low Altitude.* Various locations and dates.

National Oceanic and Atmospheric Administration. *Sectional Aeronautic Chart.* Various locations and dates.

National Transportation Safety Board. Aircraft accident statistics. Various publications and dates.

Report of AF Accident Report. U.S. Air Force, 1953.

Report of the Accident Board. Department Of Commerce, 1935.

Report of the Civil Aeronautics Board. Civil Aeronautics Board, 1943.

Report of the Governor Of Alaska. Bureau of Air Commerce, 1937.

Summary Accident Report. Department of Transport, Civil Aviation Division of Canada, 1951.

U.S. Coast and Geodetic Survey. *AAF Aeronautical Chart.* Various locations and dates.

U.S. Coast and Geodetic Survey. *World Aeronautical Chart.* Various locations and dates.

U.S.A.F. Accident/Incident Report. USAF, 1970.

U.S.A.F. Rescue Coordination Center. Aircraft crash sites and statistics, 2001.

VP-9 Navy Patrol Squadron. Accident description. Internet web site, 2001.

UNPUBLISHED WORKS

Morgan, Lael. *Flying The Alaska Bush, Wilderness Skills Required.* University of Alaska Archives, 1979.

Index

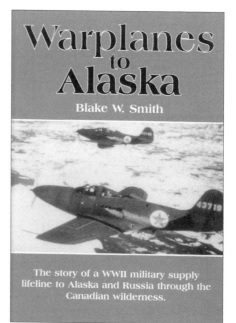
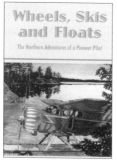